OFFICIAL 100TH RACE ANNIVERSARY EDITION

TOUR DE FRANCE

OFFICIAL 100TH RACE ANNIVERSARY EDITION

TOUR DE FRANCE

FRANÇOISE & SERGE LAGET, PHILIPPE CAZABAN, GILLES MONTGERMONT

Quercus

CONTENTS

THE BIRTH OF THE TOUR

Like all great human adventures, the Tour de France started from nothing. It sprang from a lunch, from a need for action, from a spark of inspiration. Three men were involved – all of whom worked for recently established French sports daily *L'Auto-Vélo*. They were Henri Desgrange, Victor Goddet and Géo Lefèvre.

The paper's title had emerged out of the controversy that engulfed France during the Dreyfus affair of the 1890s. Captain Alfred Dreyfus, a Jewish officer in the French army, had been unjustly condemned as spying for the Germans. Dispatched to the Devil's Island penal colony, he spent five years in solitary confinement as elements within the French army covered up his innocence on all charges. In 1898, French novelist Émile Zola took up his cause, publishing an open letter in the newspaper *L'Aurore* entitled 'J'accuse' (I accuse), highlighting the injustice that had taken place.

In the first rank of those defending Dreyfus was Pierre Giffard, a left-leaning humanist, and promoter of *Vélo*, France's first daily sports paper, which was founded in December 1892. In the wake of Zola's article, which would lead to a presidential pardon being granted to Dreyfus in 1899, Giffard took up the same fight for justice within the green pages of his own publication, *Vélo*. This provoked the displeasure of some of his advertisers and financial backers, including bike and car manufacturers such as De Dion-Bouton, Chasseloup-Laubat and Michelin, who were all in the anti-Dreyfus camp. Not content with ignoring their demands for neutrality, Giffard gladly went into all of the nasty twists and turns of the affair to the point where he antagonized his backers to such an extent that they withdrew their support and established a new title that was more favourable to those who advertised in it. That paper would be *L'Auto-Vélo*, which first appeared on 16 October 1900, printed on yellow paper.

At the helm was Desgrange, a cyclist who had set all kinds of records on the track during the 1890s, including the first officially recognized mark for the world hour record, as he established himself as one of cycling's leading performers. In addition, he also analysed the sport via a string of articles that were full of vim, passion and insight. At his side he had pernickety financial controller Goddet. Several young

HENRI DESGRANGE ET GODDET
— 155 —

The magical trio from the rue du Faubourg Montmartre: Henri Desgrange, editor of *L'Auto*; Victor Goddet, the financial director; Géo Lefèvre, the Tour's architect.

dissidents from Giffard's editorial team soon joined them, including the promising Lefèvre.

L'Auto-Vélo quickly struck a series of blows against Giffard's longer-established title, including capturing the running of Paris–Brest–Paris, a ten-yearly cycling event that Giffard had set up back in 1891. In 1902, Desgrange and his team created their own version of Paris–Bordeaux, this one faster and more widely covered than Giffard's equivalent. However, in late 1902, Desgrange and his editorial team were in the process of losing a court case that Giffard had brought against them, alleging that their paper's name had been plagiarized from his own. As a result, *L'Auto-Vélo* was about to become *L'Auto*.

Unfortunately, this jousting hadn't added a single reader to the 30,000 or 40,000 that both titles were ferociously fighting over in order to get by in this nascent and unpredictable area of sports journalism. Sales were good when there was a big city-to-city event like Paris–Roubaix to report on or a major meeting at the Vélodrome du Parc des Princes, which Desgrange and Goddet had established in 1897, but sales would then subsequently fall again. By December 1902, the situation at *L'Auto-Vélo* had become so serious that the editorial staff had been charged with coming up with the idea of the century, an idea that would lead to the establishment of something fantastic enough to compare with the popularity of wrestling tournaments, but with less fixing involved and much more adventure.

On Saturday, 20 December, Desgrange and Lefèvre met for lunch in the Brasserie du Madrid, just around the corner from *L'Auto-Vélo*'s Paris headquarters at 10 rue du Faubourg Montmartre. Their intention was to discuss an idea that Lefèvre had come up with that might save the paper. With lunch completed, Lefèvre put forward his proposal. 'And what if we were to create a Tour de France?' Lefèvre swept aside the plates, glasses and cutlery on the paper tablecloth between them, and laid out a map of France, gesturing to underline his point: 'It would only be a case of linking together our great Classic races,' he declared.

Initially a bit taken aback, Desgrange was gripped as his young lieutenant's stubby pencil flew from Paris to Lyon, from Lyon to Marseille, from Paris to Nantes, from Nantes to Bordeaux, and from Bordeaux to Toulouse. His final touch was to link Marseille to Toulouse: 'That part doesn't exist yet, boss, but we will invent it. It would only be six stages, just like a six-day event on the road, wouldn't it?' Desgrange was in a state of shock. Why hadn't they thought of this before?

The two colleagues hurried back to their newspaper's offices. All kinds of ideas were bouncing around in Desgrange's head. How could he have been thinking that the only future for racing was in velodromes? 'Yes, they are a real spectacle, but the future lies far beyond, in a much bigger setting out on the road, those same roads once carved out by the Emperor Napoleon I, his idol, his guiding light,' he thinks. Having hung up his hat and coat and glanced up at his prints of Napoleon's victories at Austerlitz, Wagram and Arcole as he did so, Desgrange then dashed across to Goddet's office to find Lefèvre already in there. 'The boy's had an idea,' he blurted

1891 – In Paris-Brest-Paris, as in just about all races before the Tour, the champion riders all had a team of pacemakers at their disposal. Jiel-Laval, from Bordeaux, poses with the back-up team who helped him finish second, eight hours behind the winner. It was Charles Terront whose name went down in posterity as the first Paris-Brest-Paris champion.

out. 'He's suggested a Tour de France for cyclists over several stages. Do you understand? I am not convinced, but what do you think?'

Goddet got up, went over to the safe and opened it. It was dreadfully empty. 'Have we got a choice?' he responded. And so began the most extraordinary meeting between three men equally driven by their passion for this emerging sport, a sport where almost everything was yet to be discovered. It should be remembered that this was a time when cars were still a rarity and more than a million cyclists were paying the tax due for owning a bike. Ideas flew around the table, got fleshed out and knocked down. In among the cries of 'impossible', 'perhaps' and 'remember that…', the initial foundations of the sport began to take shape in that room.

Was such a race feasible? Bikes had developed to the point where they weighed 15 kg instead of 30 kg as the original machines had done, and six-day riders had proved that it was possible to cover more than 3,000 km in 144 hours. In addition, road races such as Paris–Brest, Bordeaux–Paris, Lyon–Paris, Paris–Nantes, Toulouse–Bordeaux, Paris–Royan, Paris–Brussels and Paris–Saint-Malo had given rise to such excitement among the cities involved and the spectators who turned out for them that the gamble didn't seem all that crazy. Of course, they would have to find enough riders ready to plunge themselves into the unknown, 'but *Le Matin* had done just that in 1899 when it organized the first Tour de France for automobiles and had even provided vehicles for some,' Géo Lefèvre pointed out convincingly. Goddet nodded in agreement as he looked across to Desgrange, who concluded: 'It will be the cyclists' Tour de France.'

On 13 January 1903 *L'Auto*'s front page announced a mysterious 'race unlike anything before'.

OPPOSITE *L'Auto* unveils the route of the first Tour de France and profiles some of the likely contenders, including eventual champion Maurice Garin.

BELOW 1901 – Maurice Garin only needed 52 hours to cover the 1,158 km return trip between Paris and Brest, 20 hours faster than the 1891 winner.

8

L'Auto

AUTOMOBILE — CYCLISME

ATHLÉTISME, YACHTING, AÉROSTATION, ESCRIME, POIDS et HALTÈRES, HIPPISME, GYMNASTIQUE, ALPINISME

Directeur-Rédacteur en Chef :
HENRI DESGRANGE

LE TOUR DE FRANCE — LE DÉPART

Organisé par L'AUTO du 1er au 19 Juillet 1903

LA SEMENCE

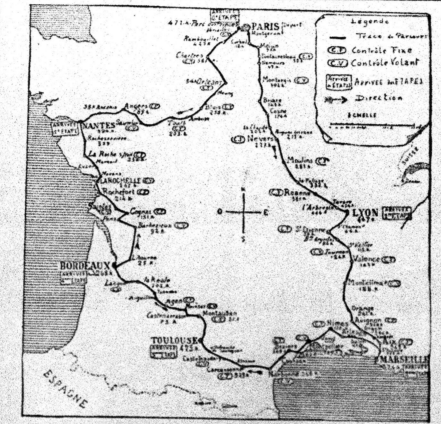

L'ITINÉRAIRE DU TOUR DE FRANCE

QUI ?

Maurice GARIN

GARIN LEADS THE WAY

Many had considered the idea of a race around France. Some had even roughed out plans. For many, though, a Tour de France was total folly. Géo Lefèvre's idea wasn't easy to get off the ground. An initial plan to start the race at the end of May and run it over six weeks was dropped. Not enough riders were interested. But the project had to be seen through. *L'Auto*'s survival depended on it.

Eventually, 60 riders registered. They were supposed to be professionals and some of them were, but a lot of them were only part-time riders, more usually working as carpenters, blacksmiths, innkeepers or even trapeze artists. They came from all over France and beyond, paying ten francs to enter. As they would be receiving five francs a day from the race organizers, they would come out of it OK, with the added incentive of a prize fund amounting to 20,000 gold francs.

Desgrange didn't have enough riders on the start line to consider eliminating those who quit during any one stage, so riders who did abandon, and were therefore no longer involved in the battle for overall victory, were allowed to keep racing and target stage victories.

On Thursday, 1 July, at 3.16 p.m., the 60 riders set off from the Réveil Matin café in Montgeron. They were heading for Lyon on bikes that weighed around 15 kg, with a brake on the front wheel and a fixed wheel at the back. They raced day and night on beaten earth roads. When it got dark, they depended on moonlight showing them the way. No fewer than 23 riders abandoned during that first stage, but after 17 hours in the saddle, during which he had suffered hunger pangs, fatigue and even indigestion caused by eating cherries, Maurice Garin was triumphant in Lyon.

By Marseille, Garin's overall lead had reached eight minutes over Léon Georget. By Toulouse, Garin had stretched it to almost two hours. In Bordeaux, Switzerland's Charles Laeser, who had been eliminated from the overall classification, became the first foreigner to win a Tour stage. Garin, meanwhile, maintained his two-hour advantage over Georget, who abandoned on the road to Nantes. Garin steamed on, winning in Nantes and in Paris's Parc des Princes to crown his overall victory.

Nicknamed 'The Little Sweep' due to his first job or 'The White Bulldog' because of his character and the colour of his jersey, Garin was the ideal victor for Desgrange. He was 32, had a palmarès as long as his arm, and, above all, he was from the La Française team. The manufacturer was one of *L'Auto*'s shareholders. It was clear that the wind of history had blown favourably on the Tour: the 21 survivors had achieved an unimaginable feat. They had inspired large sections of the French population. It was also important for *L'Auto*, which had pushed its circulation to more than 100,000 and taken a big step ahead of its competitor, *Le Vélo*.

FINAL STANDINGS

1 Maurice Garin (FRA) La Française 94:33:14
2 Lucien Pothier (FRA) La Française +2:59:31
3 Fernand Augereau (FRA) La Française +4:29:24
4 Rodolfo Muller (ITA) La Française +4:39:30
5 Jean Fischer (FRA) La Française +4:58:44
6 Marcel Kerff (BEL) no team, +5:52:24
7 Julien Lootens (BEL) Brennabor +8:31:08
8 Gustave Pasquier (FRA) La Française +10:24:04
9 François Beaugendre (FRA) La Française +10:52:14
10 Aloïs Catteau (BEL) La Française +12:44:57

AVERAGE SPEED (OF WINNER): 25.678 KM/H
TOTAL DISTANCE RACED: 2,428 KM

1 July 1903, 3.18 p.m. – because of roadworks, the actual start took place 300 m beyond the official start. Alphonse Steinès and Georges Abran accompanied the 60 starters to that point, where workers on the new Paris–Corbeil railway line witnessed the event's first pedal strokes. Few thought that these adventurers with their neck-protectors and leg-warmers would complete a circuit of France in 19 days.

RIGHT A trainee butcher, Lucien Pothier, who was second overall, looks quite the part.

OPPOSITE, CLOCKWISE FROM TOP LEFT
The winner, Maurice Garin, in his civvies. At 32, the little chimneysweep became the world's best rider. Don't be fooled by his modest appearance – he was a monster on the bike.

The Belgian rider Julien Lootens, better known as Samson and a lecturer by profession, poses with spare tubes wrapped around his neck.

A carpenter by trade, Alexandre Foureaux had a neat little saddle-bag and no brakes.

Germany's Josef Fischer, who was 15th, loved cigars and the good life.

Cliché Rigoureau. Sens

Lucien POTHIER
Champion Cycliste de l'Yonne

FLIRTING WITH DISASTER

The second Tour could easily have been the last. It might have been the Belle Époque, but the race was tough and, consequently, the riders took a few liberties with the rules. Initially, it appeared to have been a bit better than the first. There were an additional 22 starters – 82 instead of 60. It was also five days longer as the rest periods between stages were increased. It seemed Desgrange wanted to give the riders more time to recuperate, even though the start times don't suggest that: 9 p.m. for the first stage in Montgeron, 12.30 a.m. in Lyon, 8.30 p.m. in Marseille, 5 a.m. in Toulouse, 10 p.m. in Bordeaux and 7 p.m. in Nantes. The riders had to race through all or at least part of the night in order to arrive the following afternoon.

Maurice Garin won in Lyon, as he had done in 1903. But it was during the two stages that followed that the Tour was turned upside down. The first ran between Lyon and Marseille. As the riders went over the Col de la République, supporters of local champion Alfred Faure, upset by the grip the riders representing the major manufacturers had on the race, confronted them at the summit of the pass. Gunfire ended the skirmishing.

Following that stage, Ferdinand Payan was thrown off the race for cheating. This led to more trouble on the stage to Toulouse, which passed close to Payan's home in Alès. When Payan didn't appear, his supporters were so wound up that there was almost another riot. They weren't the only fans to be upset. Many had the impression that the big manufacturers and their riders felt they could carve up the race between them. Ominously for those who ended up dominating proceedings, the sport's administrators were of the same view.

They hadn't taken any action the previous year when Maurice Garin had got into an altercation with Fernand Augereau. The dispute ended with Garin smashing up his rival's bike. Augereau still finished third in 1903, but could and perhaps should have finished higher. Garin, though, had paid him to keep quiet. Garin took the title again in 1904, but on this occasion the rule-makers had the final word. On 30 November the French Velocipede Union announced that it had disqualified the first four finishers for 'violation of the rules'. There were reports of riders being paced by cars and other riders and even getting lifts from support vehicles. The title was awarded to fifth-placed Henri Cornet, who had yet to turn 20.

For a while Desgrange thought his race was finished, primarily because the guilty men had helped him to make a success of the Tour and his newspaper. Moreover, the manufacturers they rode for were his best advertisers. He considered turning his back on the race, but knew all too well that someone would step in to replace him. The solution? Route director Alphonse Steinès advised him to take the 1905 race into the mountains to toughen it up and prevent the riders forming illicit combines.

AVERAGE SPEED (OF WINNER): 26.081 KM/H
TOTAL DISTANCE RACED: 2,429 KM

OPPOSITE Henri Jardry, known as Henri Cornet and number 78 in the field, is pictured in leg-warmers and a ribbed pullover. He was nicknamed 'The Engineer' or 'The Joker' and rode for J. Conte, who was more than happy to take advantage of his protégé's unexpected success.

'TROU-TROU' SAVES THE TOUR

It was clear the Tour's original formula had limitations, so Desgrange handed over some of his responsibilities to his colleague Alphonse Steinès, who believed that the mountains would be the making of the race. Steinès picked out a totemic climb in the shape of the Ballon d'Alsace, a potent symbol because it evoked memories of the loss of Alsace-Lorraine in 1870. The 60 starters would also tackle the Côte de Laffrey and the Col Bayard in the Alps. The Tour was also 500 km longer, with an extra five stages.

There were other changes too. In order to reduce the effect of huge time gaps between the finishers, and prevent alliances between riders, the overall classification was decided on points rather than time. Consequently, the first rider home would get one point, the second man two, and so on, with the addition of another point if a rider finished more than five minutes behind the rider ahead of him. There were two categories of rider: the *coureurs de vitesse*, who were allowed to change bikes, while the *poinçonnés* had to ride the same bike during the whole race, which meant carrying out repairs themselves and replacing any faulty parts.

There was a renewed sense of unity and spirit, enhanced by the fact that riders who had been punished for cheating, such as Aucouturier, Trousselier and Petit-Breton, returned to the race. The big surprise, though, was a debutant called René Pottier, who would have won in Besançon if it hadn't been for some bad luck with punctures. His consolation was the race lead. Pottier captured everyone's attention with his performance on the Ballon. There were fears that the riders wouldn't be able to cope with the climb, but they flew up it, none more quickly than defending champion Cornet and Pottier. They produced the Tour's first great duel, riding elbow to elbow for several kilometres, which thrilled the fans who had come up from Belfort to pack the summit. Unfortunately, Pottier had a puncture on the descent, while Cornet had to wait 20 minutes at the summit for a bike change. Trousselier, who had been third to the top, attracted good reports too as a crash had left his shorts in tatters, barely covering his modesty.

The unfortunate Pottier had to quit the race on the third stage due to the injuries he had sustained when accidentally lashed by the whip of a clumsy cab driver. The race then became a duel between Aucouturier, Trousselier and Julien Maitron. Occasionally, *poinçonné* competitor Lucien Petit-Breton, a Tour debutant, got involved in their skirmishes as he finished fifth overall and first in his category.

In Paris, Louis Trousselier, the son of a florist on the Boulevard Haussmann in the French capital, was triumphant, finishing with a comfortable buffer of 26 points over Aucouturier, his partner-in-crime at Peugeot. That night, Trousselier lost almost all of his winnings playing dice. But what did it really matter? Thanks to Pottier and Trousselier, the Tour was back on track.

FINAL STANDINGS

1 Louis Trousselier (FRA) Peugeot-Wolber, 35 points
2 Hippolyte Aucouturier (FRA) Peugeot-Wolber, 61pts
3 Jean-Baptiste Dortignacq (FRA) Saving, 64pts
4 Émile Georget (FRA) Cycles JC, 123pts
5 Lucien Petit-Breton (FRA) Cycles JC, 155pts
6 Augustin Ringeval (FRA) Cycles JC, 202pts
7 Paul Chauvet (FRA) Griffon, 231pts
8 Philippe Pautrat (FRA) Cycles JC, 248pts
9 Julien Maitron (FRA) Peugeot-Wolber/Griffon, 255pts
10 Julien Gabory (FRA) Cycles JC, 304pts

AVERAGE SPEED (OF WINNER): 27.107 KM/H
TOTAL DISTANCE RACED: 2,994 KM

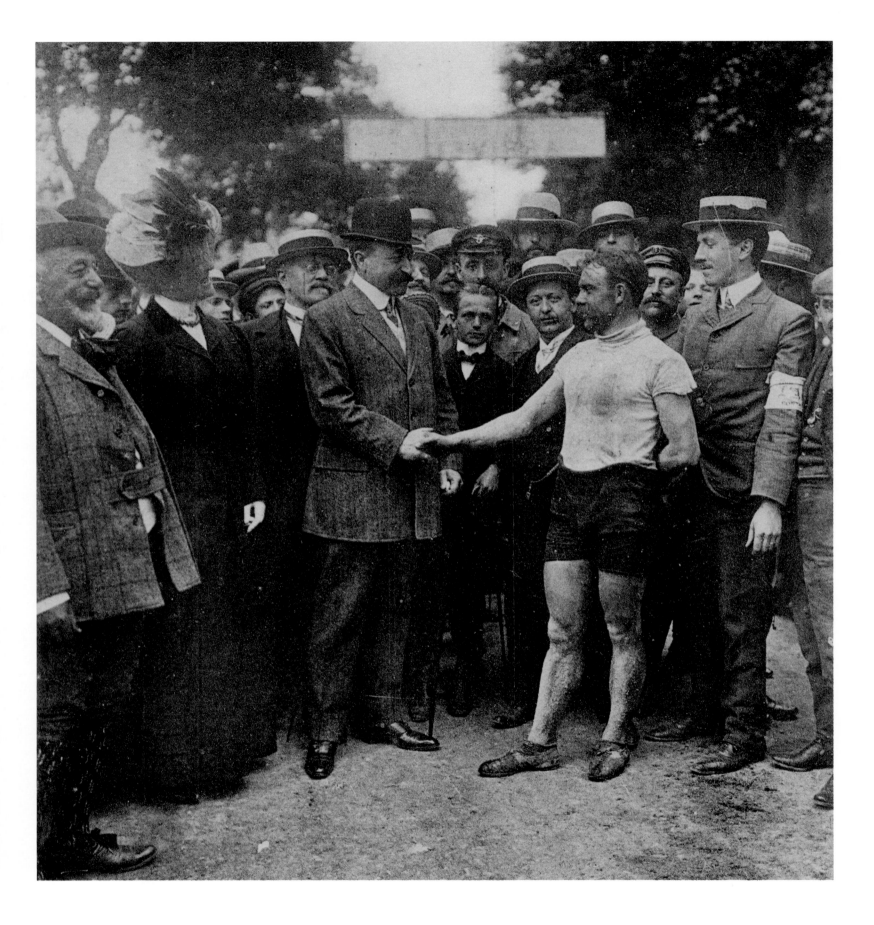

LEFT A stocky climber and fearsome
competitor, Trousselier would go
on to become a florist on Boulevard
Haussmann in Paris, like his father.

ABOVE Louis Trousselier, seen here
shaking hands with Count Zeppelin,
was an oddball and therefore exactly
the kind of character needed to get
the Tour back on its feet.

MOUNTAIN KING POTTIER MAKES HISTORY

The fourth Tour was the first to complete a full circuit of the country as Desgrange raised the race distance from 2,994 km to 4,637 km. There were now 13 stages and three small excursions over the border at Metz, Ventimiglia and Irún.

The 1906 race was all about climbing and, consequently, the best thing that could have happened was for it to be won by a climber. In fact, the race completely redefined what it meant to be a climber, thanks to the exploits of René Pottier. A miller who rode in a cotton sun hat, Pottier was a phenomenon on the climbs. Sent off course on the opening stage, he still managed to finish fourth, close behind winner Émile Georget at the end of a brutal test. Potholes and nails scattered by partisan fans forced 27 riders to abandon, leaving just 49 in the race.

Wearing number 48, Pottier showed a quick eye in avoiding hazards, and consummate skill in making repairs when required. As brown and wrinkled as a currant, Pottier won the next stage to share the lead with Georget. Ahead lay the Ballon d'Alsace. It was here that Pottier came into his own. He produced an exhibition that dazzled even the most cynical race followers. He spent 220 km on his own, reaching Dijon with an advantage of 48 minutes on his protégé, Georges Passerieu. Georget was in fifth place and now four points down on Pottier.

In order to cement his position as leader, Pottier widened the gap in the Alps by parading to victory in Grenoble and Nice. Showing cat-like suppleness, he was the first man over the Côte de Laffrey and the Col Bayard. In Grenoble he finished 14 minutes and more ahead of his pursuers, while in Nice he was 26 minutes in front of Passerieu and 41 ahead of Georget. On paper, they were only 9 and 12 points, respectively, behind King René, but in reality they were hours behind him, light years even. René had flown to victory on four consecutive stages, the hardest four of the race, finishing head and shoulders ahead of everyone.

From that point, he was able to allow the race to develop as he wished. In Marseille he let Passerieu win by a second, and he continued in that same beneficent vein all the way to Paris, allowing his friends and team-mates their moments of glory while he kept his eyes open for trouble as a good miller always would. Pottier added the final touch by winning his fifth stage in the Parc des Princes, where he received a delirious welcome because everyone knew he had left an indelible mark on the Tour. A climber had sent the race into orbit. Even his wife, Zélie, who was a bit stiff, could see that. His average speed was only 24.463 km/h, but this long Tour was extremely testing. As the organizing paper pointed out, there were just 14 'survivors' from 76 starters.

FINAL STANDINGS

1 René Pottier (FRA) Peugeot, 31 points
2 Georges Passerieu (FRA) Peugeot, 39pts
3 Louis Trousselier (FRA) Peugeot, 59pts
4 Lucien Petit–Breton (FRA) Peugeot, 65pts
5 Émile Georget (FRA) Alcyon-Dunlop, 80pts
6 Aloïs Catteau (BEL) Alcyon-Dunlop, 129pts
7 Édouard Wattelier (FRA) Labor, 137pts
8 Léon Georget (FRA) Alcyon-Dunlop, 152pts
9 Eugène Christophe (FRA) Labor, 156pts
10 Antony Wattelier (FRA) Alcyon-Dunlop, 168pts

AVERAGE SPEED (OF WINNER): 24.463 KM/H
TOTAL DISTANCE RACED: 4,637 KM

OPPOSITE TOP The fearsome Hippolyte Aucouturier had enough class and speed to win a Tour. However, he ended up getting food poisoning from lemonade, crashing over a dog, falling foul of the rules and coming up against Pottier, Petit-Breton and Trou-Trou.

OPPOSITE BOTTOM LEFT At the finish, the taciturn victor poses with his wife, Zélie. The Tour would never again see this man of the mountains. Times were hard, to the point where a sensitive soul like René Pottier ended up being blown so far off course that he took his own life one sad January day in 1907.

OPPOSITE BOTTOM RIGHT In this high-powered car, a Pipe 28 HP from Brussels, Georges Abran looked like a real pioneering spirit as he undertook his reconnaissance of the Tour de France route. One of his passengers has goggles to keep the dust out of his eyes.

VICTORY FOR 'THE ARGENTINE'

Up to this point – except when the rules had meant otherwise, with a suspension for Maurice Garin in 1905 – the Tour winner had always returned to defend his title, but this symbolic link was broken when the fifth edition started. René Pottier wasn't on the start line at the Bineau bridge in Paris and would never return again. He had committed suicide at the start of the year. He was only 27.

This Tour featured two new passes, the Porte and the Sappey, which would have been a walk in the park for the winged climber. The question now was which one of the 93 starters would be inspired by these fearsome obstacles. Another question surrounded the possibilities of the brothers in the field: Antony and Édouard Wattelier, Émile and Léon Georget, and Anselme and Lucien Mazan. The latter, better known as Petit-Breton, had been fourth the year before. The route covered 4,488 km in 14 stages, including the first ever stop in occupied Alsace-Lorraine. Once again, and rather surprisingly, the race was to be decided on points.

The formidable first stage to Roubaix gave some immediate answers to the questions being asked: Alcyon's Trousselier was clearly in form. After Trousselier and Émile Georget had jointly been awarded the stage win in Metz, 'Mimile', as Émile Georget was known, took command on the Ballon d'Alsace. Although second to his friend Marcel Cadolle in Lyon, he went on to win in Grenoble, Nîmes and Toulouse.

Partly because he was using a freewheel, which some malicious defenders of the fixed wheel referred to as 'the resting gear', Georget continued to flourish as far as Toulouse. But from then on, life wasn't so sweet. Following the stage to Bayonne, where Petit-Breton took victory, Alcyon team manager Monsieur Gentil pointed out that Georget, who had finished fourth and kept the lead, had swapped bikes with a team-mate outside the control areas after having a puncture. Gentil threatened to withdraw all of his riders from the race if Georget wasn't relegated to last place on the stage. The judges dallied and the Alcyon team quit. Only then did the judges impose the penalty, resulting in Georget dropping from first place to third behind team-mates Petit-Breton and Gustave Garrigou.

At least Georget had the consolation of the title remaining within the Peugeot family. Over the final days, with the Alcyon riders out of the picture, Peugeot's young lions went on the rampage, dividing up the spoils between them. They claimed the final four stages and filled the first five places in the Parc des Princes. Petit-Breton, dubbed 'The Argentine' due to his childhood in Latin America, won his first Tour at the age of 25, having finished fourth in 1906, when he had won the *poinçonnés* class. Garrigou finished second on his debut, while the ill-starred Émile Georget was third. He was only 25, but had had such bad luck that questions were already being asked about whether he would ever win the Tour.

FINAL STANDINGS

1. Lucien Petit–Breton (FRA) Peugeot-Wolber, 47 points
2. Gustave Garrigou (FRA) Peugeot-Wolber, 66pts
3. Émile Georget (FRA) Peugeot-Wolber, 74pts
4. Georges Passerieu (FRA) Peugeot-Wolber, 85pts
5. François Beaugendre (FRA) Peugeot-Wolber, 123pts
6. Eberardo Pavesi (ITA) Otav, 150pts
7. François Faber (LUX) Labor-Dunlop, 156pts
8. Augustin Ringeval (FRA) Labor-Dunlop, 184pts
9. Aloïs Catteau (BEL) no team, 196pts
10. Ferdinand Payan (FRA) no team, 227pts

AVERAGE SPEED (OF WINNER): 28.47 KM/H
TOTAL DISTANCE RACED: 4,488 KM

OPPOSITE Petit-Breton turns to watch the action from in among the drinks and water bottles at a feeding station.

ABOVE During an inspection before a stage start, Robert Desmarets, the future father of French actress Sophie Desmarets, checks that the wheel-nuts on the machine of Italy's Luigi Ganna are firmly fixed in place.

RIGHT In order to ensure the integrity of the race, six or seven fixed or mobile control points were scattered throughout each stage. There were also secret control points where the riders didn't have to sign in, but did receive an ink stamp on the wrist as they went past. The image shows the control point at Vire, handily situated in front of a café, where the four officials are getting the breakaway riders to sign in, with Garrigou among them.

OPPOSITE Bordeaux, Allées de Tourny. Great excitement at the start point of the stage to Nantes. Petit-Breton is the centre of attention as he prepares for action.

PETIT-BRETON TAKES AN IRON GRIP

Petit-Breton was in form, which made him the favourite to win the sixth Tour. Almost all of his rivals were on the start line, but he was set to beat them all, his crushing superiority forcing them to abandon, or pushing them into making mistakes.

In order to make sure of his win, he undertook some reconnaissance and noted the critical points on the route. His team was solid as well, but the obstacles on the route would still be a stern test, particularly the mountains. These had taken on such importance that the Labor and Hutchinson companies joined together in establishing the first mountains prize, which would be decided on four passes: the Ballon d'Alsace, the Col de Porte, the Côte de Laffrey and l'Estérel. Points and prizes would be awarded on each, while the winner of the overall mountains classification would take home 250 francs.

Émile Georget was tipped to win the mountains prize and he was among the 112 starters who signed on at the Place de la Concorde. But 'Mimile' was only a shadow of himself. He knew his legs could cope with the 4,488 km, but his problem was that Petit-Breton wanted to take his second victory in his own right, rather than thanks to a rival's relegation. On the very first stage on the cobbles of Paris–Roubaix, he broke clear with Georges Passerieu. The two Peugeot riders finished first and second. They repeated that feat in occupied Metz.

On the Ballon d'Alsace, where *L'Auto* and Desgrange unveiled a monument to the much-missed René Pottier, whose brother André was first to the top, the Peugeot riders put on another show, headlined by 'The Giant of Colombes', François Faber. Also dubbed 'The Big Man', 'The Ogre' or even 'Gargantua', Faber won the day, but Petit-Breton and Garrigou didn't let their strapping team-mate out of their sight. Faber would go on to win in Lyon, Toulouse and Brest. Peugeot's other young lions dominated everywhere else, only missing out in Grenoble and Bordeaux.

Having taken the lead in Belfort, Petit-Breton first kept the Italian Ganna at arm's length, then his team-mate 'Gargantua', who established himself as the pretender to the Tour throne. Petit-Breton claimed the final stage in Paris, his fifth of the race, and finished 32 points clear of Faber, with his Peugeot team-mates Passerieu and Gustave Garrigou third and fourth. As he was also crowned the best climber, he added a sixth success.

This time there were no questions over the rules – no doubts about his victory. He won thanks to his iron grip. Only 36 survivors made it to Paris, earning themselves the status of 'giant of the road', a title handed out only to those who completed the whole route and confirmed by a certificate that was awarded by *L'Auto*. No fewer than 78 riders had fallen by the wayside.

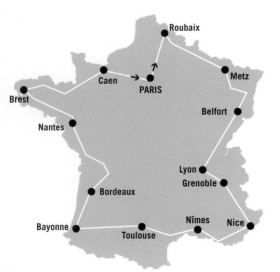

FINAL STANDINGS

1 Lucien Petit-Breton (FRA) Peugeot-Wolber, 36 points
2 François Faber (LUX) Peugeot-Wolber, 68pts
3 Georges Passerieu (FRA) Peugeot-Wolber, 75pts
4 Gustave Garrigou (FRA) Peugeot-Wolber, 91pts
5 Luigi Ganna (ITA) Alcyon-Dunlop, 120pts
6 Georges Paulmier (FRA) Peugeot-Wolber, 125pts
7 Georges Fleury (FRA) Peugeot-Wolber, 134pts
8 Henri Cornet (FRA) Peugeot-Wolber, 142pts
9 Marcel Godivier (FRA) Alcyon-Dunlop, 153pts
10 Giovanni Rossignoli (ITA) Bianchi, 160pts

AVERAGE SPEED (OF WINNER): 28.74 KM/H
TOTAL DISTANCE RACED: 4,488 KM

OPPOSITE Porte Désilles, Nancy. After a neutralized section, the riders prepare for the start: Desgrange (right) is about to unleash his champions. Thanks to their numbers, which are the size of billboards and will soon fall off, it is easy to pick out Petit-Breton (2), who is the only rider wearing glasses, the Italians Ganna (135), Pavesi (136), Galetti (101) and Cuniolo (152), as well as Garrigou (3) and Dortignacq (8).

Omer Beaugendre and Henri Cornet find it hard going in Picardy as they power their machines over the cloying road surface… The fans who have come by bike to watch the action are wearing neck-protectors just like the riders.

ABOVE At Nîmes, beneath a billowing banner, between the plane trees and boaters, after 345 km of racing and more than 12 hours in the saddle, the riders who set out from Nice overnight sprint to decide the seventh stage – Petit-Breton will get the better of Ganna.

Petit-Breton – a man in a hurry

A TWO-TIME Tour de France winner, Lucien Petit-Breton was the first modern champion and not only with regard to the Tour. The life of this Breton – born Lucien Mazan in 1882 – was packed with adventure, starting with his departure for Argentina when still a child and ending with his death in 1917 on the Western Front.

While working as a groom in Argentina, he had already got involved in cycle racing. When he returned to France, he competed in Argentina's colours on the track and took up a new name, Petit-Breton, which harked back to his Breton roots. In his new guise, he excelled as a sprinter, in hour-long races and in the 24-hour Bol d'Or events, before moving on to the Classics, to the

Tour de France and to six-day races, including some in the United States. Let's not forget that he also carried off the first mountains prize at the Tour.

As a rider, his endurance matched his quick thinking and strategic brilliance, while he was also a good mechanic, which was no bad thing at all given the standard of the materials and the roads in that period. He was interested in every aspect of the sport, a great innovator and truly gifted: he left the sport to open a bike shop in Périgueux, then returned to competition and won acclaim for introducing the derailleur to the Tour. Effectively riding alone with his magical gear-changer, he pushed Belgium's Philippe Thys right to the end of the 1913 Tour. Soon after that, he was perhaps the

first rider to publish his memoirs and, in so doing, to offer advice to budding and aspiring racers.

'The shimmering Argentine', as his son Yves referred to him, was involved in the celebrated 'taxis of the Marne' operation of 1914 that prevented the capture of Paris by German troops. In the end, he died in a senseless accident when his car was in a head-on collision with another vehicle close to the front lines in 1917. By then he was well established as the sport's first media star.

BELOW Lucien (left) with his brother Anselme Mazan, who abandoned on stage seven of the 1907 Tour and would also die at the front.

1909
FRANÇOIS FABER
ALCYON

'THE OGRE' CRUSHES HIS RIVALS

The route was the same in every way as the previous year's. However, there was no chance of the same rider winning – for the good reason that Petit-Breton was a non-starter. There were, however, two clear pretenders to his thone: François Faber and Gustave Garrigou, who were both now part of a revamped and very ambitious Alcyon team, managed by Alphonse Baugé.

Although there had been a reshuffling of the established order and there were 150 starters, making it the biggest field yet, wintry temperatures were set to make the race even more of a test. It wasn't the kind of weather many relished, but it mattered little to 'The Ogre'. Standing out from the rest as a quite extraordinary performer, that man was François Faber, who hailed from Luxembourg and lived in the Paris suburb of Colombes, where he was a docker. He was such an impressive figure, so sturdy and muscular, that he was quickly dubbed 'The Giant of Colombes'. He may only have been 5'10", but in that era that made him very big indeed. In addition, the giant tipped the scales at 200lbs. He didn't seem to feel the cold – he simply covered himself with a thin layer of grease.

He was reaching maturity as a rider and, thanks to his four stage wins during the 1908 Tour, he had also gained in confidence, having previously been a bit of a gentle giant who was most comfortable when in the presence of his half-brother, Ernest Paul. He won in Metz, then in Belfort,

then in Lyon, then in Grenoble, then in Nice. Add them up – five stages in a row, a feat never seen before, better than René Pottier in 1906. Like René, he led over the Ballon, the Laffrey and the Bayard, thanks to his brute power.

Whether wrapped up in a jute sack or exposed to the elements, he simply powered along. When he had problems with his bike, as he did in Lyon when his chain broke, he ran with it in his hands. He was happy undertaking solitary breaks of 200 km and more, building up huge gaps even though this didn't benefit him because the classification was decided on points.

He could have plotted a steady path back to Paris, but 'The Ogre' wasn't like that. He had panache, as well as his half-brother and team-mates to think about. Consequently, he set about distributing the bouquets – a stage for his little brother Paul in Nîmes, two for Jean Alavoine, one for Trousselier in Nantes, one for Garrigou in Brest, and one on home ground in Caen for Norman rider Paul Duboc.

Witnessing this orgy of success, Desgrange's right-hand man Steinès was afraid that this monster of a man was going to devour every stage. In the Parc des Princes, he finished 20 points clear of Garrigou and didn't seem the slightest bit tired. He also pulverized the record average for the race by setting a mark of 28.658 km/h. This strapping man who, in his yellow and black jersey resembled a huge bumble bee, was only 22 years old.

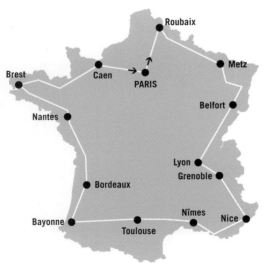

FINAL STANDINGS

1 François Faber (LUX) Alcyon, 37 points
2 Gustave Garrigou (FRA) Alcyon, 57pts
3 Jean Alavoine (FRA) Alcyon, 66pts
4 Paul Duboc (FRA) Alcyon, 70pts
5 Cyrille van Hauwaert (BEL) Alcyon, 92pts
6 Ernest Paul (FRA) no team, 95pts
7 Constant Ménager (FRA) Le Globe, 102pts
8 Louis Trousselier (FRA) Alcyon, 114pts
9 Eugène Christophe (FRA) no team, 139pts
10 Aldo Bettini (ITA) no team, 142pts

AVERAGE SPEED (OF WINNER): 28.658 KM/H
TOTAL DISTANCE RACED: 4,488 KM

OPPOSITE A well-organized control point provided much more spectacle than seeing the riders flash by. Everyone is done up in their Sunday best and the police are out in force. The parasols indicate that the weather is good. Faber leads the way ahead of Trousselier and Faber's half-brother, Ernest Paul.

ABOVE Luxembourg's François Faber with his compatriot, the journalist Alphonse Steinès.

RIGHT Fans, policemen, border officials and race judges await the arrival of the riders at a control point on the stage into German-occupied Metz.

Night riders

IN ITS EARLY years large parts of the Tour used to take place at night. This added significantly to the difficulty of what was already an extraordinary race, but also boosted the sense of adventure. Stages used to start at different times of night – sometimes in the late evening, on other occasions at three in the morning. Riders had to eat beforehand, when they probably weren't feeling all that good anyway.

Racing at night was essential as stages had to finish the following afternoon. It meant the riders spent between 12 and 17 hours in the saddle, assuming they

didn't get lost in the dark. Riders wouldn't ride all that quickly, but would move steadily along, waiting for dawn to break. Fortunately, because the race took place in July it wasn't too cold and the moon was often out. Some clever riders would attach lamps to their forks, while Maurice Garin used to wear a white jacket so that his La Française team-mates and bosses could spot him. Riders who were dropped, were struggling or on the verge of abandoning were dubbed 'the shadows', but night-time riding reduced all of the racers to shadows, both the big guns and the also-rans.

ABOVE 1909, Grenoble. A night start for the stage to Nice, during which the riders will depend on the light of the moon or on weak lamps that just about illuminate roads that are more or less white. With their eyes full of stars from the magnesium flash of the camera, they will head off into the dark almost blind until their eyes get accustomed to the gloom. Nice is 345 km away. It will take Faber 12 hours to get there, while the last man to finish, Italy's Augusto Pasquali, will need almost 18!

LAPIZE IS CROWNED IN THE PYRENEES

The 1910 Tour took a huge step into the unknown by sending the riders into the high mountains of the Pyrenees, which was an unprecedented test in the sport. Would the riders make it, many wondered? Alphonse Steinès, Desgrange's right-hand man, who had pushed for the innovation, was short and to the point: 'They will get over it.' Desgrange, though, was worried.

Steinès wanted to revitalize a race that François Faber had dominated to the extent that he had killed all suspense. The riders now coped all too easily with the small passes in Alsace and the Alps, so Steinès was determined to raise the bar. After creating a sense of epic adventure, the Tour was now looking for heroic acts. Early on the morning of 3 July, lined up at the Pont de la Jatte, the field of 110 comprised 80 *isolés* and three big teams put together by leading manufacturers: Alcyon, with Faber, Garrigou, Lapize and Trousselier in its ranks, Legnano with Petit-Breton and Émile Georget, and Le Globe with Cornet and Crupelandt, who won the first stage to Roubaix.

From then on, though, Alcyon maintained a vice-like grip. Alphonse Baugé's riders filled the first three places on stage two as Faber took the lead. The climbers from the Legnano and Globe teams, Émile Georget and Crupelandt, managed to unsettle Alcyon on the climbs in the Vosges and Alps, but on the descents there was always a sky blue Alcyon jersey to bring

them back into line, usually Octave Lapize. Best known for his sprint at that point, Lapize showed that he could climb and get back up to the leaders on descents. That combination of talents won him the stage into Grenoble. Nevertheless, he was still 20 points behind Faber, his friend, team-mate and, now it also appeared, his rival.

The stopover in Nice produced one of the race's first great tragedies when Adolphe Hélière died after suffering a stroke while swimming in the sea. The 69 riders who set off for Nîmes left under a cloud, but little changed on the race as Faber continued to dominate. Until, that is, the stage to Perpignan, where Lapize finished third and picked up six points on his team-mate. Was Faber cracking?

The Pyrenees loomed. There were 11 passes on the menu and just 15 points between the Alcyon pair. The duel between them started straight away on the Portet d'Aspet: Lapize dropped everyone to win on his own in Luchon ahead of Georget and Faber, who had recovered well after crashing on the descent off the Portet d'Aspet. Next up was tenth stage, the prospect of which was so daunting that Desgrange fled back to Paris to avoid any flak.

Riding in the dark, Lapize attacked and at 7.30 in the morning he walked over the summit of the Tourmalet, where about 100 bike fanatics had gathered. Even though he was

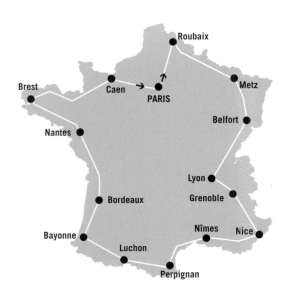

The tight battle he had with François Faber ensured that Lapize's popularity grew no end, especially at the control points. Right behind him stands Desgrange. On the left is the official starter Abran with his flag.

leading, Lapize had found it tough. At the summit he railed against Desgrange's assistants, Victor Breyer and Alphonse Steinès, branding them 'assassins'. He was on the point of throwing in the towel when providence intervened in the shape of local rider François Lafourcade. He emerged from nowhere and passed Lapize, who hadn't seen him coming.

How could this be? It was totally out of order for an Alcyon rider to be bested by an independent *isolé*, so Lapize started to chase. Lafourcade achieved a notable success by leading over the Aubisque, but Lapize eventually caught up and passed him, and went on to win in Bayonne. Faber, showing even more grit than had been expected, came in ten minutes later in third place. 'The Ogre' still led by more than ten points,

but Lapize was nibbling away at his advantage. By Nantes, where Faber struggled after falling over a dog, his lead was just a single point. Their duel had driven sales of *L'Auto* to beyond 200,000 copies a day.

The turning point came at Brest. Lapize gained another four points on Faber, who had been weakened by his fall. On the run to Caen, Faber attacked and opened a gap of 20 minutes. But he lost his momentum after a puncture and fell another three points behind. Going into the final stage into Paris, Lapize led by six points, but was soon waylaid by a puncture that left him at the back of the pack. Forced into a hellish chase, Lapize failed to catch Faber, but did come back from the dead to finish sixth and win the race by four points.

LEFT Pont-Audemer. There's tension at the control point 183 km from Paris: Lapize, seen with André Blaise, is 11–40 down on Faber on the final stage.

ABOVE François Faber, the 'giant of Colombes', was a huge man in every sense of the word, the very archetype of the first giants of the road.

GARRIGOU FOILS GALLANT DUBOC

The Pyrenees had given the Tour wings and Desgrange immediately wondered whether his race could get another lift by adding the Alps. Alphonse Steinès had been exploring the range since 1903, but had stuck to smaller climbs on the edge of the massif. In 1911, however, they did not hold back. The Allos (2,250 m), Aravis (1,498 m), Galibier (2,556 m), Lautaret (2,058 m) and Télégraphe (1,566 m) all featured on the route, which was also 600 km longer.

Perhaps not surprisingly, taking into account what was ahead, only 88 riders lined up at the Pont de la Jatte, well below the 110 who had started the previous year. The race would effectively pit everyone against the Alcyon team, who had snapped up every prize on offer since Alphonse Baugé had started managing them. They had lost defending champion Octave Lapize to La Française, but could still count on former winners François Faber and Louis Trousselier, the stylish Gustave Garrigou, and budding star Eugène Christophe.

The Alcyon riders didn't waste any time taking control. They filled the first three places in both Dunkirk and Longwy. Faber then destroyed everyone on the stage over the Ballon d'Alsace. He took the lead in Belfort, ahead of team-mates Garrigou and Masselis. La Française struck back in the Alps, where Crupelandt and Émile Georget were victorious, the latter becoming the first man to conquer the Galibier. Although Lapize abandoned, Paul Duboc moved up La

Française's hierarchy and the classification. Lying third, he steadily closed in on Alcyon's leaders. Nicknamed 'The Apple' due to his origins in cider-producing Normandy, Duboc beat Garrigou in Perpignan, then Luchon, and went into the big Pyrenean stage just ten points down on the race leader.

Duboc took control as the race went over the Aspin, Peyresourde and Tourmalet. But suddenly he came to a stop and vomited in the ditch. He had been poisoned. There had been something sinister in the bottle he had been given at the feeding station. Garrigou passed the stricken Duboc and went on to win the stage in Bayonne following the disqualification of Brocco, who had accepted money to help other riders earlier in the race. Duboc recovered but struggled to get over the Aubisque, finished three hours down on the winner and, crucially, lost 17 points.

His Tour hopes had gone, but the Norman continued to fight like a lion, winning in La Rochelle. Garrigou countered with a victory in Cherbourg. Duboc responded with another success on home ground in Le Havre, where Garrigou wisely decided to swap his blue Alcyon jersey for a neutral one in order to avoid being lynched by Duboc's supporters. Duboc's team-mate Godivier provided La Française with another success in Paris, but it was too late. Garrigou and Baugé provided Alcyon with their third success in a row. The unfortunate Duboc finished 18 points down, 17 of which he lost in Bayonne...

FINAL STANDINGS

1 Gustave Garrigou (FRA) Alcyon, 43 points
2 Paul Duboc (FRA) La Française, 61pts
3 Émile Georget (FRA) La Française, 84pts
4 Charles Crupelandt (FRA) La Française, 109pts
5 Louis Heusghem (BEL) Alcyon, 135pts
6 Marcel Godivier (FRA) La Française, 141pts
7 Charles Cruchon (FRA) La Française, 145pts
8 Ernest Paul (FRA) Alcyon, 153pts
9 Albert Dupont (BEL) Le Globe, 158pts
10 Henri Devroye (BEL) Le Globe, 171pts

AVERAGE SPEED (OF WINNER): 27.332 KM/H
TOTAL DISTANCE RACED: 5,344 KM

OPPOSITE Eight times a top-five Tour finisher, Gustave Garrigou became an ironmonger after retiring from racing.

Three smaller Tours as well as the big one

IF SOMEONE TELLS you: 'My grandfather rode the Tour de France', then be slightly suspicious and don't waste time looking through the Tour's official record books because you have probably got very little chance of finding the name of this 'giant of the road'. There is a threefold reason for this: between 1910 and 1911 there were three smaller Tours that were open only to independent riders, a category created in 1909 and comprising riders in between the professional and amateur ranks. It is more than likely that your friend's forefather was one of the thousand or so competitors who took part in these almost entirely forgotten stage races.

These were the three most important events in this category, although in 1911 Peugeot also organized an edition of Paris–Toulouse and one of Paris–Turin along the same lines. Peugeot, believing that it had already shown what it could do by winning five Tours with Trousselier, Pottier and Petit-Breton (who won three, one in the *poinçonné*

category), decided that it didn't need to depend on *L'Auto* and Desgrange, and organized races of its own, recruiting young riders from all over France. It started with the Circuit Français in 1909, which comprised 15 different races, then in 1910 it put on its first Tour, which took place in August, just after Desgrange's big race, and featured 575 starters, of whom 313 finished. The prizes came from Peugeot's range of cars, motorbikes and bicycles.

Peugeot's move in this new direction didn't pass unnoticed by its major rival, Alcyon, and that team's *directeur sportif*, Alphonse Baugé. They were also in the business of selling bikes, cars and motorcycles. Consequently, in 1911, the two companies organized their own versions of the Tour running at almost the same time. Peugeot's version was more successful because the company had more experience, a bigger network of dealers and had plenty of champions. After two preparation events, Peugeot's Circuit Français blew Alcyon's Eight Days out of

the water in terms of length, quality of riders and level of competition. Peugeot also got the riders onside by offering cash prizes, while its rival stuck with offering prizes from its product range. As a result of this, despite suffering 21 punctures, Philippe Thys pocketed 6,000 francs, while another Belgian rider, Félicien Salmon, came away from Alcyon's race with a small collection of cars, motorbikes, bicycles and stopwatches that he had to sell off his own back.

Thys, who had his expenses covered by Peugeot as one of their development riders, went on to turn professional and win three Tours de France, while Salmon was no more than an also-ran. Henri Pélissier was also unearthed by Peugeot in this same way. These races, which were organized to provide riders with some experience in the sport, were so easygoing that some of those taking part, including the illustrious Oscar Egg, abandoned because they had overindulged at the many receptions during the race.

LEFT This independent tour was a great sporting and popular success. Léon Vallotton (centre) finished it in second place.

OPPOSITE The unfortunate Paul Duboc, nicknamed 'The Apple', was poisoned.

DEFRAYE HITS THE HEIGHTS

The 1912 race was a carbon copy of the previous year's, although on this occasion there were 131 starters. With Garrigou and Duboc lining up for Alcyon, Cornet at Le Globe, Faber at Automoto, Petit-Breton and Thys at Peugeot, and Lapize at La Française, all of the recent Tour heroes were set to participate. A lot was also being said about two Belgian riders: Peugeot's Philippe Thys, who had won the first three big stage races he'd taken part in as an independent the previous year when he was only 21, and Odile Defraye, who had dominated the Tour of Belgium to such an extent that Alcyon's Belgian representative had pushed the sky blue team into taking him on.

Charles Crupelandt got things under way by winning in Dunkirk. On the second stage, and coincidentally the one on which he had abandoned in 1909, Defraye led the field home in front of his team-mate Garrigou. Italy's Vicenzo Borgarello, from the J. B. Louvet team, took over as leader, but that only lasted as far as Belfort, where Defraye, who finished just behind Eugène Christophe (Armor), knocked him off top spot. It was a great year for Christophe, who won both of the major Alpine stages in Chamonix and Grenoble, where he tied Defraye for the lead.

Although Octave Lapize and Borgarello fought like demons, Alcyon and Defraye's grip was complete once the race left the Alps. Later on, the Belgian would tell a story that said much about his form at that moment: 'Early one morning I was almost an hour and a half behind Lapize and Christophe. I had punctured several times in the night, but the thought of abandoning never occurred to me. I kept on riding and, seven hours later, I caught Lapize and Christophe on a pass; they were climbing it on foot and pushing their bikes. When the stage finished I was 12 minutes ahead of them.'

Lapize was only two points behind in Perpignan, but however much he pressed he could not break the understanding between Alcyon and its affiliates, between Defraye and his Belgian compatriots. This led to him quitting the race in Luchon, where Defraye claimed his third win. There may have been collusion between the Belgians but Defraye was also in the form of his life, and Lapize, who only liked to win, realized that this was going to be beyond him.

By the finish in Paris, Defraye's advantage over Christophe had extended to 59 points, making him the first Belgian to win the Tour. Although Defraye would go on to win Milan–San Remo in 1913, this was his last great stage race victory. He made five more appearances in the Tour, but never finished the race again. Like Lapize and Henri Pélissier, he only completed the Tours that he was in with a chance of winning. Strangely, in 1924, 15 years after his first Tour appearance, he returned to the race in the second-category competition! By now a brush salesman, he abandoned on stage six.

FINAL STANDINGS

1 Odile Defraye (BEL) Alcyon, 49 points
2 Eugène Christophe (FRA) Armor, 108pts
3 Gustave Garrigou (FRA) Alcyon, 140pts
4 Marcel Buysse (BEL) Peugeot, 147pts
5 Jean Alavoine (FRA) Armor, 148pts
6 Philippe Thys (BEL) Peugeot, 148pts
7 Hector Tiberghien (BEL) Griffon, 149pts
8 Henri Devroye (BEL) Le Globe, 163pts
9 Félicien Salmon (BEL) Peugeot, 166pts
10 Alfons Spiessens (BEL) J. B. Louvet, 167pts

AVERAGE SPEED (OF WINNER): 27.763 KM/H
TOTAL DISTANCE RACED: 5,319 KM

OPPOSITE The first Belgian winner gives a smile – for once. After the 1912 Tour, Desgrange saw a report saying that the winner, Odile Defraye, had completed the course in 11,434 minutes, while the runner-up, Eugène Christophe, had taken 11,441 minutes, or a mere seven minutes more over 5,319 km. Desgrange realized that something wasn't quite right with the points system because the winner had finished with 49 points, while the runner-up had 108.5. In other words, the gap between them was 59.5 points, giving the impression of a crushing victory when this wasn't the case at all.

OPPOSITE TOP As well as being able to count on the support of his compatriots, Defraye also received backing from Louvet riders such as Luxembourger François Faber, who is pictured leading him towards the summit of the Galibier.

OPPOSITE BOTTOM With Alphonse Baugé pulling the strings, the Alcyon team was invincible: after Faber in 1909, Lapize in 1910 and Garrigou in 1911, it was the turn of Belgium's Odile Defraye.

RIGHT Caen. Feverish action at a control point and feed station where Tiberghien (18), Spiessens (27), Courcelles (127), Borgarello (29) and Christophe (21) are among those stopping to take on supplies.

BELOW Odile Defraye later shed some light on the salaries paid to riders in that era: 'We were very well paid. Personally, I received a monthly salary of 500 francs. I don't know how much that is worth now, but at the time that salary was three or four times as much as a policeman's...' To provide another perspective, Defraye went on to earn 3.5 francs a day in his next career as a brushmaker.

RONDE VAN FRANKRIJK, door O. Defraye

ODIEL DEFRAYE   Prijs : 0.15 fr.

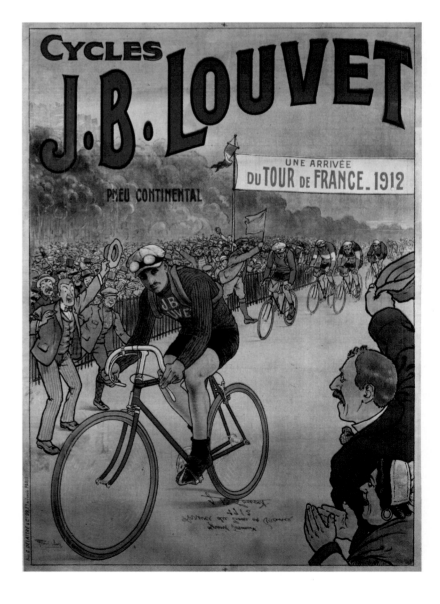

CYCLES J.B. LOUVET

PNEU CONTINENTAL

UNE ARRIVÉE DU TOUR DE FRANCE. 1912

'THE BASSET' BOUNDS TO VICTORY

Having noted the problems of a points-based classification, Desgrange judged that the race would benefit from a return to a classification based on time. This worked out well for Peugeot, who had been sulking since losing their stranglehold on the race in 1909. Having returned to the Tour in 1912, Peugeot signed up Alphonse Baugé and put together a line-up able to respond to the firepower of Baugé's former team, Alcyon, which still had Defraye at its hub. As well as past winners such as Faber and Garrigou, the Peugeot team featured precocious talent in the shape of Belgian Philippe Thys. Only 23, he was nicknamed 'The Basset Hound' because he sat very low over his bike and could be a bit cantankerous.

For the first time, the Tour followed an anti-clockwise route around France, which helped Thys, as it meant that he wasn't at a disadvantage compared to experienced campaigners. New Peugeot recruit Eugène Christophe commented: 'The race really begins in Luchon.' By that point, 96 of the 140 starters had already abandoned, as Thys led two other Peugeot riders, Marcel Buysse and Garrigou. The tide had turned in favour of riders bearing Peugeot's rampant lion.

Dubbed 'the lion cubs', Baugé's Peugeot riders could have won the race with three different riders: Buysse, Garrigou or Thys. Buysse took the lead in Marseille, then lost it to Thys in Nice after his handlebars broke and he lost three hours. He was the second Peugeot champion to suffer mechanical mishap. Christophe's chances had gone during the horrific Bayonne–Luchon stage. He had gone into it only 4-55 down on Defraye and led the field over the Aubisque. But on the descent of the Tourmalet, Thys overtook him and then Christophe's forks broke, forcing him to walk 14 km down the mountain before he found a forge at Sainte-Marie-de-Campan, where the former locksmith repaired the forks himself. He should perhaps have abandoned like Defraye, but he persisted and arrived in Luchon almost four hours down on Thys. When asked why he had pressed on, he replied: 'For the team, for the race…'

In the Alps and all the way in to the finish, Peugeot took complete control. Buysse won four times and Faber twice. However, the Peugeot riders did have to keep an eye on one man: 'old' Petit-Breton, who was only 30 and had got a new lease of life at Automoto, where he was making very good use of a derailleur gearing system, one of the few riders to do so. With just two stages remaining, he had unexpectedly cut Thys's lead back to an hour and three minutes. Everyone knew that anything could happen on the cobbles that followed, and it did: Petit-Breton went on the attack and opened up a gap of an hour on Thys. But he crashed and was forced to abandon. Thys crashed too, but managed to continue. In the Parc des Princes, 'The Basset Hound' claimed victory in a race that was so brutal that only 25 riders crossed the finish line.

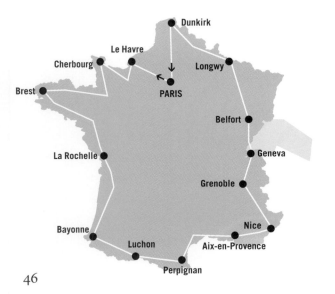

FINAL STANDINGS

1 Philippe Thys (BEL) Peugeot 197:54:00
2 Gustave Garrigou (FRA) Peugeot +8:37
3 Marcel Buysse (BEL) Peugeot +3:30:55
4 Firmin Lambot (BEL) Griffon +4:12:45
5 François Faber (LUX) Peugeot +6:26:04
6 Alfons Spiessens (BEL) J. B. Louvet +7:57:52
7 Eugène Christophe (FRA) Peugeot +14:06:35
8 Camillo Bertarelli (ITA) no team +16:21:38
9 Joseph Vandaele (BEL) J. B. Louvet +16:39:53
10 Émile Engel (FRA) Peugeot +16:52:34

AVERAGE SPEED (OF WINNER): 27.22 KM/H
TOTAL DISTANCE RACED: 5,388 KM

OPPOSITE The Parc des Princes saw another Belgian winner, this time Thys.

ABOVE Young shepherds look on rather perplexed
as Firmin Lambot takes to his feet on the goat track
that doubles as the road over the Aubisque pass
in the Pyrenees.

OPPOSITE A rider in the process of abandoning the Tour.
In 1913, 115 out of the 140 starters quit the race.

THYS UNDER THREAT

The 12th edition of the Tour de France was almost a carbon copy of the 11th, both in terms of distance (5,405 km), starters (145 instead of 140) and protagonists. Baugé's Peugeot team was still built around Thys, with Faber, Garrigou and Christophe as back-up. But it had been strengthened by the arrival of Émile Georget, Firmin Lambot and Henri Pélissier. These moves meant La Française and Alcyon had been weakened, although the sky blues had kept Defraye and re-signed Marcel Buysse and his brother Lucien. The Italian *campionissimo* Constante Girardengo was also among the starters. Another surprise was the presence of the Phébus team, which included two Australians.

The various forces gathered for battle in Saint-Cloud on 28 June, the same day that Archduke Franz Ferdinand, heir to the Austro-Hungarian empire, was assassinated in Sarajevo by Serb nationalist Princip. For the time being, though, the only thing on the riders' minds was reaching Le Havre, 388 dusty and difficult kilometres away. Twenty-seven riders failed to reach the port, where Thys led in ten of the favourites.

Peugeot maintained an iron grip on proceedings, winning every stage except those into Cherbourg, Marseille and Nice – 12 out of 15 in total. At the same time, the sound of war drums was building and the race was effectively fighting a rearguard action. The order for general mobilization didn't come until 3 August, but the clouds of war were already gathering when, on 26 July, 54 riders completed a lap of honour at the Parc des Princes, where Thys was once again hailed as the champion.

It was perhaps his easiest Tour success. He was the leader from the off, although for one brief moment he did share that position with Alcyon's Rossius. He regularly demonstrated the edge he had on his rivals. In Luchon, he finished 34 minutes ahead of team-mate Henri Pélissier and 46 clear of another Peugeot rider, Jean Alavoine. In Grenoble, the four leading Peugeot riders finished 12 minutes clear of the rest, resulting in Defraye and Lapize throwing in the towel. From that point on, Peugeot's grip on the podium places wasn't threatened.

At Longwy, ahead of the stage over the fearsome northern cobbles, second-placed Pélissier was more than half an hour down on Thys, but ready to spring an ambush. There had been plenty of drama on the same stage the previous year, when Thys had struggled. He did so again. Thys suffered a broken wheel and had to replace it, picking up a time penalty of 30 minutes, which left Pélissier just one minute and 50 seconds behind the Belgian. The final stage was very tense. Pélissier won it, but Thys was right on his heels. There were no less than eight Peugeot riders in the top ten, the top two of them split by the narrowest winning margin in the race's history. That feat was, however, overshadowed by dark clouds rolling in from the east. Cycling jerseys were about to be swapped for army trenchcoats.

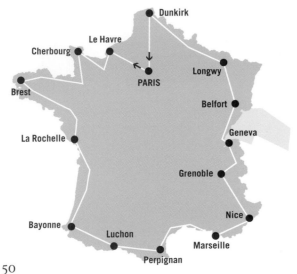

FINAL STANDINGS

1 Philippe Thys (BEL) Peugeot-Wolber 200:28:48
2 Henri Pélissier (FRA) Peugeot-Wolber +1:50
3 Jean Alavoine (FRA) Peugeot-Wolber +36:53
4 Jean Rossius (BEL) Alcyon-Soly +1:57:05
5 Gustave Garrigou (FRA) Peugeot-Wolber +3:00:21
6 Émile Georget (FRA) Peugeot-Wolber +3:20:59
7 Alfons Spiessens (BEL) J. B. Louvet-Continental +3:53:55
8 Firmin Lambot (BEL) Peugeot-Wolber +5:08:54
9 François Faber (LUX) Peugeot-Wolber +6:15:53
10 Louis Heusghem (BEL) Peugeot-Wolber +7:49:02

AVERAGE SPEED (OF WINNER): 26.96 KM/H
TOTAL DISTANCE RACED: 5,405 KM

OPPOSITE TOP Used since 1911, the Col de Valgelaye or d'Allos (2,250 m) is still a test for the best riders. Here, Faber, Garrigou and Thys, each of them Tour champions, tackle it.

OPPOSITE BOTTOM The top riders at the 1914 Tour, the likes of Thys, Pélissier, Jean Alavoine, Rossius, Garrigou, Émile Georget, Lambot, Faber etc, all drank 'Koto wine containing Peruvian coca', according to an advertorial that appeared in *L'Auto*. Less irritating than tea and coffee, and with extraordinary stimulating properties, the Koto restaurant in Paris produced it by soaking Peruvian coca in port and adding a number of other products scientifically proven to be of benefit. Once the preserve of millionaires, it had become accessible to all with a bottle costing 3.50 francs.

The Tour emerges stronger than ever

ON 3 AUGUST 1914, Germany declared war on France. The conflict was expected to last just a few months – there were plenty of people around over-optimistically claiming that 'we will be in Berlin tomorrow' – but it would develop into 'The Great War', a conflict that was characterized by the trenches, mud and cold, and by the use of planes, tanks and gas. At the end of hostilities, millions were dead on both sides, millions more were injured. On 11 November 1918, the armistice signed at Rethondes would bring an end to the slaughter as Germany surrendered.

The 12th Tour had only just finished on 26 July when riders started to receive their orders for mobilization. The crisis that led to war had begun on 28 June, the same day that the Tour had started in Saint-Cloud. It was on that day that Archduke Franz Ferdinand of Austria was assassinated in Sarajevo. As a result of the alliances and treaties in force at the time, the entire world, and Europe in particular, moved unstoppably down the road towards death and destruction.

There would not be another Tour for some years, and by the time the next one did come around, the war had taken a heavy toll on the cycling fraternity. Tour winners François Faber, Octave Lapize and Henri Petit-Breton all perished. Petit-Breton played an important role in the 'taxis of the Marne' operation in September 1914. Realizing that Paris was under threat of capture by German forces, the governor of Paris, General Galleni, commandeered taxis to ferry troops up to the front, saving the French capital. Petit-Breton remained on active service at the front until, in 1917, he fell

victim to the kind of car accident that could have happened absolutely anywhere. His great rival and friend, Octave Lapize, perished in that same year. Having become a pilot, he was shot down during a mission on 14 July after engaging three enemy planes in combat. Faber died in the trenches in 1915 in the Battle of Carency as he attempted to save a friend.

In the end, more than 50 Tour riders paid the ultimate price, and paying tribute to them all is difficult, but we would like to pick out two for special mention: Pierre-Gonzague Privat and François Lafourcade. The former was an artist, a caricaturist and poster-designer of great talent who rode four Tours, finishing 11th in 1907. He also acted as a soigneur on the race and, more famously, as an illustrator. With regard to Lafourcade, who died when learning to fly in 1917, he was 13th in 1907 and stood out even more when he was 14th in 1910, which was the year that the Pyrenees were tackled for the first time. It was Lafourcade, riding on home terrain, who saved the Tour that year. Heading over the summit of the Tourmalet, Lapize, who was out on his own at the front, had just accused the organizers of being 'assassins' and was on the point of abandoning, a move that would have thrown the whole race into doubt, when Lafourcade, a rather modest performer, caught up with and overtook the champion, pricking Lapize's pride to the extent that he soon got back up to racing speed.

It wasn't only the riders who went beyond the call of duty. Their boss did too. Although he was 52, Henri

Desgrange enlisted in 1917. He became an officer, wearing his legion of honour medal in combat.

The Tour restarted on 29 June 1919 with its 13th edition in very difficult conditions. But at least it got back under way. It provided the whole country with a morale boost. Eugène Christophe and Firmin Lambot, the heroes of 1913 and 1914, were on the start line. The race didn't feature the Ballon d'Alsace, but did stop in Strasbourg and Metz, which had both been liberated. A new jersey appeared, yellow in colour, which made the race leader stand out and would light up the race and the world. Christophe was the first to wear it, but lost it when his forks broke on the cobbled roads of the north. That area, between Dunkirk and Valenciennes, was dubbed 'The Hell of the North' because it had been completely torn apart by shelling. Roads that had been full of potholes and treacherous even before the war had become completely hellish. But the Tour would emerge stronger than ever from having tackled them.

OPPOSITE At Caen, during his ride to victory in the Tour, Octave Lapize experienced his first flight. Léon Morane was at the controls of a Blériot. This was the starting point for his vocation, as 'Tatave' would go on to become a fighter pilot during the Great War. He disappeared in combat on 14 July 1917.

Capuze & Morane sur Blériot

THE REBIRTH OF THE TOUR

Although the Treaty of Versailles had been signed the evening before the race started, officially putting an end to the First World War, traces of conflict were everywhere. There had been so many losses within the professional ranks that only 69 riders set out from the Parc des Princes, and the Tour limped along through the ruins and general shortages. The bicycle manufacturers had been making weapons and were still returning to 'civilian' production, so they grouped their meagre resources into a consortium – La Sportive, which was managed by Alphonse Baugé. Most of the starters wore the team's grey jersey.

The Tour set off towards Le Havre, where the Belgians Thys and Rossius had completed a double six years earlier. Rossius was victorious, but later received a 30-minute penalty for trying to help Thys, who was one of 26 riders to abandon. Henri Pélissier took over as the leader. Pélissier won again at Cherbourg, but racing was hard for men who had not been in the habit of competing. At Les Sables-d'Olonne, the standings were tipped upside down: Jean Alavoine won and Eugène Christophe took the lead. Now 34, 'the old Gaul' had an 11-minute lead on Henri Pélissier as the race's 20 survivors set out on the 482-km stage to Bayonne.

Feeling that victory was slipping away from them, Henri Pélissier and his brother Francis both abandoned. The field, still led by Christophe, was now just 17-strong. As well as dwindling numbers, the Tour had another problem: it was hard for anyone to pick out the race leader as the whole peloton was wearing grey. Desgrange and his team decided to find some way of distinguishing the leader and livening up the race. In the end, it was Baugé who suggested: 'What if we gave a yellow jersey to the leader? Yellow just like your paper.' Desgrange hardly paused for thought. He immediately put in an order for some yellow jerseys and announced its introduction in *L'Auto*'s yellow pages.

On 17 July, as the race reached Grenoble, a package of yellow jerseys finally arrived, enabling Desgrange to proceed with a formal presentation. Two days later, feeling both proud and moved, Christophe set out for Geneva in the yellow jersey, the first rider to race in it. He had gone close to victory in 1913, but now felt his time had come. However, on the penultimate stage to Dunkirk there was a final twist. Christophe crashed, but quickly remounted. He began to chase Firmin Lambot, who was 30 minutes behind in the standings, but realized his forks had snapped. He managed to get a new set at a bike shop in Raismes and fitted them himself in the adjoining workshop. But the repair had taken him more than an hour. Chasing forlornly, he crashed again at a level crossing. That evening, now lying third, Christophe took the yellow jersey to Lambot's room.

Fortune was on the side of Firmin Lambot, who won the Tour on his fifth attempt. However, Christophe, viewed as the moral victor, received the most rapturous welcome at the Parc des Princes. The average speed was the slowest in Tour history and only ten riders were classified. But what mattered most was that the Tour was off the ground again.

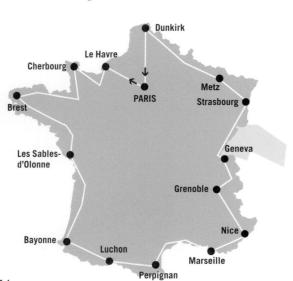

FINAL STANDINGS

1 Firmin Lambot (BEL) 231:07:15
2 Jean Alavoine (FRA) +1:42:54
3 Eugène Christophe (FRA) +2:26:31
4 Léon Scieur (BEL) +2:52:15
5 Honoré Barthélémy (FRA) +4:14:22
6 Jacques Coomans (BEL) +15:21:34
7 Luigi Lucotti (ITA) +16:01:12
8 Joseph Van Daele (BEL) +18:23:02
9 Alfred Steux (BEL) +20:29:01
10 Jules Nempon (FRA) +21:44:12

AVERAGE SPEED (OF WINNER): 24.056 KM/H
TOTAL DISTANCE RACED: 5,560 KM

OPPOSITE TOP At 33 years old, this was an unexpected success for Firmin Lambot.

OPPOSITE BOTTOM LEFT Jean Alavoine sprints to take his fifth stage on the Parc des Princes track. Were it not for the multiple punctures and a major breakdown, he might have won the Tour.

OPPOSITE BOTTOM RIGHT Eugène Christophe didn't win, but received some consolation in having his portrait painted by Pico. He did wear the yellow jersey again in 1922 at the age of 37. In 1970 he was buried in that jersey.

AN ARMCHAIR RIDE FOR THYS

The La Sportive team was still the dominant force at the Tour, which featured 113 starters divided between first- and second-class riders. The Italian Luigi Lucotti wasn't there, nor was Paul Duboc, but all of the other protagonists from 1919 were. Once again, they set off towards Normandy for 5,500 km and 15 stages of racing. From the outset the Belgians set the pace, taking the top three places in Le Havre – they would go on to fill the top seven in Paris!

The Pélissier brothers, who considered themselves thoroughbreds and took pleasure in referring to the Belgians as 'workhorses', yet again bowed out of the Tour, declaring that the Belgians were invincible. Francis Pélissier withdrew in Brest, and Henri followed after taking victories in Brest and Sables. He quit in open countryside after being penalized for throwing a tyre, a gesture of pique that led Desgrange to comment: 'He doesn't know how to suffer, he will never win the Tour.' A number of French riders tried to shake up the Belgians, notably Chassot, Bellenger, Dhers and Jacquinot, but their efforts were in vain. Firmin Lambot, Jean Rossius, Louis Heusghem and his brother Hector shared the bouquets with Léon Scieur and Philippe Thys.

For the most part, the riders were acclaimed by garrisoned troops and huge crowds. However, as they passed what had been the Great War's front line in Montdidier and Abbeville,

the pavements of the devastated towns and villages were often deserted. But whatever the setting and terrain, the Belgians were almost complete in their domination. Only Honoré Barthélémy managed to unsettle them briefly after Eugène Christophe, beset by a problem in his kidneys, had to throw in the towel in the Pyrenees.

Lambot set the pace over virtually every pass. The Heusghem brothers and Léon Scieur were never far behind, nor was Philippe Thys, who would have worn the yellow jersey almost from start to finish if the organizers had thought to bring it to the race. Instead, a torn sweater had to make do as far as Nice, where the organizers conjured up a replacement. The Belgians continued relentlessly on, their winning run only briefly halted by Félix Goethals, who was victorious in his hometown of Dunkirk. Out of 15 stages, the Belgian champions bagged 12…

Thys's average speed was a meagre 24 km/h as he became the first rider to win the Tour three times, following his victories in 1913 and 1914. 'I never suffered in this Tour, because I had prepared myself to race it,' said the Belgian. French honour was saved to some extent by the diminutive figure of Honoré Barthélémy, who finished eighth of the 22 survivors, despite a fractured shoulder and a dislocated wrist. Although he finished five hours down on the winner, he was carried in triumph around the Parc des Princes.

FINAL STANDINGS

1 Philippe Thys (BEL) 231:07:15
2 Hector Heusghem (BEL) +57:21
3 Firmin Lambot (BEL) +1:39:35
4 Léon Scieur (BEL) +1:44:58
5 Émile Masson (BEL) +2:56:52
6 Louis Heusghem (BEL) +3:40:47
7 Jean Rossius (BEL) +3:49:55
8 Honoré Barthélémy (FRA) +5:35:19
9 Félix Goethals (FRA) +9:23:07
10 Joseph Vandaele (BEL) +10:45:41

AVERAGE SPEED (OF WINNER): 24.072 KM/H
TOTAL DISTANCE RACED: 5,503 KM

OPPOSITE José Pelletier, who was 12th in the final standings, led home the second-class riders, providing an unexpected success for his small bike manufacturer.

OVERLEAF At 2,250 m, the Col d'Allos takes a lot of climbing, but in 1920 it wasn't a problem for the Belgians, who dominated in the mountains as much as they did everywhere else. The yellow jersey of Thys leads the way, but Lambot will be the first over the summit.

CYCLES

Cl. Delage

RABOISSON

DORFEUILLE

5.400 Kilomètres SANS AUCUN ACCIDENT de MACHINE

TOUR DE FRANCE 1920

1er José PELLETIER

(Cat B)

4. PARTANTS _ 3. ARRIVANTS

AGENT :

BELGIAN 'LOCO' GETS THE TOUR BACK ON TRACK

The 15th Tour de France closely resembled the previous year's race. There were 123 starters in the Parc des Princes, but it was hard to see anyone denying Belgium another victory. Although the French riders Barthélémy, Christophe and Goethals gave their all, the Pélissier brothers were absent because their feud with the organizers was continuing. Could the Italian climber Luigi Lucotti, who was back at the Tour, step into their shoes and show he was strong enough to upset predictions? Well, in short, no he couldn't.

The differences from the 1920 race were slight. Belgian riders didn't fill the top seven places in the final standings this time, but there were seven of them in the top ten. The winner was Léon Scieur, who came from Florennes, just as 1919 winner Firmin Lambot did. Another coincidence is that he won at the age of 33, the same age Lambot had been when he won. They were both Pisces as well.

The greatest threat to Scieur came from other Belgians, notably Hector Heusghem, who finished second in 1920 and established himself as runner-up to Scieur in the Pyrenees. However, he failed to trouble Scieur unduly. Nicknamed 'The Locomotive', Scieur was simply too strong. He took the yellow jersey on the second stage and continued to extend his lead as far as Luchon, where Heusghem cut his advantage to four minutes. But Scieur powered clear again. He did have some

problems on the cobbles during the penultimate stage when he had to change a wheel. The rules at the time meant that he had to ride for 300 km with the damaged wheel strapped to his back, which left him injured and permanently scarred.

The fact that Belgians only triumphed in nine of the fifteen stages was down to the French scooping five of them. Félix Goethals won three, while Honoré Barthélémy, Romain Bellenger and the Italian Lucotti took one each. However, the dominance of the Flemish and Walloon riders was almost total, even though Rossius, Louis Heusghem and Philippe Thys, who had been hit by illness, abandoned on the second stage. Pictures from the race back up this assessment. Whatever the surface of the road, whether it was steep or not, wherever they were in France, the same riders are almost always at the front: Heusghem, Lambot, Lucotti, Mottiat and Scieur.

In the Alsatian town of Dalstein, the little Swiss rider Henri Collé surprised the locals by stopping to enjoy a tankard of beer. When you are 17th and 15 hours behind Scieur, 5 minutes doesn't matter too much, although this may no doubt have upset Desgrange, who thought Scieur's rivals had given up and tried various schemes to force them onto the offensive. However, there was no stopping 'The Locomotive'. Although he only learned to ride a bike at the age of 22, Léon Scieur got the Tour back on track.

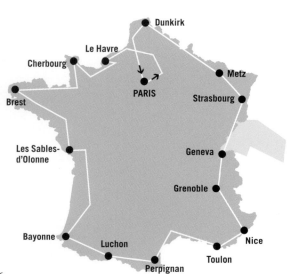

FINAL STANDINGS

1 Léon Scieur (BEL) 221:50:26
2 Hector Heusghem (BEL) +18:36
3 Honoré Barthélémy (FRA) +2:01:00
4 Luigi Lucotti (ITA) +2:39:18
5 Hector Tiberghien (BEL) +4:33:19
6 Victor Lenaers (BEL) +4:53:23
7 Leon Despontin (BEL) +5:01: 54
8 Camile Leroy (BEL) +7:56:27
9 Firmin Lambot (BEL) +8:26:25
10 Félix Goethals (FRA) +8:42:26

AVERAGE SPEED (OF WINNER): 24.72 KM/H
TOTAL DISTANCE RACED: 5,484 KM

OPPOSITE, CLOCKWISE FROM TOP LEFT
Léon Scieur with his wife.

Dalstein. Swiss riders Collé and Parel knock back a beer.

Hector Heusghem climbs the Galibier, where he will be the fourth rider to reach the summit.

Barthélémy flies down the Galibier just as he had done in 1919.

THE OLDEST TOUR WINNER

Bad luck was the dominant theme of the 16th Tour. But bad luck for some meant good luck for others, and Belgium's Firmin Lambot had some past history in that respect having won the 1919 Tour thanks to Eugène Christophe's broken forks. Would fortune shine for a second time on the man from Florennes? It would require a miracle to do so since he was 36.

As well as luck, the other guiding theme was experience. Apart from the Pélissier brothers, who were absent once again, all of the old stagers were on the start line, including all of the winners from 1914 onwards. Christophe, Hector Heusghem and Jean Alavoine added to the strength of the field that faced fearsome new summits such as the Col de Vars and the Col d'Izoard. Thys and French riders Robert Jacquinot, Christophe, Romain Bellenger and Alavoine were on form right from the start. They shared the bouquets and the yellow jersey between them as the race passed through the Pyrenees and Alps. Others fared less well. Scieur was eliminated straight away with a broken bike. By the time the race had reached Luchon, almost 70 others had joined him on the sidelines.

Well into his 35th year, Jean Alavoine was in the form of his life. He shook up the peloton on the marathon stage between Les Sables-d'Olonne and Bayonne and followed up by winning both stages in the Pyrenees, where he climbed like a rocket. He didn't lead over the Tourmalet, but only because the summit was covered in snow, otherwise he surely would have done. His main victim during this run was 37-year-old Christophe, who ceded the yellow jersey to his slightly younger compatriot. Christophe's hopes disappeared in the Alps when, once again, his forks broke – this time on the Galibier.

Thanks to Thys and Émile Masson, the Belgians took the reins in the Alps. Like Alavoine, Thys took three stages in a row and rattled the French yellow jersey by romping over the Vars and the Izoard. Under huge pressure, Alavoine panicked and crumbled, his cause not helped by punctures and mechanical problems. He couldn't withstand the Belgian wave led by Masson and Heusghem that engulfed him on the road to Strasbourg. He lost the yellow jersey and dropped back to third place, just behind Lambot, who couldn't stay with the Frenchman in the Pyrenees, but had performed much better in the Alps.

New race leader Heusghem's grip on the yellow jersey was, however, short-lived. He crashed on the next stage and, contrary to the rules, continued with a new bike. He was hit with a one-hour time penalty, which meant the yellow jersey found its way onto Lambot's shoulders. Two stages away from Paris, the veteran had the race won. Firmin Lambot remains the oldest winner of the Tour at 36 years, 4 months and 9 days. To those who talked of miracles, Firmin responded: 'To win the Tour, firstly you need good health, then luck. Knowing how to climb only gets you third place.'

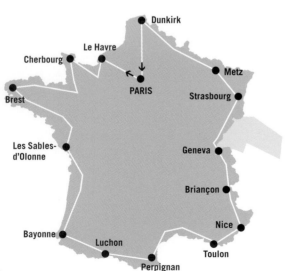

FINAL STANDINGS

1 Firmin Lambot (BEL) 222:08:06
2 Jean Alavoine (FRA) +41:15
3 Félix Sellier (BEL) +42:02
4 Hector Heusghem (BEL) +43:56
5 Victor Lenaers (BEL) +45:32
6 Hector Tiberghien (BEL) +1:21:35
7 Léon Despontin (BEL) +2:24:29
8 Eugène Christophe (FRA) +3:25:39
9 Jean Rossius (BEL) +3:26:06
10 Gaston Degy (FRA) +3:49:13

AVERAGE SPEED (OF WINNER): 24.196 KM/H
TOTAL DISTANCE RACED: 5,375 KM

OPPOSITE TOP At 36 years and four months, Firmin Lambot remains the oldest winner of the Tour.

OPPOSITE BOTTOM Parc des Princes. A second victory for modest Lambot.

Lambot 1° Classement

ABOVE A line of climbers head around a hairpin bend. It's hard to establish who the riders hidden by the musettes are but it could well be Alavoine, Thys and Christophe.

LEFT Geneva. At the entrance to the city's velodrome, assistant race director Robert Desmarets runs behind Belgium's Émile Masson, who is the first man into the arena. Assuming he doesn't slip over and no one runs out in front of him, victory should be his.

OPPOSITE Nice–Briançon. Riders stopped either to change gear by flipping their rear wheel over as Théophile Beeckman and Hector Heusghem (above) are seen doing here, or to repair a puncture like Jean Alavoine (below). The two Belgians were wearing jerseys loaned by clubs in Nice, since their soigneurs had packed their jerseys with their bags and sent them on to the next stop.

A FRENCH WINNER AT LAST

The manufacturers finally returned to the race, which was divided into three categories. Francis and Henri Pélissier returned too with the Automoto team for the first time since their abject abandon in 1920. Would they see it through on this occasion with team boss Pierre Pierrard driving them on? He had recruited a little-known Italian, Ottavio Bottecchia, to the team, to goad them into unleashing their fabulous prowess. Whatever their state of mind, they would once again have to deal with a mass of Belgian talent. The likes of Thys, Lambot, Scieur, Heusghem and Rossius would not give way easily.

Robert Jacquinot led off by winning in Le Havre. Bottecchia was second. Surprisingly, the revitalized Pélissier brothers were up there too. Their new team-mate surprised them, and even more so when he won in Cherbourg and took the yellow jersey. On the following stage to Brest the Pélissier brothers completed a brotherly one-two under the watchful eye of Bottecchia, who kept the lead. Romain Bellenger did capture the jersey for a couple of stages, but Bottecchia regained control of it in the Pyrenees, where Jean Alavoine won both stages again while the Italian showed himself to be a superb climber.

Although Lucien Buysse did win in Toulon, the Belgians steadily fell by the wayside. Lambot and Scieur didn't reach Perpignan. Philippe Thys also abandoned before the Alps.

Bottecchia still led heading into the range, but neither he nor anyone else could resist Henri Pélissier's magnificent attack on the Izoard. The Italian lost 40 minutes, the yellow jersey and the Tour. The Pélissier brothers had finally shown what they were made of.

The pair completed another double in Geneva and from then on French riders dominated, despite Alavoine's departure in the Alps. As Henri Pélissier cruised towards Paris in the yellow jersey, his compatriots took all of the victory bouquets. At the Parc des Princes, where Félix Goethals took his second consecutive stage win, Pélissier's unexpected victory provoked scenes of hysteria. Sales of *L'Auto* had already risen to 600,000 copies, but the story of Pélissier's success pushed them to more than a million, a figure not seen since Gustave Garrigou had taken the last French victory in 1911.

To emphasize the tightness of Automoto's grip on the race, Bottecchia was second, while faithful Francis Pélissier was 23rd. Automoto splashed the name of the Pélissier brothers on posters and commemorative books, capitalizing on the euphoria of a French victory. Only one man wasn't convinced by Automoto's triumph. Two-time winner Lambot believed he would have won if he hadn't been halted by a broken pedal in the Pyrenees. However, Lambot had already leaned heavily on Lady Luck…

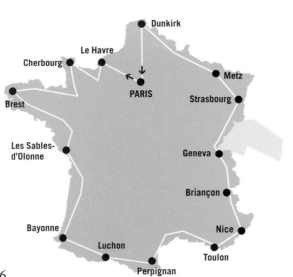

FINAL STANDINGS

1　Henri Pélissier (FRA) Automoto 222:15:30
2　Ottavio Bottecchia (ITA) Automoto +30:41
3　Romain Bellenger (FRA) Peugeot-Wolber +1:04:43
4　Hector Tiberghien (BEL) Peugeot-Wolber +1:29:16
5　Arsène Alancourt (FRA) Armor +2:06:40
6　Henri Collé (SWI) Griffon +2:28:43
7　Léon Despontin (BEL) Peugeot-Wolber +2:39:49
8　Lucien Buysse (BEL) Automoto +2:40:11
9　Eugène Dhers (FRA) Armor +2:59:09
10　Marcel Huot (FRA) Griffon +3:16:56

AVERAGE SPEED (OF WINNER): 24.233 KM/H
TOTAL DISTANCE RACED: 5,386 KM

OPPOSITE Saint-Étienne-based bike manufacturer Automoto, although clearly delighted at having taken first and second place thanks to Pélissier and Bottecchia, seem to have been taken by surprise by the success – judging by the minimalist nature of this poster.

UN FRANÇAIS GAGNE
LE
TOUR DE FRANCE 1923

5600 Kilomètres

1er H. PÉLISSIER   2ème BOTTECCHIA

SUR
BICYCLETTE
AUTOMOTO
PNEUS HUTCHINSON

CYCLES AUTOMOTO _ 152, Avenue Malakoff. PARIS

BOTTECCHIA CROWNED AS PÉLISSIERS QUIT

In the euphoria of his 1923 victory, Henri Pélissier predicted Ottavio Bottecchia would be his successor. However, Pélissier couldn't have imagined that it would happen the following year when he was the favourite for the title. As he had been the previous year, Bottecchia was on song from the start. He won in Le Havre to take the yellow jersey. Now 30, the former builder from Fruili was on the road to Tour domination.

He had assisted the Pélissier brothers in 1923 and now it appeared to be their turn to return the favour. However, they didn't see things that way. On the third stage they quit with a typical show of pique at the control point in Coutances. Their complaint? They objected to a rule stating riders had to finish with all the kit they had started with, including clothing. Henri Pélissier could not throw away jerseys he had worn to keep off the early morning chill.

Their decision to quit took on greater significance when, as they shared a hot chocolate with team-mate Maurice Ville who had also been dragged into the mess, they were approached by a reporter. Albert Londres was a special correspondent from *Petit Parisien*. He noted down an outpouring of accusations from the two brothers. Under the headline 'The convicts of the road', Londres' paper revealed the reality of the Tour to the public. The Pélissier brothers talked of suffering, pills and potions, saying, 'We keep going on dynamite.' While they weren't wrong about everything, they certainly exaggerated and distorted the facts.

Yet all that made no difference to Bottecchia. The Pyrenees were the springboard for his victory as he triumphed at Luchon and Perpignan. A hard worker who was as strong on the flat as he was in the mountains, he stretched his lead to 50 minutes over his nearest rival, Alcyon's Luxembourg champion, Nicolas Frantz. His margin was such that in the Alps Bottecchia only needed to control attacks made by his compatriots Aimo and Brunero. Frantz, who was marvellous on the Galibier, did pull back some time on Bottecchia, but didn't trouble the Italian, who was well supported by Belgian team-mate Lucien Buysse. On the final day Bottecchia showed he hadn't exhausted his reserves by claiming his fourth stage win.

The battle between Automoto in purple and Alcyon in sky blue had been a gripping one and was set to continue. For now, Automoto boss Pierre Pierrard and Bottecchia held the upper hand. Where Automoto had failed in 1914 with *campionissimo* Costante Girardengo, it had succeeded with Ottavio Bottecchia, transforming him from an almost unknown rider, who had only come fifth in the 1923 Giro d'Italia behind Girardengo, into the new *campionissimo*. He was the first Italian to win the Tour and the first champion to wear the yellow jersey from beginning to end. The Tour's sparkle had been restored and Automoto naturally profited from it, as sales of the bike that carried its champions to victory soared.

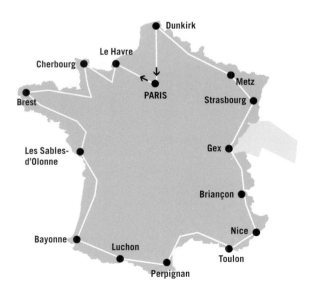

FINAL STANDINGS

1 Ottavio Bottecchia (ITA) Automoto 226:18:21
2 Nicolas Frantz (LUX) Alcyon +35:36
3 Lucien Buysse (BEL) Automoto +1:32:13
4 Bartolomeo Aimo (ITA) Legnano +1:32:47
5 Théophile Beeckman (BEL) Griffon +2:11:12
6 Joseph Muller (FRA) Peugeot +2:35:33
7 Arsène Alancourt (FRA) Armor +2:41:31
8 Romain Bellenger (FRA) Peugeot +2:51:09
9 Omer Huyse (BEL) Lapize +2:58:13
10 Hector Tiberghien (BEL) Peugeot +3:05:04

AVERAGE SPEED (OF WINNER): 23.971 KM/H
TOTAL DISTANCE RACED: 5,425 KM

Legend has it that Bottecchia never laughed. This picture shows that's wrong as the Italian (right) jokes with team-mate Lucien Buysse. He has just found out that a policeman from Montreuil-sur-Mer has retrieved the knee-bandage he threw away.

AUTOMOTO STEAMROLLER THE OPPOSITION

If you had cast an eye over the 130 riders on the start line in Vésinet on 21 June, you would have been hard pushed to pick a winner. Although some worried that the race would be nothing more than a procession for Automoto, the ongoing war between Ottavio Bottecchia's team and Alcyon was set to be fiercer than ever. Automoto lined up with three former champions, as Philippe Thys and Henri Pélissier joined Bottecchia. Alcyon, who wanted to return to its pre-war glory days, was counting on Nicolas Frantz, Bartolomeo Aimo and Félix Sellier. With old campaigners such as Christophe and Alavoine also in the field, the scene was set for an epic encounter.

Bottecchia claimed the first bouquet in Le Havre, but this was to be no start-to-finish romp. Alcyon attacked in bursts and pinched the yellow jersey from the Italian in Brest, or at least Adelin Benoît, from the Alcyon subsidiary Thomann, did. Bottecchia was just as concerned by the early loss of the Pélissier brothers and Thys. He could, fortunately, rely on Lucien Buysse in the Pyrenees, where he believed he could win the Tour. However, having reclaimed the yellow jersey with victories in Bordeaux and Bayonne, he lost it again to Benoît on the first day in the range. Although Bottecchia missed out again on the stage to Perpignan, his conqueror was Frantz and not Benoît, who was hampered by a knee injury.

Bottecchia had the jersey back and defended it in the Alps, largely thanks to Buysse, who was in the form of his life while his leader seemed below his best. However, the Belgian stuck to team orders. His turn would surely come. Alcyon did pull off a fine victory in the mountains thanks to Aimo, but the Bottecchia-Buysse tandem had them under control. Alcyon's attempt to unsettle their rivals all but ended when Frantz fell ill and lost more than 35 minutes. His team-mate Aimo inherited his podium place, but at the finish he was 56 minutes behind his compatriot Bottecchia, who confirmed his status as the *campionissimo* by completing his second Tour victory with a prestigious stage win in the Parc des Princes.

Many suggested that Bottecchia had not had it so easy as the previous year, partly because Buysse had closed the gap between them, finishing 54 minutes behind instead of 90 as had been the case the year before. However, his average speed improved markedly. None of this bothered him, though. The Tour was won and he spent the final afternoon smiling as he handed out mountains of postcards with fellow Italian Alfonso Piccin. The French had little reason to smile. The first Frenchman to place, and the only one to have won a stage, was Romain Bellenger in 11th position. At 37, Alavoine was 13th and, aged 40, Eugène Christophe finished his last Tour in 18th place. A new generation was coming…

FINAL STANDINGS

1 Ottavio Bottecchia (ITA) Automoto 219:10:18
2 Lucien Buysse (BEL) Automoto +54:20
3 Bartolomeo Aimo (ITA) Alcyon +56:37
4 Nicolas Frantz (LUX) Alcyon +1:11:24
5 Albert Dejonghe (BEL) J. B. Louvet +1:27:42
6 Théophile Beeckman (BEL) Thomann +2:24:43
7 Omer Huyse (BEL) Armor +2:33:38
8 Auguste Verdyck (BEL) Christophe +2:44:36
9 Félix Sellier (BEL) Alcyon +2:45:59
10 Federico Gay (ITA) Météore +4:06:03

AVERAGE SPEED (OF WINNER): 24.775 KM/H
TOTAL DISTANCE RACED: 5,430 KM

OPPOSITE Although the Tour could be won on the climbs, it could also be lost on the descents. Bottecchia, who was a poor downhiller, knew this all too well and always tried to take a good lead in the mountains.

BUYSSE'S MOMENT FINALLY ARRIVES

The 20th Tour was always likely to be special. The war between Automoto and Alcyon was still raging and would be fought over the longest Tour in history at 5,745 km. In addition, this was the first Tour to start outside Paris, in Évian to be precise. The drama began on the very first stage when Italian favourite and defending champion Ottavio Bottecchia finished 34 minutes behind his Automoto teammate Jules Buysse, brother of Lucien. Fatigue couldn't be an issue this early on, but it seemed motivation was. Fortunately for Alcyon, Lucien Buysse could not have been more fired up. This was his sixth Tour and it had become his obsession. Belgian journalist Karel Steyaert wrote: 'Lucien lives only for the Tour. He knows all of its roads and pitfalls. He remembers all the difficult sections, he has pinpointed the bridge or tree where you need to flip your wheel over and change gear.'

Initially, the heat was unrelenting and the dust unspeakable, so bad that the riders' goggles could barely cope with it. Despite the conditions, the 33-year-old Belgian's strength increased as the race progressed, while Bottecchia's stalled. He bided his time until the Pyrenees, enabling his compatriot Gustaaf Van Slembrouck, a horse dealer and blacksmith in normal life, to take command of the yellow jersey.

The fun really started the night the race's 76 survivors (out of 126 starters) set off from Bayonne for Luchon. They were immediately assaulted by rain, wind and cold, and

enveloped in fog. Lucien Buysse led over the Aubisque, but trailed compatriot Odile Taillieu on the Tourmalet. Their positions were reversed on the Aspin, where Taillieu, who had drunk some icy water, stalled. The mud and ruts forced him off his bike. He found it impossible to change his tyre without a helping hand. Freezing cold and dripping wet, the riders were more concerned with survival than the race. Bottecchia and 21 other riders abandoned, while others reached the finish in coaches and cars.

Victory went to Lucien Buysse, who had attacked again on the Peyresourde. After 17 hours and 22 minutes in the saddle, he finally donned the yellow jersey. He'd had no punctures, hadn't got off his bike once, but had finished absolutely shattered. He needed to be helped to the control table to sign his name. More than 25 minutes passed before Bartolomeo Aimo took second place. As for Van Slembrouck, he finished almost two hours after Buysse. The conditions had been so bad that race organizer Desgrange had to extend the cut-off time to 40% of the winner's total.

In Perpignan, the yellow jersey and his brother Jules confirmed their superiority, as Lucien moved more than an hour clear of his rivals. The race was over. All Lucien had to do was control Alcyon's attacks in the Alps and then make it to Paris. Later in life, Lucien Buysse opened a café he called l'Aubisque, in tribute to the mountain pass where he had forged his success.

FINAL STANDINGS

1 Lucien Buysse (BEL) Automoto-Hutchinson 238:44:25
2 Nicolas Frantz (LUX) Alcyon-Dunlop +1:22:25
3 Bartolomeo Aimo (ITA) Alcyon-Dunlop +1:22:51
4 Théophile Beeckman (BEL) Armor-Dunlop +1:43:54
5 Félix Sellier (BEL) Alcyon-Dunlop +1:49:13
6 Albert Dejonghe (BEL) J. B. Louvet-Wolber +1:56:15
7 Léon Parmentier (BEL) Jean Louvet-Hutchinson +2:09:20
8 Georges Cuvelier (FRA) Météore-Wolber +2:28:32
9 Jules Buysse (BEL) Automoto-Hutchinson +2:37:03
10 Marcel Bidot (FRA) Thomann Dunlop +2:53:54

AVERAGE SPEED (OF WINNER): 24.063 KM/H
TOTAL DISTANCE RACED: 5,745KM

ABOVE Mountain passes, mud, cold, punctures – nothing stops Buysse who wins the Tour on one stage between Bayonne and Luchon.

LEFT Chasing after Lucien Buysse, the peloton is led by Aimo, Frantz, Jules Buysse, Parmentier and Omer Huyse as it arrives at the summit of the Col du Puymorens in the Pyrenees.

OVERLEAF The riders are in relaxed mood as the peloton gathers for a stage start.

FRANTZ SIGNALS ALCYON'S RETURN

The 21st Tour saw numerous changes and innovations. The race distance was reduced and the start moved back to Paris. More notably, Automoto did not field a team out of respect to Ottavio Bottecchia, who had died in mysterious circumstances just days before the race. Lucien Buysse and Bartolomeo Aimo were also missing from the field, leaving Alcyon and team leader Nicolas Frantz with a clear run at the title, particularly as they were backed up by subsidiaries Thomann, Armor and Labor. The primary innovation was the running of 16 flat stages as team time trials, because Henri Desgrange believed riders would have to race flat out as they would not know how their rivals were faring.

Frantz had every reason to believe his time had come, but he was wary of a return to form by Francis Pélissier. Although his Tour-winning brother Henri was absent, Pélissier looked a man transformed in the blue and gold colours of his new Dilecta team. Now 33, he had a strong line-up around him, which suited the new format. He took the lead from the off in Dieppe and kept it until Brest on stage six, where he passed it on to team-mate Ferdinand Le Drogo.

Heading south, the J. B. Louvet team took control and the yellow jersey moved onto the shoulders of Hector Martin, who led all the way to the Pyrenees. Finally, Frantz stamped his mark on the race. Having allowed Italian independent rider Michele Gordini to lead over the Aubisque, Frantz set the pace over the Tourmalet, Aspin and Peyresourde to win alone in Luchon and take the lead. His team-mate Maurice Dewaele now lay second, with Martin more than an hour and a half down in third. The Tour had all but been decided on one stage.

Wearing his trademark beret and riding with cowhorn bars and mudguards, Nicolas Frantz only needed to keep his rivals in check and himself out of trouble. He had been afflicted by saddle boils in the past and, consequently, did all he could to stay as clean and hygienic as possible. He amused himself by listening to the adverts belting out of the loudspeaker on the car sponsored by Kaplan and the jousting between his *directeur sportif*, Ludovic Feuillet, distinctive in his white jacket, and Léopold Alibert, *directeur* of French hope Antonin Magne's Alléluia team. Feuillet delivered his instructions through a megaphone, while Alibert used a whistle, perhaps too much as at one point he drove over Magne's bike, injuring his rider's knee.

Frantz remained unflustered. During the rest day in Pontarlier he was seen pushing his team-mates around in a wheelbarrow. In the end, in the Parc des Princes, where André Leducq grabbed a final bouquet for Alcyon, Frantz was all smiles, having claimed the title, brought Alcyon back to centre stage and recorded the fastest average speed since the war. Thanks to the elated Luxembourger, the Tour had regained some of its zest.

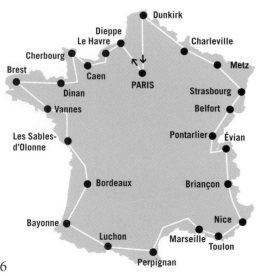

FINAL STANDINGS

1 Nicolas Frantz (LUX) Alcyon-Dunlop 198:16:42
2 Maurice Dewaele (BEL) Labor-Dunlop +1:48:21
3 Julien Vervaecke (BEL) Armor-Dunlop +2:25:06
4 André Leducq (FRA) Thomann-Dunlop +3:02:05
5 Adelin Benoît (BEL) Alcyon-Dunlop +4:45:01
6 Antonin Magne (FRA) Alléluia-Wolber +4:48:23
7 Pé Verhaegen (BEL) J. B. Louvet +6:18:36
8 Julien Moineau (FRA) Alléluia-Wolber +6:36:17
9 Hector Martin (BEL) J. B. Louvet +7:07:34
10 Maurice Geldhof (BEL) J. B. Louvet +7:16:02

AVERAGE SPEED (OF WINNER): 26.931 KM/H
TOTAL DISTANCE RACED: 5,340 KM

OPPOSITE Frantz as portrayed on the cover of weekly magazine *La Pédale* by cartoonist Abel Petit, who has depicted the beret-wearing Luxembourger riding over the famous Pyrenean passes.

REVUE HEBDOMADAIRE DE LA BICYCLETTE ET DES INDUSTRIES QUI S'Y RATTACHENT

:::: SPORT ::::
TOURISME
—
Directeur :
Aug. DELERIVE
Rédacteur en Chef :
Marcel GENTIS
Secrétaire Général :
Claude TILLET

La Pédale

||||||||||||||||||||||
17, Faubourg Montmartre — PARIS (9ᵉ)
Fondateur : HENRY ETIENNE

PRIX DE L'ABONNEMENT
FRANCE
Un an .... 45 fr.
Six mois .... 24 fr.
Trois mois .... 14 fr.
ETRANGER
Un an .... 60 fr.
Six mois .... 34 fr.
Trois mois .... 20 fr.
Chèque postal : Nᵒ 715-24

nos phénomènes

Nicolas FRANTZ, vainqueur des vrais Çols pyrénéens

ABOVE Riders had to carry tyres everywhere as they might have up to ten punctures during a stage, and Italian *touriste-routier* Michele Gordini (1896–1970) certainly has plenty to keep him going – in his bottle cages, under his saddle and around his shoulders. This giant of a man, who was 6'5" tall, had showed real guts when he launched a night-time attack on the Bayonne–Luchon stage and led over the Aubisque, before Frantz passed him on the Tourmalet.

OPPOSITE TOP The champion (centre) receives congratulations from his peers.

OPPOSITE BOTTOM Heading for Dinan, the second group of the Alcyon team, with Leducq and Hamel either side of the struggling Marcel Bidot, are being urged on by team manager Ludovic Feuillet, dressed in white on the right.

FRANTZ RULES FROM START TO FINISH

Such was the domination that Nicolas Frantz and his team Alcyon showed at the 1927 Tour that it was hard to see how their supremacy could be challenged a year later. Some did suggest a surprise might come from the regional teams formed by grouping together the *touristes-routiers* riders, notably from Victor Fontan. However, he was 36 and it was only his second Tour. Australia's 24-year-old Hubert Opperman came to the race with a strong record as well. Yet, Frantz's toughest task was overcoming the talent within the Alcyon armada.

The sky blues dominated from the outset, immediately putting Frantz in yellow in Le Havre. The team time trials that followed all the way to Hendaye highlighted their ruthlessness and power. It wasn't until the fourth stage in Brest that J. B. Louvet's Pé Verhaegen loosened their grip, although Alcyon still filled the top three places overall. Frantz was soon back in winning form in Les Sables-d'Olonne. Then the climber Fontan emerged. First, he proved himself with victory in Bordeaux, setting up a duel with Frantz in the Pyrenees. Their head-to-head fully lived up to expectations. The old Frenchman gave the yellow jersey a lesson on his favoured terrain, although without upsetting the established order.

Frantz picked up the bouquets in Nice, Metz and Paris, and had only two punctures on the way. Conscious of his tendency for saddle sores, he changed his shorts every day. The musette he was handed during each stage always contained four sandwiches, four eggs, four bananas, five tartlets and 30 sugar cubes. He drank Vittel and black coffee, and sucked on raisins and prunes.

His only scare was a technical one: his bike broke on stage 19 to Charleville, which he had to finish on a much smaller borrowed bike. Even though he came in 38 minutes behind the winner, he still had a substantial lead over his team-mates Leducq and Dewaele, who were his most dangerous rivals. He finished in glorious fashion with victory in the Parc des Princes having worn the yellow jersey from start to finish. Behind him were four riders either from Alcyon or an affiliate. The first non-Alcyon was Antonin Magne, who came home in sixth more than two-and-a-half hours behind the winner. One place behind him was old Fontan, who completed the Tour for the first time. As for the Antipodeans taken under the wing of Ravat-Wonder of Saint-Étienne, three out of the four finished: Opperman in 18th, Watson in 28th and Osborne in 38th.

Although there was no doubting the impressiveness of Alcyon's performance, their stranglehold created a good deal of frustration and debate. Some called for national teams to be introduced in 1929. But Desgrange wasn't convinced – yet…

FINAL STANDINGS

1 Nicolas Frantz (LUX) Alcyon-Dunlop 192:48:58
2 André Leducq (FRA) Alcyon-Dunlop +50:07
3 Maurice Dewaele (BEL) Alcyon-Dunlop +56:16
4 Jan Mertens (BEL) Thomann-Dunlop +1:19:18
5 Julien Vervaecke (BEL) Armor-Dunlop +1:53:32
6 Antonin Magne (FRA) Alléluia-Wolber +2:14:02
7 Victor Fontan (FRA) Elvish-Wolber +5:07:47
8 Marcel Bidot (FRA) Alléluia-Wolber +5:18:28
9 Marcel Huot (FRA) Alléluia-Wolber +5:37:33
10 Pierre Magne (FRA) Alléluia-Wolber +5:41:20

AVERAGE SPEED (OF WINNER): 28.4 KM/H
TOTAL DISTANCE RACED: 5,476 KM

OPPOSITE TOP LEFT Nicolas Frantz – as smart off his bike as he was on it.

OPPOSITE TOP RIGHT The Australian escapade in France led to the publication of a postcard. Watson, Bainbridge and Osborne surround 'Oppy' in the centre. At the bottom, Bruce Small sings about their exploits.

OPPOSITE BOTTOM On the Col d'Allos, Dewaele, yellow jersey Frantz and Fontan battle it out at the front of the lead group. Fontan and Frantz would cross the summit together.

FRANTZ

This old lady was about to cross the main street in her village when a noisy and colourful pack of bicycling men with eyes like frogs surged through. Out of wisdom and prudence, she lets them pass. She's still worried. Should she look at them? Applaud them? She appears disoriented.

DEWAELE TRIUMPHS IN ALCYON'S SWANSONG

Desgrange had tried everything to reduce the influence of the Alcyon team but he couldn't stop them clinching another victory, although this would be their last. It was close run and eventually won by a 'corpse'. This finally convinced Desgrange of the need for national teams at a time when nations were competing against each other in tennis's Davis Cup and football's first World Cup.

The Tour was changing in other ways too. French radio was now covering the race and more companies were using the Tour to promote their products. On the road, the riders were divided into two classes – the *As* or Aces and the *touristes-routiers*. Alcyon still dominated, though. Four riders were tied for the lead as far as Brest, where Alcyon's Maurice Dewaele claimed the yellow jersey outright. Defending champion Frantz pinched it in Bordeaux. Gaston Rebry maintained Alcyon's grip on the jersey in Bayonne.

The race then came to life when Victor Fontan rode away from the peloton on the big Pyrenean stage he knew like the back of his hand. His friend Salvador Cardona won it as Fontan took a ten-minute lead over Dewaele. News of Fontan's success was transmitted to more than two million radios. Everyone expected Fontan to increase his lead on the second stage in the Pyrenees, but as they raced through the night his bike broke in a gutter. His world caved in. He no longer knew where he was, how to pedal or how to repair the bike. Almost everyone overtook him. With a heavy heart, he abandoned the race on the brink of glory.

The three Belgians Demuysere, Delannoy and Dewaele powered on almost as one and finished in that order in Perpignan, where Dewaele retook the yellow jersey. It was only the midway point of the Tour, but he looked to have the race won. He was 14 minutes up on Demuysere and 22 minutes up on the Italian Pancera. It became even clearer that there was no chance of Dewaele losing the race when he collapsed prior to a stage in the Alps and had to be helped onto his bike. Riders from Alcyon and its affiliates kept him outright and the other riders in check, effectively turning the race into a non-contest, much to Desgrange's dismay.

A number of riders were penalized for the assistance they had given to Dewaele, but it didn't change the result. In Paris, the Belgian's lead had stretched to 44 minutes over Pancera and 57 minutes over Demuysere, who would have been second but for a 25-minute penalty for taking on drinks outside specified points. Branded a 'corpse' by Desgrange, Dewaele had won at the same average speed as Frantz a year earlier. For many, though, Fontan was the moral victor. He was named best climber by *L'Auto*, while a national subscription no doubt softened his huge disappointment just a little.

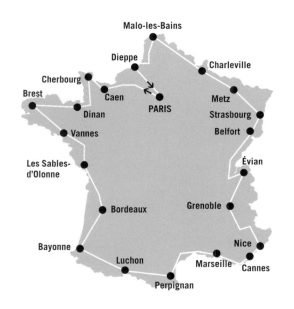

FINAL STANDINGS

1 Maurice Dewaele (BEL) Alcyon 186:39:15
2 Giuseppe Pancera (ITA) La Rafale +44:23
3 Joseph Demuysere (BEL) Lucifer +57:10
4 Salvador Cardona (SPA) Fontan-Wolber +57:46
5 Nicolas Frantz (LUX) Alcyon +58:00
6 Louis Delannoy (BEL) La Française +1:06:09
7 Antonin Magne (FRA) Alléluia-Wolber +1:08:00
8 Julien Vervaecke (BEL) Alcyon +2:01:37
9 Pierre Magne (FRA) Alléluia-Wolber +2:03:00
10 Gaston Rebry (BEL) Alcyon +2:17:49

AVERAGE SPEED (OF WINNER): 28.159 KM/H
TOTAL DISTANCE RACED: 5,256 KM

Maurice De Waele

(Lovendegem, 27.12.1896 - Maldegem, 14.02.1952)

ABOVE The peloton is getting stretched out as it leaves La Grave heading for the Lautaret pass, which Rebry would cross first. André Leducq has just had a severe ear-bashing from Alcyon team manager Ludovic Feuillet because he was eating an ice-cream.

TOP Maurice Dewaele participated in four Tours, finished them all and always in the top five. To an extent Dewaele's great mistake was reclaiming the yellow jersey after French favourite Victor Fontan had quit in the Pyrenees. Desgrange wanted the Tour to be a testing ground for equipment as well as athletes and Dewaele indirectly benefited from that.

RIGHT Maurice Dewaele, the 'corpse' who enraged Desgrange.

LEDUCQ RESTORES FRENCH PRIDE

France had become a power in world sport thanks to the likes of boxer Georges Carpentier, tennis star Suzanne Lenglen, and the 'Four Musketeers' who had won the Davis Cup in the USA in 1927. Henri Desgrange wanted to capture that mood at the Tour, which had been dominated by manufacturer-teams who had transformed him into little more than a stooge. The antics of the Alcyon team and its leader Maurice Dewaele in 1929 proved to be the tipping point.

Desgrange's principal concern was finance as *L'Auto* would have to assume all the costs for staging the race. It was an audacious gamble. Forty champions were gathered in five teams of eight. The Belgians were a real force, as were the Italians with Binda and Guerra, the Spanish had their eyes on the mountains prize, while the Germans could not be overlooked. As for the French, they placed their faith in Charles Pélissier (the younger brother of Tour veterans Henri and Francis Pélissier), Victor Fontan, Jules Merviel, Marcel Bidot, Antonin Magne, André Leducq, Pierre Magne and Joseph Mauclair. Nine regional teams of five riders and a selection of *touristes-routiers* including 1926 champion Lucien Buysse completed the line-up.

One hundred riders were equipped with identical yellow bikes designed by *L'Auto*, which also provided all of their other equipment. Desgrange negotiated hard with the manufacturer that provided the bikes, with the towns and hotels along the route, and with new advertisers. Some finance was raised by

the introduction of a publicity caravan, featuring chocolate company Menier, who gave their wares to fans on the route.

Desgrange was taking a huge risk, but it paid off, in part due to the success of the French team, which won 12 stages, 8 of which were taken by Pélissier. Leducq claimed the yellow jersey as France also swept up the team classification. The pre-race favourites were Binda and Guerra, Belgium's Demuysere and France's Fontan, so unlucky the previous year. On this occasion, Fontan crashed at a level crossing in Bordeaux right in front of Binda. Fontan struggled on to Luchon before quitting, while the Italian, who lost an hour due to the fall, made a last stand in the Pyrenees before abandoning, with Leducq now in the lead.

After Binda quit, Guerra wanted to prove he was more than simply his leader's lieutenant. He took one stage in the Alps and had his eye on the next, particularly when Leducq crashed on the descent of the Galibier and the Télégraphe. 'Dédé' was in tears on the side of the road, but was saved by Antonin and Pierre Magne and Bidot. They took a pedal off a spectator's bike and got the yellow jersey back in the saddle. With Pélissier setting the pace as they chased after Guerra, the French wiped out a deficit of 15 minutes in 75 km and Leducq won the sprint in Évian. Pélissier cleaned up the final four stages as French fans turned out in their hundreds of thousands to cheer them home. The Tour had got its second wind.

FINAL STANDINGS

1 André Leducq (FRA) France 172:12:16
2 Learco Guerra (ITA) Italy +14:13
3 Antonin Magne (FRA) France +16:03
4 Jef Demuysere (BEL) Belgium +21:34
5 Marcel Bidot (FRA) France +41:18
6 Pierre Magne (FRA) France +45:42
7 Frans Bonduel (BEL) Belgium +56:19
8 Benoît Fauré (FRA) South-East +58:34
9 Charles Pélissier (FRA) France +1:04:37
10 Adolf Schön (GER) Germany +1:21:39

AVERAGE SPEED (OF WINNER): 27.978 KM/H
TOTAL DISTANCE RACED: 4,818 KM

In Évian, where he has just strengthened his grip on the yellow jersey having almost lost it, Leducq congratulates the main players in the revival of his fortunes: Pierrot and Tonin Magne, Charles Pélissier and Marcel Bidot.

PYRENEAN PREP PAYS OFF FOR MAGNE

In spite of the previous year's success, the French team had a makeover as upcoming talents Louis Péglion, Jean Maréchal, Léon Le Calvez and Benoît Fauré joined André Leducq, Charles Pélissier, Antonin Magne and Joseph Mauclair in the defence of the title. Everyone assumed Leducq would win again, but he was below his best having competed in a hugely testing French time trial championship. Instead, Antonin Magne emerged as France's lead man. Magne had regained his form in the Pyrenees. He had been working with the experienced Victor Fontan and had rediscovered the art of climbing by tackling the same passes time and time again, learning when to press and when to ease off.

Early in the race, however, the hardworking *touristes-routiers* outflanked the national teams. Desgrange set the two groups of riders off at separate start times to spice up the race, the national riders starting ten minutes before the rest. Consequently, in Dinan it appeared that Pélissier had won, but in fact Austrian *touriste-routier* Max Bulla had covered the ground quicker and took the yellow jersey. That forced the big guns to up their game. Between Les Sables and Pau, two of them, Pélissier and Raphaël Di Paco, wore the yellow jersey. As expected, Magne then wasted little time in taking advantage of all of the training he had undertaken in the mountains. He not

only won in Luchon, but his lead was large enough for him to dream of holding it all the way to Paris. Bulla shone again in Montpellier, but the main danger for Magne would come in the Alps.

Unlike the Pyrenees where he was dominant, Magne struggled to contain his rivals in the Alps and had to depend on the powerful Pélissier to survive constant attacks from the Belgians and Italian. The last hope for the Belgians was to launch an attack on the cobbles in the north, which were often more difficult than a mountain stage. Heading for Malo-les-Bains, Rebry and Demuysere rode without caution and flat out. Magne held on to them for 200 km and kept the famous yellow jersey.

At the finish in the Parc des Princes, Pélissier delighted the fans as he beat Leducq and Di Paco in the final sprint. The French team then completed a lap of honour arm in arm, before Magne, a teetotaller, celebrated his victory with water. On his return to his farm at Livry Gargan, Magne went to the bottom of his garden to seek out his lucky stone. As a test of his moral fortitude, he carried it non-stop from one end of the garden to the other like Sisyphus, demonstrating how he married superstition, discipline and technique into a winning formula. Of course, he had more than a pinch of class too.

FINAL STANDINGS

1 Antonin Magne (FRA) France 177:10:03
2 Jef Demuysere (BEL) Belgium +12:56
3 Antonio Pesenti (ITA) Italy +22:51
4 Gaston Rebry (BEL) Belgium +46:40
5 Maurice Dewaele (BEL) Belgium +49:46
6 Julien Vervaecke (BEL) Belgium +1:10:11
7 Louis Péglion (FRA) France +1:18:33
8 Erich Metze (GER) Germany +1:20:59
9 Albert Büchi (SWI) Switzerland +1:29:29
10 André Leducq (FRA) France +1:30:08

AVERAGE SPEED (OF WINNER): 28.758 KM/H
TOTAL DISTANCE RACED: 5,095 KM

After an epic Tour, Antonin Magne savours victory, flanked by Rosine Picquart, the 'mother of the riders', and Henri Manchon.

OPPOSITE This illustration of a control point, as depicted by *Le Petit Journal*, shows that yellow jersey Antonin Magne is well protected by the French team. Thirst and dust constantly trouble the throats and eyes of the peloton.

SECOND SUCCESS FOR LEDUCQ

Two pillars of the victorious French teams of 1930 and 1931 were missing from the 26th Tour: Antonin Magne and Charles Pélissier. Henri Desgrange was none too pleased as he had overhauled the bonus system in order to help Pélissier win the title. By awarding a bonus of four minutes to the stage winner, two minutes to the rider in second and one minute to the man in third, Pélissier was the odds-on favourite. After all, he had won 13 stages, come second 11 times and third three times in two years. But Desgrange had forgotten how unpredictable the Pélissier brothers could be.

Eighty riders set off for Normandy, but on this occasion there would be no stopover in either Brittany or the Basque Country. The organization's preparations were better than ever and this year included 6,000 sandwiches, 9,600 bananas, 10,000 biscuits/rusks, 200 kg of peaches, 100 kg of grapes and 50 kg of butter sachets. With all that food stocked up, there was little chance of riders running out of rations.

Belgium's Jean Aerts won the opening stage, but fell victim to splits between the Flemish and Walloon members of his team. At the finish in Nantes, Germany's Kurt Stöpel took advantage and the lead. However, he too only managed to hold the yellow jersey for a stage. The German got a puncture 2 km from the finish in Bordeaux, where Leducq won and pinched the lead. He kept it for the rest of the race despite some finish-line battles with Italy's Raphaël Di Paco, Pélissier's old rival.

Leducq benefited from the system designed to suit Pélissier. He waltzed off with six stage wins, came second twice and third three times… He did receive a five-minute penalty and relegation in Charleville for getting a push from Barthélémy after being dropped. His task was made easier by the philosophy of his German rival Stöpel, who 'feared losing second place more than he desired taking first'. Leducq was also strongly supported by his French team-mates, notably Archambaud on at least two occasions in the Pyrenees, as well as Moineau and Speicher in the Alps.

At the newly renovated Parc des Princes in Paris, Leducq savoured his second triumph and presented his wife with the bouquet he received for his sixth stage win. Now 28, he was stronger than he had been in 1930. He told radio listeners: 'I am so happy to have returned to Paris with this beautiful and rather weighty yellow jersey on my shoulders.'

FINAL STANDINGS

1 André Leducq (FRA) France 154:11:49
2 Kurt Stöpel (GER) Germany/Austria +24:03
3 Francesco Camusso (ITA) Italy +26:21
4 Antonio Pesenti (ITA) Italy +37:08
5 Georges Ronsse (BEL) Belgium +41:04
6 Frans Bonduel (BEL) Belgium +45:13
7 Oskar Thierbach (GER) Germany/Austria +58:44
8 Jef Demuysere (BEL) Belgium +1:03:24
9 Luigi Barral (ITA) individual +1:06:57
10 Georges Speicher (FRA) France +1:08:37

AVERAGE SPEED (OF WINNER): 29.313 KM/H
TOTAL DISTANCE RACED: 4,520 KM

OPPOSITE TOP Assistant race director Robert Desmarets guides André Leducq on his lap of honour in the Parc des Princes.

OPPOSITE BOTTOM LEFT Although absent from the race, Antonin Magne was still at the roadside to encourage his friend Leducq as he battles here through the mud in the Pyrenees. On the brink of collapse on the way up, he would fall in the mud on the way down.

OPPOSITE BOTTOM RIGHT A rider receives attention from race followers following a crash in the mountains.

ABOVE AND RIGHT The Tour is a unique experience both for the eyes and the ears. This rather surreal image (above) shows a coach full of the Paul Beuscher accordionists, who entertained fans during the race. In the image on the right, spectators defy the Pyrenean cold to get the best view of the climbers twisting up the hairpins.

OPPOSITE TOP AND BOTTOM The peloton ignores the gate that is coming down at a level crossing (top), while (bottom) fans who are well wrapped up against the rain and cold encourage the riders as they climb through cloying mud towards the summit of a pass.

CANNY SPEICHER PLAYS THE RULES

Twenty years after the Tour had last run clockwise around France, the race set off towards Lille and then the Alps. Once again it would result in victory for the French national team, as Georges Speicher brought a fourth consecutive success. His glory continued at the World Road Championships in Montlhéry, where he added the rainbow jersey to his yellow – the first man to achieve that double.

It was also a double success for Alcyon, although they were not totally happy as Speicher's Tour-winning bike was painted yellow, the colour of organizing newspaper *L'Auto*. The manufacturers, who had never been happy with the change from trade to national teams in 1930, were boosted by Speicher's Worlds success. At the end of 1933 they had thoughts of setting up their own Tour, like Peugeot and Wolber had done from 1910. However, the French cycling federation declared the idea a pipedream, announcing that there was only one Tour and only one organizer – Desgrange.

The danger to Desgrange had been averted, but all was not right with the Tour. Although Speicher took the title, he did so thanks to the bonus time on offer at stage finishes – two minutes to the stage winner and one to the rider in second. Without these bonuses victory would have gone to Italian *touriste-routier* Giuseppe Martano, who actually finished third. He would have beaten Speicher by two minutes and his compatriot Learco Guerra, who took second, by nearly ten

minutes. Desgrange had introduced the bonuses to give his protégé Charles Pélissier an advantage, but he abandoned the race on the third stage. Thanks to that, the Tour floundered, even though little Maurice Archambaud was a great yellow jersey.

Another concern was the rules. They were applied strictly to Altenburger, who was disqualified for hanging on to a car on the Ballon d'Alsace. However, they were not applied in the same unbending way in Nice and Cannes, where the cut-off times were changed from 8% to 10% and from 10% to 15%, respectively. If the rules had been adhered to in Nice, the whole of the peloton from seventh place on would have been eliminated, leaving Trueba in the yellow jersey, with Cornez, Fayolle, Pastorelli, Bulla and Le Calvez ranked behind him. In Cannes, where Archambaud won and regained the yellow jersey, five more riders benefited, including Cornez.

The fuss was all but forgotten in Marseille, where Speicher took the yellow jersey. Well supported by Archambaud, Le Grèves, Magne, Leducq, Le Calvez, Lapébie and Cornez, who was raging a gruelling war to win the bonus time against Belgium's Aerts and Italy's Guerra and Martano, Speicher edged clear. Although he suffered some injuries due to acts of madness on descents, he rarely looked likely to lose, given the strength of the team behind him. As Speicher celebrated, Spain's Trueba, who had led the race over the Galibier and Tourmalet, was crowned first official King of the Mountains.

FINAL STANDINGS

1   Georges Speicher (FRA) France 147:51:37
2   Learco Guerra (ITA) Italy +4:01
3   Giuseppe Martano (ITA) individual +5:08
4   Georges Lemaire (BEL) Belgium +15:45
5   Maurice Archambaud (FRA) France +21:22
6   Vicente Trueba (SPA) individual +27:27
7   Léon Level (FRA) individual +35:19
8   Antonin Magne (FRA) France +36:37
9   Jean Aerts (BEL) Belgium +42:53
10 Kurt Stöpel (GER) Germany/Austria +45:28

AVERAGE SPEED (OF WINNER): 29.724 KM/H
TOTAL DISTANCE RACED: 4,395 KM

OPPOSITE TOP On the mountain roads that were always hellish and decisive, France's Antonin Magne keeps the Italians, Belgians and Germans in check.

OPPOSITE BOTTOM In Marseille, Georges Speicher wins and takes the yellow jersey that he will keep for the rest of the race.

TO VIETTO THE CHEERS, TO MAGNE THE SPOILS

The final result of the 28th Tour didn't reflect the concerns of the French team going into it. Although they could still count on Magne, Speicher, Archambaud and Pélissier, they had lost André Leducq. Would youngsters Roger Lapébie and René Vietto be able to fill his shoes? They would certainly be up against some fierce opposition, led by Spain's Trueba, Germany's Stöpel, Belgium's Rebry and Italy's Martano and Di Paco.

The French response had been made by the halfway mark in Montpellier. By that point, as Georges Speicher recorded his third stage win, Antonin Magne had held the yellow jersey since the second stage. Tour debutant Vietto, sprinter René Le Grèves and Roger Lapébie had each taken three stage wins as well, so the French clearly had the race under control. Guiseppe Martano, the winner in Gap, was the biggest threat as he lay 3-42 down going into the Pyrenees.

Even though Magne knew the area well, like any other rider he was always at the mercy of a fall or a puncture. Heading for Ax-les-Thermes, he fell on the descent of the Puymorens and broke his wheel. Vietto gave him a wheel, but ultimately it was Speicher's bike that got Magne back in the race. The next day, on a small descent after the Portet d'Aspet, the yellow jersey's back wheel jammed and his chain got caught between the cranks.

'I really thought it was all over,' admitted Magne. 'Then I saw René Vietto had turned around and was bringing me his bike. I got on it and rejoined Roger Lapébie, who was waiting for us and led all the way to the summit of the Col des Ares. He continued to set the pace on the descent. To this day I don't know which of them I owe more to – Vietto or Lapébie.' That evening, only Italy's Vignoli finished ahead of Lapébie and Magne.

Between Luchon and Tarbes, a corner of France that he knew by heart, Magne was imperious. He all but killed off the opposition. The selfless Vietto took another victory in Pau, which ensured his success in the mountains classification. Slightly irritated by his team-mate's success, Magne took advantage of the Nantes time trial to widen his advantage on Martano and, more notably, on Vietto, who some people saw as the race's moral victor.

Although Vietto had worked twice as hard as most on the team, he had lost too much time to have the slightest chance of winning the Tour and finally ended up fifth in the Parc des Princes, where the lap of honour he undertook with Magne received the most rapturous reception. As well as showing chivalry and panache, the French team had walked away with 19 of the 23 stages.

FINAL STANDINGS

1 Antonin Magne (FRA) France 147:13:58
2 Giuseppe Martano (ITA) Italy +27:31
3 Roger Lapébie (FRA) France +52:15
4 Félicien Vervaecke (BEL) individual +57:40
5 René Vietto (FRA) France +59:02
6 Ambrogio Morelli (ITA) individual +1:12:02
7 Ludwig Geyer (GER) Germany +1:12:51
8 Sylvère Maes (BEL) individual +1:20:56
9 Mariano Cañardo (SPA) Switzerland/Spain +1:29:02
10 Vicente Trueba (SPA) Switzerland/Spain +1:40:39

AVERAGE SPEED (OF WINNER): 29.633 KM/H
TOTAL DISTANCE RACED: 4,363 KM

OPPOSITE The taciturn Magne smiles while answering questions from radio journalists.

ABOVE Revelation of the Tour, young Vietto was the best climber, Magne's best team-mate and the best mechanic. In the Parc des Princes he shared a wonderful lap of honour with his leader.

RIGHT Before setting off, Antonin Magne enjoys some quiet time at the back of the Latil technical van while Dizy, the mechanic, tests his brakes. Note the small mudguard at the front. He is wearing glasses and carrying the two compulsory tyres – one across his chest, the other under the saddle.

OPPOSITE Riders stock up with Ovomaltine, as Ovaltine is known in France, which has been prepared in a bath at a stage start.

MAES SHAPES HIS DESTINY

Since the switch to national teams in 1930, the French had won every Tour and that run should have continued in 1935 because all of their winners during that period – Leducq (1930/32), Magne (1931/34) and Speicher (1933) – were on the start line. What's more, they had Archambaud, Vietto and Le Grèves backing them up. However, no one was counting on a little-known Belgian.

The Belgians, who had been off centre stage since Dewaele's success in 1929, were growing in strength. Much was expected of Félicien Vervaecke and Sylvère Maes, fourth and eighth, respectively, in 1934, but unforeseen incidents with level crossings and cars allowed another Belgian to come into the picture. Sylvère's namesake Romain Maes emerged, largely because he was the most audacious rider in the field.

Knowing he could impose himself as leader of his team on the tough first stage between Paris and Lille, Romain Maes attacked. As he went through the level crossing at Méru, panic had already spread through the peloton, which was scattered across the countryside. At Bray, in the midst of the slagheaps, he had two minutes on the still faltering peloton. Four riders counter-attacked: Maes's compatriots de Calume and Aerts, and France's Magne and Pélissier. They would have caught the lone leader if they hadn't found the gates at the level crossing in Haubourdin were down. Maes had just slipped through. In Lille, he finished a minute ahead. Time bonuses gave him

a lead of 2-31 on de Calume and more than 3 minutes on Aerts, Magne and Pélissier. Speicher was almost 6 minutes down, Lapébie 8 and Vietto 21.

The previous year Maes had quit the race in the Alps, but with the yellow jersey now on his shoulders he consolidated his lead and gained confidence. He also benefited from Magne leaving the race after being hit by a car. In the Alps, tragedy hit the Tour when Spanish climber Francisco Cepeda suffered a fatal fall on the descent of the Galibier due to brake failure. The race continued under a cloud.

Victory for Maes in Cannes underlined his position as the race's outstanding performer, backed up by strong performances from Vervaecke, who was the best climber. The only sustained threat came from Italian Ambrogio Morelli, but he lost several minutes over the final few stages, enabling Maes a comfortable run-in, even though Morelli did respond with victory in the final time trial.

After Bottecchia (1924) and Frantz (1928), Romain Maes was the third champion to wear the yellow jersey from start to finish. Like them, after taking the first stage he made it a point of honour to clinch the final one. Just 22 and the 13th child in a family of 15, Maes was a totally deserving champion. He had overcome 28 punctures, three bad moments when he struggled, and had posted the best average speed in Tour history (30.65 km/h). The only surprise was that he never finished the Tour again.

FINAL STANDINGS

1 Romain Maes (BEL) Belgium 141:32:00
2 Ambrogio Morelli (ITA) individual +17:52
3 Félicien Vervaecke (BEL) Belgium +24:06
4 Sylvère Maes (BEL) individual +35:24
5 Jules Lowie (BEL) individual +51:26
6 Georges Speicher (FRA) France +54:29
7 Maurice Archambaud (FRA) France +1:09:28
8 René Vietto (FRA) France +1:21:03
9 Gabriel Ruozzi (FRA) individual +1:34:02
10 Oskar Thierbach (GER) Germany +2h:00:04

AVERAGE SPEED (OF WINNER): 30.65 KM/H
TOTAL DISTANCE RACED: 4,338 KM

OPPOSITE TOP Spanish champions Francisco Cepeda and Vicente Trueba lead the way in their preferred terrain. Soon after this image was taken Cepeda suffered a fatal crash.

OPPOSITE BOTTOM Maes, lining up on the far left with his team-mates, was only an outsider for Belgium, but his talent and his eye for a chance made the difference.

SYLVÈRE MAES – MR TOURMALET

The organizers wanted the 30th Tour to be more captivating after what had been a fairly humdrum race in 1935. In this they were helped to an extent by France's Popular Front government, which introduced paid holidays for workers, resulting in a big increase in spectators along the route. This being the Tour, there was little chance of those fans feeling the race was an anti-climax. Indeed, there was a hugely significant change in the opening days when health problems forced Henri Desgrange to hand over the reins of power to Jacques Goddet.

Thanks to a deluge on the road to Lille, Switzerland's Paul Egli became the first rider from that country to wear the yellow jersey. The Tour's field was also developing more of an international feel as Romanian and Yugoslav teams made an appearance, although the four-man Romanian team all quit by the time the race reached Metz. They were in good company, though, as defending champion Romain Maes and 1933 victor – and most people's pre-race favourite – Georges Speicher both quit in Grenoble.

By that point, Sylvère Maes, who had very ably supported his namesake Romain in 1935, and Maurice Archambaud, without whom Georges Speicher would not have reigned supreme in 1933, were leading the way. When Archambaud failed to stay with the main contenders on the road to Briançon, Maes took the yellow jersey. Although rival teams tested the Belgians, Maes's men demonstrated their power and unity before the Pyrenees over a series of stages run as team time trials.

Although France had been having plenty of success in the sprints thanks to René Le Grèves, who bagged six stage wins, Antonin Magne now had just one realistic chance of removing the yellow jersey from Maes. The stage to Pau crossed the Peyresourde, Aspin, Tourmalet and Aubisque on roads Magne knew extremely well. That knowledge didn't help him, though, as Maes romped over the Tourmalet and Aubisque in dazzling fashion to win alone in Pau, where his advantage stretched to 26 minutes over Magne. The Frenchman's only consolation was victory in the penultimate stage, which enabled him to split Maes and compatriot Vervaecke on the final podium. Just behind these three were the Clemens brothers from Luxembourg. Pierre and Mathias Clemens finished fourth and seventh, respectively, displaying the same understanding and power as the compatriots the Schlecks today.

A more complete rider than his namesake Romain, Sylvère Maes also recorded a better average speed (31.108 km/h). His café in Gistel, where the beer flowed freely, was renamed 'The Tourmalet' to commemorate his best moment on the Tour. There was joy for the Spanish too as Julián Berrendero reclaimed the mountain classification for them three years on from Vicente Trueba's success.

FINAL STANDINGS

1 Sylvère Maes (BEL) Belgium 142:47:32
2 Antonin Magne (FRA) France +26:55
3 Félicien Vervaecke (BEL) Belgium +27:53
4 Pierre Clemens (LUX) Spain/Luxembourg +42:42
5 Arsène Mersch (LUX) Spain/Luxembourg +52:52
6 Mariano Cañardo (SPA) Spain/Luxembourg +1:03:04
7 Mathias Clemens (LUX) Spain/Luxembourg +1:10:44
8 Leo Amberg (SWI) Switzerland +1:19:13
9 Marcel Kint (BEL) Belgium +1:22:25
10 Léon Level (FRA) individual +1:27:57

AVERAGE SPEED (OF WINNER): 31.108 KM/H
TOTAL DISTANCE RACED: 4,442 KM

Lille
Charleville
Metz
Vire
Caen
PARIS
Belfort
Angers
Cholet
La Roche
-sur-Yon
La Rochelle
Évian
Saintes
Aix-les-Bains
Bordeaux
Grenoble
Briançon
Digne
Nîmes
Nice
Montpellier
Pau
Narbonne
Marseille
Cannes
Luchon
Perpignan

Sylvère MAES
Belge
offert par les Bonbons
Vanluydt de Wattrelos

N° 7

TOP Lille looked more like Venice as the riders made for the finish. Egli and Archambaud managed to stay afloat.

LEFT Maes and his team-mates in Belgium's team kitted out completely in black were royally received on their return to Brussels.

ABOVE Maes later named his cafe 'Le Tourmalet' in tribute to his feats in the Pyrenees.

Behind the scenes at the Tour

THE ORGANIZATION OF the Tour during this period when the big names were separated into national rather than trade teams was the complete responsibility of *L'Auto*. From Desgrange's yellow bikes to tubeless tyres, pumps and raincoats, everything was handed out to riders as they set off from the Vel d'Hiv velodrome, which, like the Parc des Princes, was part of *L'Auto*'s empire.

The 1936 Tour, which featured 90 riders, 21 stages and 6 rest days, cost Henri Desgrange 1,500,000 francs. The daily cost of hotels including food was 5,000 francs. The cost of all the supplies needed for the race was 60,000 francs. The pharmacy needed 20,000 francs worth of disinfectants, dressings and medicines. The race organizers also had 500 extra jerseys, 1,000 pairs of sunglasses with mica lenses, 150 suitcases, 100 raincoats, 80 bikes and 2,000 spare tyres. In addition, 3 special

L'Auto vehicles transported 100,000 posters, 5,000 leaflets and 1 million special race programmes that listed the riders, start numbers and the race's roll of honour.

With regard to personnel, in 1936 the caravan numbered 500 people, who would spend 300,000 francs between them at every stage town. These 500 people comprised 90 riders, 12 mechanics, 11 masseurs, 6 drivers for the Hotchkiss trucks and 5 for the Latil trucks. There were also 4 policemen permanently on the race to organize local gendarmes, as well as someone responsible for the race convoy, a bursar, a dispatch rider, a timekeeper, 2 men in charge of diversions, and 5 *L'Auto* editors. In addition to this core group, there were a further 150 people in the growing publicity caravan, which featured 50 vehicles and was led by a supervisor and a motorcycle liaison officer.

The third level of the hierarchy comprised journalists, photographers, French filmmakers and foreign journalists. They were provided with up to 70 cars. Some members of the organization also travelled by train and there was even an aeroplane.

There were between three and six rest days during the Tour. The towns chosen for them tended to be Royan, Cannes, Pau, Évian and Nice. At that time, most riders believed, like Antonin Magne, that the Tour was won in bed, and exercise should be limited to leafing through the papers. Consequently, for many the rest day was spent stretched out. The down side of this, according to Frenchman Victor Cosson, was that the next day 'you needed more than 150 km to get rid of the water retained'. It was rare for any of the riders to head out on a bike for a spin. As for the rest of the caravan, they tended to get into party mode.

LEFT Oubron, Ducazeaux and Gallien laze on the beach in Nice.

OPPOSITE CLOCKWISE FROM TOP LEFT In Luchon, the Spanish climbers including Ezquerra swap bike saddles for the equivalent on the back of a donkey.

Mauclair, Moorels, Le Drogo and Aerts listen to music outside a bar.

Their donkey jaunt complete, Ezquerra and his Spanish team-mates look for another way to divert themselves on a rest day.

Assistant Tour director Robert Desmarets (right) celebrates at the end of the Tour with his team.

Büchi and Wanzenried weigh themselves in Évian.

VICTORY FOR THE DERAILLEUR KING

Napoleon Bonaparte preferred a lucky general to an intelligent one. In this, the 31st Tour, the lucky man who would have suited Napoleon perfectly was Frenchman Roger Lapébie. Use of the derailleur was becoming increasingly widespread, and it was Lapébie who first used it to winning advantage. The title could have gone to another derailleur-user in the shape of Italy's Gino Bartali, who held the yellow jersey in the Alps, but, as an old Italian tradition dictated, he crashed out of contention. In Digne, where Lapébie triumphed, Bartali handed his yellow jersey on to defending champion Sylvère Maes. Could he retain his title?

Not if the organizers had anything to do with it. They started tinkering with the route, cancelling the team time trials that were likely to favour Maes and the Belgians. In the midst of the four Pyrenean stages, there was huge tension as Lapébie was only 2-18 down on Maes and found his bike had been sabotaged. Belgian and French riders, their relatives and fans were set against one another. On the road to Pau, cars muscled in behind riders in order to push them along; Lapébie copped a 90-second penalty, leaving him 3-03 behind Maes.

The Tour then arrived on Lapébie's home turf. The stage to Bordeaux was dreadful as far as fair play was concerned. After puncturing, Maes was paced back into the race by two Belgian independent riders, for which he was handed a 15-second penalty. Closing on Bordeaux, Maes and his team were held up at a level crossing just after Lapébie had sped through. Even worse, the locals threw pepper at them! Nose to the handlebars, Lapébie charged on to take the bonus awarded for second place on the stage. The gap between the two leaders was now a mere 25 seconds.

The race was set for the most gripping of showdowns. However, Maes, together with Belgian team manager Karel Steyaert, decided he couldn't win and abandoned the race with the yellow jersey still on his back. This was a first. His team showed a united front and abandoned with him. Thrust unexpectedly into the lead, Lapébie widened his advantage over the three sections of the 17th stage, before wrapping victory in the final two time trials.

L'Auto journalist Jean Leulliot, who was also manager of the French team and always capable of spinning a good yarn, explained: 'The ability to change gear played a vital part in Lapébie's victory as he was always able to find the right speed at the right time.' The proof of that was that Lapébie recorded a new best for the Tour's average speed – 31.768 km/h. That pace was too much for more than half of the starters, including Britain's first two Tour riders, Charles Holland and Bill Burl, competing as a Great Britain/Canada team with Pierre Gachon, who failed to finish stage one. Burl lasted just a day longer, but Holland made it as far as the Pyrenees – a good effort but not a Napoleonic one.

FINAL STANDINGS

1 Roger Lapébie (FRA) France 138:58:31
2 Mario Vicini (ITA) Italy +7:17
3 Leo Amberg (SWI) Switzerland +26:13
4 Francesco Camusso (ITA) Italy +26:53
5 Sylvain Marcaillou (FRA) France +35:36
6 Edouard Vissers (BEL) individual +38:13
7 Paul Chocque (FRA) France +1:05:19
8 Pierre Gallien (FRA) individual +1:06:33
9 Erich Bautz (GER) Germany +1:06:41
10 Jean Frechaut (FRA) individual +1:24:34

AVERAGE SPEED (OF WINNER): 31.768 KM/H
TOTAL DISTANCE RACED: 4,415 KM

ABOVE Lapébie leads the charge across this level crossing just before the train trundles by.

LEFT Although not as good a climber as Berrendero, Bartali or Félicien Vervaecke, Lapébie fought like a lion and limited his losses, as seen here on the Col de Port.

ABOVE A fan checks on Leo Amberg following a crash on the descent of Col de la Croix.

RIGHT Félicien Vervaecke carries his bike with its broken wheel, but he has found someone with whom to share his suffering.

OPPOSITE TOP Following a fall in front of the Hotel des Alpes, the rider inspects his knee as an onlooker straightens his wheel.

OPPOSITE BOTTOM Cars can also cause crashes, even the one containing the Tour boss. But help is always quickly at hand, underlining that spectators on the road are by no means ordinary.

THE ANGEL OF THE MOUNTAINS

Even though Gino Bartali and Sylvère Maes were on the hunt for revenge following events in 1937, the French should never have lost this race. There were no fewer than 36 French riders at the start, comprising the national team with former winners Magne and Speicher, the Cadets (France B) with another ex-champion Leducq, and Les Bleuets (France C) featuring Dante Gianello. There was a problem, though. The French leaders were too old and the up-and-comers were too young.

France's A team was under pressure right from the start, losing riders in crashes before the mountains, then having to say goodbye to Georges Speicher in the Pyrenees when he was disqualified for holding on to a car. The biggest man in the peloton, Luxembourg's Jean Majerus, held the yellow jersey until Bayonne, where old warhorse André Leducq snatched it for one stage. It then passed to Belgium's Félicien Vervaecke. The best climber in the 1935 and 1937 Tours, he was also on the hunt for revenge. The snag was that on this occasion he wasn't the best climber.

Although Vervaecke won the main Pyrenean stage into Luchon, Bartali was hard on his heels. The Belgian gave himself some breathing space by winning the Narbonne time trial, extending his lead to 3-45, but that was as big as his advantage got. From that point it seemed that Bartali was almost riding the 1937 Tour in reverse. A year earlier

he had abandoned in Marseille, but now he won there. In 1937, he had lost the yellow jersey at Digne in the Alps. Heading into the same town from the other direction, he almost regained it. Vervaecke's lead was little more than a minute after he picked up a 30-second penalty for hampering the Italian on the corkscrewing Braus pass.

Clearly in the ascendant, Bartali was untouchable on the road to Briançon. He attacked on a whim on a stage that crossed the Allos, Vars and Izoard passes and finished more than five minutes clear. Vervaecke was 20 minutes behind. The Belgian made it a point to conquer the Iséran, the newest peak on the Tour and hitherto the highest ever at 2,770 m, but a flat tyre prevented him from putting Bartali under any undue pressure. Vervaecke did finally gain some time in the time trial at Laon, but it only meant his deficit on the Italian was 18 minutes.

Thoroughly outclassed by Bartali, who became the first rider to take the yellow jersey and win the mountains title, the French did gain some satisfaction from Victor Cosson's performance. The 23-year-old Parisian finished third, but almost half an hour behind the incredible Bartali. Home fans were also dazzled by Antonin Magne and André Leducq's emotional farewell on the Parc des Princes track. The two former winners shared the final stage victory as they rode into retirement.

FINAL STANDINGS

1 Gino Bartali (ITA) Italy 148:29:12
2 Félicien Vervaecke (BEL) Belgium +18:27
3 Victor Cosson (FRA) France +29:26
4 Ward Vissers (BEL) Belgium +35:08
5 Matt Clemens (LUX) Luxembourg +42:08
6 Mario Vicini (ITA) Italy +44:59
7 Jules Lowie (BEL) Belgium +48:56
8 Antonin Magne (FRA) France +49:00
9 Marcel Kint (BEL) Belgium +59:49
10 Dante Gianello (FRA) France C +1:06:47

AVERAGE SPEED (OF WINNER): 31.612 KM/H
TOTAL DISTANCE RACED: 4,694 KM

ABOVE Gino Bartali (second in line) was in a class of his own in the mountains and would become the first rider to win the yellow jersey as well as the mountains title.

LEFT Overcome with emotion, Bartali receives congratulations from Italian team manager Alfredo Binda.

1939
SYLVÈRE MAES
BELGIUM

MAES WINS AS WAR LOOMS

The situation in Europe meant there were no Germans, Italians or Spaniards on the start line in 1939. In the absence of defending champion Gino Bartali and so many others, would the Tour lack spice? There were only the Belgians – even though they had two former winners – a small number of Swiss, the great riders from Luxembourg, the Dutch, and no less than five French teams – the national squad led by Cosson, Gianello and Marcaillou, plus four regional outfits featuring the likes of Archambaud and Vietto.

Spectators didn't seem too concerned by the missing riders. They turned out in bigger numbers than ever – at the top of the small climbs, on telegraph poles and in Vésinet, where 79 riders started.

The first team at the centre of the action was North-Île de France, who claimed the yellow jersey in Caen thanks to Amédée Fournier's victory. The main actors, however, would be the Belgians, even though they would lose Romain Maes (yellow jersey in Vire), Félicien Vervaecke and Lucien Storme. They allowed Breton Jean Fontenay to take the yellow jersey on his home turf, then left René Vietto (South-East) in control of it for two weeks until the race reached his home ground at the foot of the Alps. This was too long for a rider who lived on his nerves.

In the Alps, Sylvère Maes had a rendezvous with history. On the Izoard, race leader Vietto started to crumble under the pressure. At the finish he came in 17 minutes behind Maes, who was now in the yellow jersey. The next day's racing was split into three sections. The riders had to get up in the early-morning cold for a stage over the Galibier, then ride a time trial over the Iséran. Sylvère Maes destroyed his opposition over this immense pass, gaining another ten minutes on 'King René', now 27 minutes behind the Belgian, who pushed out his lead even more on the way into Paris. As Vietto dropped out of contention for the yellow jersey, the French team finally freed his team-mate Archambaud from his shackles. He flew in the Dijon time trial but it was too late.

At the Parc des Princes, Marcel Kint, 'The Black Eagle', provided the final touch to a Belgian victory that was absolute. The three best climbers were Belgian, with Maes the pick of them. They had six riders in the top ten and both of their two teams finished on the podium. At 30 years old, Sylvère Maes had averaged almost 32 km/h, the Tour's top speed so far, and had won his second victory, just like his compatriot Philippe Thys in 1914. By strange coincidence, both those Belgian victories were followed by war. It would be eight years before the Tour returned, and much would have changed…

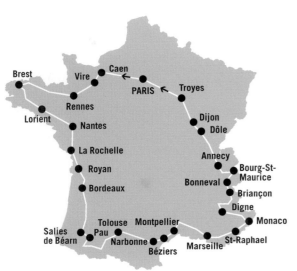

FINAL STANDINGS

1 Sylvère Maes (BEL) Belgium 132:03:17
2 René Vietto (FRA) South-East +30:38
3 Lucien Vlaeminck (BEL) Belgium B +32:08
4 Mathias Clemens (LUX) Luxembourg +36:09
5 Edward Vissers (BEL) Belgium +38:05
6 Sylvain Marcaillou (FRA) France +45:16
7 Albertin Disseaux (BEL) Belgium B +46:54
8 Jan Lambrichs (NED) Netherlands +48:01
9 Albert Ritserveldt (BEL) Belgium B +48:27
10 Cyriel Vanoverberghe (BEL) Belgium B +49:44s

AVERAGE SPEED (OF WINNER): 31.986 KM/H
TOTAL DISTANCE RACED: 4,224 KM

OPPOSITE TOP RIGHT The peloton provided a touch of optimism to a country where major military operations were in full swing.

OPPOSITE BOTTOM AND TOP LEFT Whether in the fog on his beloved Tourmalet (bottom) or in the rain as he replenishes his reserves (top left), Sylvère Maes is a man apart. Runner-up René Vietto would end up half an hour behind him.

Looking at this stony track near the top of a mountain pass you have to wonder why there weren't more punctures. The rider carrying out the repair is Sylvère Maes, while the man looking on closely is former Tour director Henri Desgrange, who appears to have a watch in his left hand. It should take Maes two to three minutes to carry out the repair. Desgrange no doubt let him know how he had fared.

Racing in the war years

AFTER FRANCE DECLARED war on Germany on 3 September 1939 following its invasion of Poland, several French riders competing in the swiftly halted Circuit de l'Ouest suddenly found themselves in the front line. They included André Leducq, Antonin Magne and Maurice Archambaud. That December, there was an even stranger occurrence at a meeting between two former Tour riders: Robert Oubron, 20th in 1937, arrested Kurt Stöpel, who was 2nd in 1932. Shortly afterwards, the UCI (the International Cycling Union) released the dates for the 1940 Tour: it would take place between 26 June and 21 July and would include several of the Tour's great mountain passes.

Despite the occupation, Henri Desgrange dreamed of having the first Americans among the starters for the 33rd Tour, but any such thoughts were about to be dashed. Indeed, by that point Desgrange was so unwell that he had forgotten that the 33rd Tour had already taken place. Sadly, he would not live to see the 34th. The father of the Tour died on 16 August 1940. His successor, Jacques Goddet, was adamant that the Tour would not take place during the conflict, but other races did take place including what was effectively a mini-Tour known as the Circuit de France. Organized by *La France Socialiste*, a right-wing publication run by former *L'Auto* journalist Jean Leulliot, and run between 28 September and 4 October 1942, the race was shameful and a failure.

L'Auto's wartime activities were almost as dubious. The paper was closed after the liberation of France for printing articles that were regarded as being too close to the Germans. Jacques Goddet defended the paper by saying that its presses had also been used for printing copies of speeches and posters of General de Gaulle. As for the yellow jersey, it still fluttered thanks to the Grand Prix de France, a series of races based on the one-day classics. Jo Gourtorbe took the first one in 1943 and the Belgian Maurice Desimpelaere the second in 1944. In the aftermath of the war, a number of competing titles were in the running to organize the Tour. All of them wanted to convince the government of their suitability to take on what was by now a well-established French institution.

LA RONDE DE FRANCE

DE BORDEAUX
A GRENOBLE
PAR LES COLS DES PYRENEES ET DES ALPES

DISTRIBUTION
PARISIENNE DE FILMS

UNE PRODUCTION BONNETERRE
14, Cours de l'Intendance - BORDEAUX

After *L'Auto* had been closed down, *L'Équipe* appeared in its place at the end of February 1946. However, the news-papers *Sports* and *Record* were ahead of it in the running to take on the Tour, as was *Élans*. Each put on a five-day race, which was all that was permitted by the government due to post-war shortages.

The communist-leaning *Sports* appeared to be the best placed to take over the Tour after it organized the Ronde de France (10–14 July 1946). The race ran between Bordeaux and Grenoble via the Pyrenees and the Alps. It was only a partial success as the winner of the yellow jersey was an unknown, Giulio Bresci. New riders who would soon become household names did emerge such as Fachleitner, Apo Lazaridès and Brambilla.

Meanwhile, *L'Équipe* delegated the task of getting the The Race of the Tour de France and Monaco–Paris up and running to the Parc des Princes Velodrome Society and its sister paper *Le Parisien*. The former took place on 23–28 July. Featuring five national teams and five regional teams, with René Vietto as the standard-bearer, it was a popular success. Although not perfect, the organization of this race was better than the rest. Consequently, the right to organize the 34th Tour was assigned to Desgrange's successors: Jacques Goddet and Jacques May.

LA JOIE ÉCLATE SUR LES VISAGES DE BRESCI ET BERTOCCHI, RESPEC-TIVEMENT 1ᵉʳ ET 2ᵉ DE LA « RONDE DE FRANCE »

ABOVE The unknown Bresci and Bertocchi finished first and second in the Ronde de France but the success failed to raise their profile.

ABOVE TOP As for the Circuit de France, it resembled the Tour and rekindled some of the fever of the Tour, but was never likely to be a resounding success.

OPPOSITE The Ronde de France gave riders a little taste of the Tour by featuring some of the race's famous mountain passes.

ROBIC BY A KNOCK-OUT

The Tour looked very different coming out of the war. *L'Équipe* had replaced *L'Auto* as the organizing newspaper. Jacques Goddet, the pre-war Tour director, had taken over as the paper's editor-in-chief following the death of Henri Desgrange in 1940. The Tour had also been organized by the Parc des Princes Vélodrome and *L'Équipe*'s sister paper *Le Parisien*, who put together a route of 4,640 km over 21 stages.

There were 100 starters, but not a single pre-war winner among them. Defending champion Sylvère Maes was due to start but an outbreak of boils prevented him from doing so. Fortunately, 1939 runner-up René Vietto was there and looking to go one better. He had the French team fully behind him, while the Belgians backed Raymond Impanis, the Italians Pierre Brambilla and Aldo Ronconi, and the Swiss Ferdi Kübler. The French regional teams were also fired up, especially Jean Robic, a 26-year-old Breton who was recently married and had the cheek to promise his wife victory in the Tour by way of a dowry.

Youth and freshness would be essential requirements during a race run in scorching weather. The favourites, Pierre Cogan and Vietto were 33 years old, which is quite an age when you haven't embarked on such a great adventure since 1939. A real opportunist, Kübler won in Lille and took the yellow jersey. But Vietto was clearly champing at the bit

as the next day he launched a crazy 140-km attack and reclaimed the yellow jersey he had last worn eight years before. He had, though, made a novice's mistake by using up vital reserves early on. He used up even more defending the jersey.

Waiting patiently in the wings were Édouard Fachleitner and Robic, who showed on the Lyon–Grenoble stage that he was both a pure climber and a fighter. He showed this again on the big Pyrenean stage, where he took back more than ten minutes from the yellow jersey. In Nice he was 25 minutes behind Vietto. By Saint-Brieuc, following a mammoth 139-km time trial, he was third and less than three minutes behind the new race leader, Brambilla. Vietto was in a mess.

Robic failed to reduce the gap on the penultimate stage, but would not admit defeat. On the final day he attacked on the hill at Bonsecours near Rouen. Fachleitner, who was four minutes behind overall, was with him and, perhaps unwisely, helped the faltering Robic over the top of the hill. He could have won the Tour, but let Robic recover. The Breton then proposed the following deal: 'If you work with me, I win the Tour and you are second. If not, you let it slip, Brambilla wins, I'm second and you're third.' Fachleitner went to work with Robic. Their advantage ballooned on the 130 km into Paris. The disconsolate Brambilla lost 13 minutes and fell to third overall as Robic seized the title, just as he had promised his wife he would.

FINAL STANDINGS

1. Jean Robic (FRA) West 148:11:25
2. Édouard Fachleitner (FRA) France +3:58
3. Pierre Brambilla (ITA) Italy +10:07
4. Aldo Ronconi (ITA) Italy +11:00
5. René Vietto (FRA) France +15:23
6. Raymond Impanis (BEL) Belgium +18:14
7. Fermo Camellini (ITA) Netherlands/Foreign +24:08
8. Giordano Cottur (ITA) Italy +1:06:03
9. Jean-Marie Goasmat (FRA) West +1:16:03
10. Apo Lazaridès (FRA) South-East +1:18:44

AVERAGE SPEED (OF WINNER): 31.311 KM/H
TOTAL DISTANCE RACED: 4,640 KM

The Pyrenees were Robic's playground, in particular the Tourmalet. In the midst of a huge crowd that loved and encouraged him, the Breton set the race on fire in order to achieve his goal of overall victory.

BARTALI RISES IN THE MOUNTAINS AGAIN

Unable to defend his title in 1939 due to global tensions, Gino Bartali was back in the game ten years later. Like Vietto, Bartali was now 34 and could see how much the younger riders had dominated in 1947. He was also aware of the strength of a French team that featured Vietto, Robic, Fachleitner, Apo Lazaridès and Louison Bobet.

The 12 teams of 10 were set to cover 4,922 km during a race that took in four countries. Like Vietto in 1947, Bartali showed a touch of impatience as he won the first stage in Le Havre. However, unlike his French rival, the Italian had no thoughts of hanging on to the yellow jersey. The *campionissimo* and his team director, Alfredo Binda, were experienced enough to know that the mountains would decide the jersey's final destination. Consequently, they let the young Bobet carry the weight of leading the race.

The Frenchman took the lead in La Rochelle, lost it immediately, then regained it in Biarritz, where he was almost 21 minutes up on the Italian. Bobet then clung on brilliantly as Bartali took back-to-back wins in the Pyrenees, losing only three minutes to the Italian. However, Bobet lacked support on the French team and was hampered by a boil on his foot. He almost abandoned in San Remo, but responded to his difficulties with a sensational victory in Cannes after he had broken away with Lazaridès. Bartali was 21 minutes down once more, but his favourite terrain was just ahead.

He had taken the lead in 1937 and 1938. Back in Italy there was a turmoil following an assassination attempt on Communist Party leader Palmiro Togliatti. As Bartali prepared for the Alps, Italian Prime Minister Alcide de Gasperi called him to say: 'You must win to help us forget the crisis that has struck Italy.' Robic controlled Bartali over the Allos and Vars passes, but could not follow when the Italian surged clear on the Izoard, winning the stage and cutting Bobet's lead to little more than a minute.

On the 14th and 15th stages, which featured seven passes between them, including the Galibier, Croix de Fer and Forclaz, Bartali was majestic in adding two bouquets to his collection. The ailing Bobet was beaten. The Breton lost the yellow jersey, then his podium place as Bartali triumphed again in Mulhouse and then once more in Liège, giving him seven stage wins in total. The first TV broadcast from the Parc des Princes showed the extent of Italy's success. The *campionissimo* had returned victorious ten years after his first success, his team-mate Giovanni Corrieri won in the Parc, while Bartali had also claimed the mountains title and set the best average speed (33.442 km/h) in history. Belgium's Briek Schotte was 26 minutes behind in second. Binda took great pleasure in saying, 'If I had been Bobet's manager, the young Frenchman would have won.' In the end he was fourth, but no one could surely have beaten the great Gino that year.

FINAL STANDINGS

1 Gino Bartali (ITA) Italy 147:10:36
2 Briek Schotte (BEL) Belgium +26:16
3 Guy Lapébie (FRA) Centre/South-East +28:48
4 Louison Bobet (FRA) France +32:59
5 Jeng Kirchen (LUX) Netherlands/Luxembourg +37:53
6 Lucien Teisseire (FRA) France +40:17
7 Roger Lambrecht (BEL) Internationals +49:56
8 Fermo Camellini (ITA) Internationals +51:36
9 Louis Thiétard (FRA) Paris +55:23
10 Raymond Impanis (BEL) Belgium +1:00:03

AVERAGE SPEED (OF WINNER): 33.442 KM/H
TOTAL DISTANCE RACED: 4,922 KM

Bartali was at least one level
above his rivals in the mountains,
and maybe even two.

Posters

RIGHT FROM THE very first editions of the Tour, the bicycle manufacturers engaged in an advertising war in order to take the best advantage of the shop window that the race offered them. They battled to sign up the best riders, whose exploits were used to sell bikes to as many as six million bike owners in France alone. In fact, this market was so large that the contest to gain a significant slice of it produced a good deal of ill-feeling between the brands when they tried to poach each other's champions. But the discord was often well worth the effort. For example, when the Pélissier brothers moved to Dilecta, their sales increased tenfold.

The Tour was also a springboard to hugely increased sales for Alcyon, whose sky blue colours claimed seven Tour titles, and for Automoto, the purple brand who had nudged them off top spot from 1923 to 1926. J. B. Louvet, La Française, Allélulia, Dilecta, Christophe, Elvish, Armor, Lucifer and La Rafale shared the crumbs available by taking stage wins or receiving honourable mentions.

In the pre-war, pre-radio age, companies depended on advertising campaigns in newspapers such as *L'Auto*, with often gloriously colourful posters that highlighted the exploits of their star riders. The designs tended towards the basic in the Tour's early years, but quickly developed into something much more eye-catching, produced with a good deal of canny finesse. For example, the poster produced to celebrate Peugeot's crushing success in the 1908 race carries the headline 'Two Great Victors'. Beneath it stands race winner Lucien Petit-Breton holding a roll of honour listing the successes taken by the famous lion brand that year. Next to him is Napoleon Bonaparte, who is flourishing a list of his famous victories. No doubt Peugeot were very well aware that Napoleon was Tour organizer Henri Desgrange's inspiration and idol.

In the inter-war period, the posters put across the manufacturers' message more cleverly using designers such as Mich, who had become celebrated for their artistry and humour. J. B. Louvet's poster for 'a bike that climbs everything' is a classic of this type, showing a rider scaling a pair of stepladders (see below). In the post-war period, as first radio and then television became the pre-eminent way of promoting bikes and other products, promotional posters rapidly disappeared as a means of promoting manufacturers, leaving them indelibly associated with such long-extant names as Alcyon, La Française and Elvish.

COPPISSIMO!

According to Tour sprinting great Charles Pélissier, the favourites for the title in 1949 were Italy's Fausto Coppi and Gino Bartali, and the Bretons. By a quirk of circumstance, Brittany almost marked the end of the race for Coppi. He was already lagging in the standings but was away in a break with Jacques Marinelli, when the two men tangled and fell while taking on food. Marinelli escaped unscathed and went on to claim the yellow jersey, but Coppi remained on the ground with his forks and wheel broken. The Italian had to wait for the peloton to arrive before he could get a new bike, then refused it because it wasn't his personal spare. Feeling that Bartali was getting more support from team manager Binda, Coppi crawled along 18 minutes behind the winner and had to be persuaded by Binda to continue.

Marinelli, meanwhile, had become a national hero. Not because he had clashed with Coppi but because of his diminutive stature – he was 5'1½" – and his nickname of 'The Parrot' due to his green jersey and headgear. *L'Équipe* built him up, focusing on his determination to battle with the big guns, which helped push their sales up to more than 600,000 copies. 'The Parrot' became a sensation, although Coppi quickly struck back by winning the La Rochelle time trial and gaining seven minutes on Marinelli, who finally lost the lead in Pau to a third Italian, Fiorenzo Magni.

At this point, Coppi was 19th and 32 minutes behind Magni. Fresh from victory in the Giro d'Italia, Coppi tested himself on the Aubisque and the Tourmalet, then let Robic go and claim the stage while reducing his deficit to 14 minutes. Magni held firm until the Alps, when his two great compatriots seized control. Coppi and Bartali finished alone together in Briançon, the defending champion taking the yellow jersey, with his team-mate and rival now just 1-22 behind overall. The conditions had been so cold on the Izoard that one rider had to warm his feet up on a car radiator. Nothing seemed to slow the Italians, though – or at least Coppi. Heading to Aosta in Italy the following day, Bartali punctured when with his rival, who rode on to win alone and take a five-minute lead.

The Italians' grip on the race continued until Coppi sealed his victory by a 7-minute win over Bartali in the 137-km Colmar to Nancy time trial, which boosted the 29-year-old Coppi's advantage over 35-year-old Bartali to 11 minutes overall, with 23-year-old Marinelli a very impressive third. Described in one paper as 'the man with the hammer', Coppi had turned a 28-minute deficit on Marinelli in Pau to a 25-minute lead in Paris. He also claimed the mountains title for good measure. After having almost lost the Tour, Fausto had stunned everyone.

FINAL STANDINGS

1 Fausto Coppi (ITA) Italy 149:40:49
2 Gino Bartali (ITA) Italy +10:55
3 Jacques Marinelli (FRA) Île de France +25:13
4 Jean Robic (FRA) West/North +34:28
5 Marcel Dupont (BEL) Belgian Aiglons +38:59
6 Fiorenzo Magni (ITA) Italian Cadets +42:10
7 Stan Ockers (BEL) Belgium +44:35
8 Jean Goldschmit (LUX) Luxembourg +47:24
9 Apo Lazaridès (FRA) France +52:28
10 Pierre Cogan (FRA) West/North +1:08:55

AVERAGE SPEED (OF WINNER): 32.121 KM/H
TOTAL DISTANCE RACED: 4,808 KM

OPPOSITE Whether in time trials or in the mountains, Coppi is sublime, excelling at every turn. Against the clock in La Rochelle and Nancy he was unmatchable, while in the mountains only his great rival Bartali could compete with him.

OVERLEAF The Tour flies through the feed zone in Brussels, where home favourite Roger Lambrecht will go on to win the stage and take the yellow jersey. Note the race organization's jeeps on the left, a relic perhaps of the still not too distant war.

KÜBLER 'THE EAGLE' FLIES HIGH

To say that this 37th Tour was open as a result of the absence of Fausto Coppi, who had fractured his pelvis in the Giro, is an understatement – such was the Italian's domination of the sport at that time. However, the field still included two former champions in Bartali and Robic, as well as several wearers of the yellow jersey, notably Italy's Magni, France's Bobet and Switzerland's Kübler.

The Tour came to life during the sixth stage time trial, where Kübler was triumphant and climbed to third overall, less than a minute down on leader Jean Goldschmit of Luxembourg. A bit of a maverick, Kübler had abandoned the 1947 and 1949 races after winning stages in both. On this occasion, Swiss team manager Alex Burtin had brought his riders closer together and got them fully behind Kübler. He was still prone to some odd decisions such as changing into a silk jersey during the time trial, which earned him a 15-second penalty. Little matter, though, as he had gained a huge psychological boost by beating everyone, notably the Italians.

Heading to the Pyrenees, the Italians tightened their grip. Magni won a stage and Bartali came to the fore with victory in Saint-Gaudens. But there was trouble en route. Partisan crowds were angry at the Italians, particularly on the Col d'Aspin, where Bartali, blocked by a car, collided with Robic and crashed. He recovered to win the stage as Magni took the yellow jersey, but the *campionissimo* had been frightened by

his time on the road, by the kicks and punches directed at him. That night he announced he was abandoning the race, and he wanted his team to quit with him. But was he actually more afraid of his young team-mate Magni winning the title?

Although the French government apologized to the Italians and their government, Bartali was adamant. The Italians left, leaving second-placed Kübler in yellow. However, the Swiss refused to wear the jersey on the road to Perpignan, as a mark of respect for his departed rivals. He put it on for the following stage to Nîmes and, in scorching heat, produced a devastating attack with Belgium's Stan Ockers. Bobet, perhaps distracted by an ice-cream, lost ten minutes. This heatwave is best remembered for two unforgettable Tour moments: the collapse of the Algerian rider Abdel-Kader Zaaf due to sunstroke and the peloton running into the Mediterranean to cool down.

Bobet responded by attacking on the Turini and Izoard passes, regaining four minutes on Kübler. Heading for Saint-Étienne, knowing he still needed to press, he attacked again at a feeding station and didn't take on supplies. He paid for his rashness by losing five more minutes, then another nine in the subsequent time trial. It was all over.

Kübler, known as 'The Eagle of Adliswill', was cheered all the way into Paris, where he was crowned Switzerland's first Tour champion. Ockers was second, while Bobet had to be content with third and the mountains title.

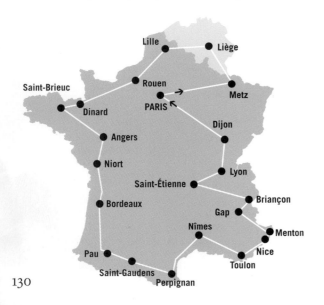

FINAL STANDINGS

1 Ferdi Kübler (SWI) Switzerland 145:36:56
2 Stan Ockers (BEL) Belgium +9:30
3 Louison Bobet (FRA) France +22:19
4 Raphaël Geminiani (FRA) France +31:14
5 Jean Kirchen (LUX) Luxembourg +34:21
6 Kléber Piot (FRA) Île de France/North-East +41:35
7 Pierre Cogan (FRA) Centre/South-West +52:22
8 Raymond Impanis (BEL) Belgium +53:34
9 Georges Meunier (FRA) Centre/South-West +54:29
10 Jean Goldschmit (LUX) Luxembourg +55:21

AVERAGE SPEED (OF WINNER): 32.791 KM/H
TOTAL DISTANCE RACED: 4,775 KM

OPPOSITE The unpredictable Swiss transformed himself into a worthy champion thanks to two stunning time trial performances.

KOBLET'S CLASS SHINES THROUGH

For the second time in its history the Tour started in the provinces, this time in the eastern city of Metz. Fausto Coppi was back in the Italian team with Gino Bartali, now 37, but Coppi was in mourning following the tragic death of his brother, Serse, in the Giro del Piemonte just a few days earlier. Defending champion Ferdi Kübler was missing due to exhaustion, so the Swiss team was led by debutant Hugo Koblet, winner of the Giro d'Italia the previous year.

Pre-race favourite Louison Bobet knew Koblet might be a threat, but he was also well aware that the Giro is not the Tour. He hoped to continue his progression: fourth in 1948, third in 1950… However, Koblet was confident and so was his team, overseen by *directeur sportif* Alex Burtin. As had been the case in 1950, the first time trial kickstarted the action. Koblet judged his effort perfectly over an 85-km course to Angers, despite having woken starving hungry at two that morning and quelled those pangs with a jellied chicken.

The star of the first part of the race was a certain Roger Levêque, from the West/South-West team. The winner as the race passed through Paris, he took the yellow jersey in Rennes and was still holding it in Brive, where boxer Sugar Ray Robinson started the stage. Perhaps it was the boxer's presence that inspired Koblet to deliver a tremendous blow to his rivals. With 140 km remaining of the stage between Brive and Agen

he attacked on his own. Surely, it was pure madness. Coppi, Bobet, Robic, Geminiani and Ockers pursued him in vain. On the line, where he still had enough energy left to comb his hair and check his watch, Koblet's lead was 2-35 moving him to third overall, well ahead of the other favourites.

Everyone expected him to collapse in the Pyrenees, but instead the spotlight fell on the first Dutch wearer of the yellow jersey, Wim Van Est. He crashed off the road and into a ravine on the descent of the Aubisque and had to abandon the race. In the key mountain stage between Tarbes and Luchon, Koblet allowed Coppi and Bartali free rein, before reeling them in on the Aspin and outsprinting Coppi for a stage win that put him in the yellow jersey. Two days later the Swiss romped to another win in Montpellier, gaining 5 minutes on Bobet and more than 30 on a sickening Coppi.

The Italian made a last stand in Briançon, but Koblet was not far behind and was naturally more concerned with his nearest rivals, Raphaël Geminiani and Lucien Lazaridès, Apo's older brother who had been the first man to lead the race over the Ventoux. He crushed both Frenchmen and everyone else in the 97-km time trial that finished on his home turf in Geneva, enabling him to enjoy a triumphal march into Paris, where old Bartali was fourth and happy to have beaten Magni (7th), Coppi (10th) and Bobet (20th).

FINAL STANDINGS

1   Hugo Koblet (SWI) Switzerland 142:20:14
2   Raphaël Geminiani (FRA) France +22:00
3   Lucien Lazaridès (FRA) France +24:16
4   Gino Bartali (ITA) Italy +29:09
5   Stan Ockers (BEL) Belgium +32:53
6   Pierre Barbotin (FRA) France +36:40
7   Fiorenzo Magni (ITA) Italy +39:14
8   Gilbert Bauvin (FRA) East/South-East +45:53
9   Bernardo Ruiz (SPA) Spain +45:55
10 Fausto Coppi (ITA) Italy +46:51

AVERAGE SPEED (OF WINNER): 32.999 KM/H
TOTAL DISTANCE RACED: 4,697 KM

OPPOSITE TOP Hugo Koblet shines thanks to sterling efforts of the well-drilled Swiss team.

OPPOSITE BOTTOM Against the clock, Koblet (right), 'The Pedaller of Charm', is astonishing. In Angers over 85 km he gains six minutes on Geminiani (left) and nearly double that in Geneva over 97 km. 'Gem', who is runner-up, is 22 minutes behind but also the best climber…

As furnace-like heat descends on the race, Italian champion Fiorenzo Magni is happy to be doused with water by a fan at the roadside.

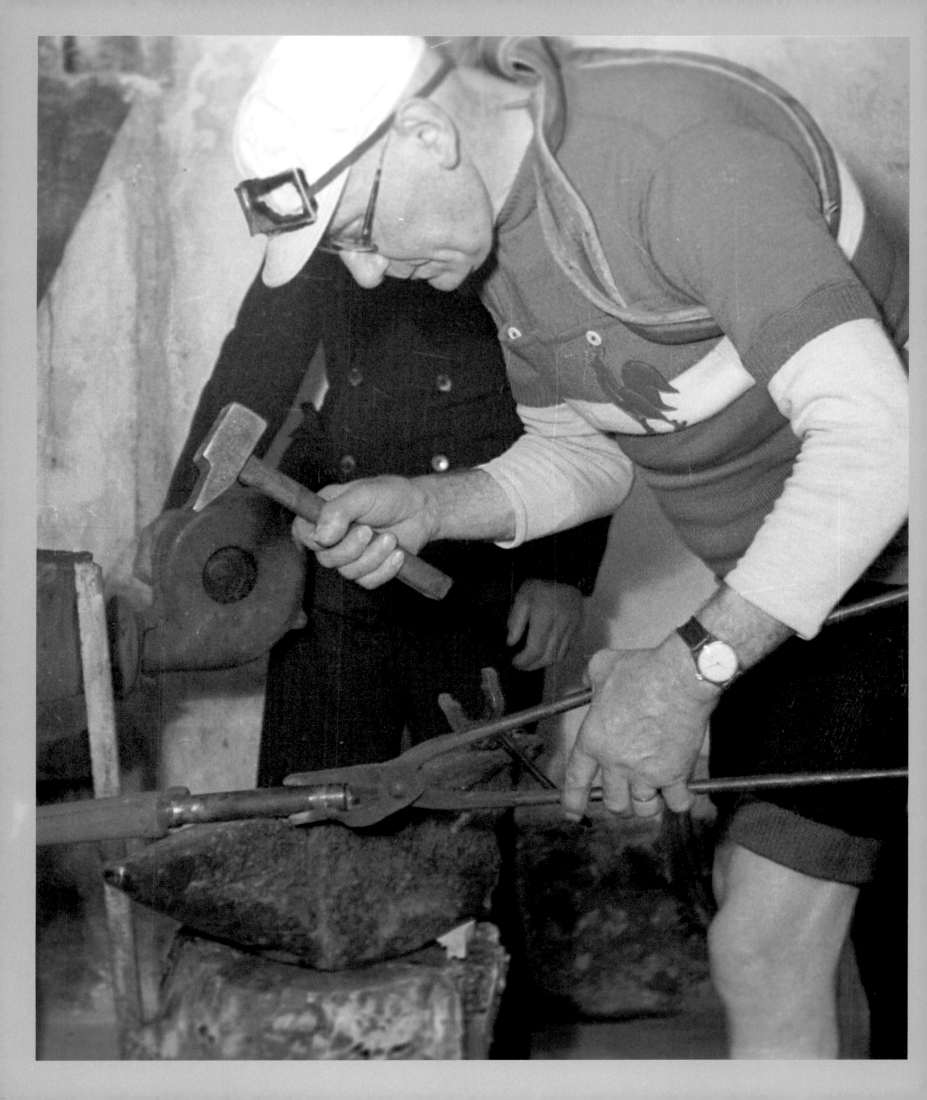

Christophe at the forge

THE LEGENDARY HISTORY of the Tour is based upon the riders' exploits, the epic races and dramas involved. Broken forks have been a regular occurrence on the Tour, particularly in the pre-war years when what were still fairly rudimentary bikes were used on hellish roads. One man in particular was unforgettably affected by this type of breakdown: Eugène Christophe, known as 'Cri-Cri' and 'The Old Gaul', twice suffered a broken fork when poised to win the Tour.

The first incident took place in 1913 when he broke his fork prior to the start of the descent of the Tourmalet. Christophe was the leader on the road, but his team-mate Philippe Thys understandably made the most of it by taking the lead as Christophe descended on foot to the forge at Sainte-Marie-de-Campan to carry out a repair. The second incident was in 1919 when he was wearing the yellow jersey near Dunkirk, just one stage from the finish.

The first time, the former locksmith took more than two hours to repair his forks in the forge he had fortunately found, although he was penalized because someone else operated the bellows as he did it. In those heroic days the riders were completely dependent on themselves and were not allowed to receive any assistance at all. The Tour was a testing ground for men and equipment. Six years later it was the cobblestones of the north that caused the same malfunction. Fortunately, there was a factory nearby with a workshop. Christophe barely took an hour to repair it, but the Belgian Firmin Lambot, who had been on his heels, was long gone. Victory disappeared once again.

What was terrible was that there was no authentic record of these two dramas that have since become epics. There were some rare photos at the finish lines but nothing of the improvised work of the forger. Paradoxically, that lack of evidence has contributed to the strengthening of the legend. There was a remarkable drawing done by Paul Ordner, but it was done a long time afterwards.

However, on 3 June 1951, the mayor of Sainte-Marie-de-Campan invited Christophe and the Tour organization to relive the episode from 1913. It took place under the watchful eye of Marie Despiau, who had been 49 on 9 July 1913 when the original incident took place and had shouted, 'Go in there' at Christophe. She was now 84. Also present was young Tornay, now 49, who had shown Eugène the forge and had then helped him work the bellows. Also on hand was race judge Henri Lecomte who was in tears as he watched Christophe re-enacting the scene. Did he regret being so severe with the French rider? By now 66, Christophe tapped, tapped, tapped – again and again.

Clearly moved, Christophe had the last word. 'At least I won the Tour de France of your hearts, long live Desgrange…' he declared. A plaque presented by the French cycling federation and *L'Équipe* still marks the spot in Sainte-Marie-de-Campan today.

" J'ai mesuré, ajusté, forgé.... "

Now 66, Christophe re-enacts one of the Tour's most celebrated incidents, which had taken place 38 years earlier.

COPPI JOINS THE GREATS

The 39th Tour de France started in Brest, which could have provided Breton hero Louison Bobet with the inspiration he needed to win the race. However, after five defeats, Bobet chose not to take part. Instead, he listened to it on five transistor radios he had at home while sipping Coca-Cola. Another Breton, Jean Robic, replaced him in the French team, together with Jean Dotto. France's line-up looked capable of dealing with the challenge presented by the hugely powerful Italian team featuring Bartali, Coppi and Magni. Other teams looked well equipped too, although Switzerland were unable to count on either Kübler or Koblet.

Coppi bided his time initially, as the yellow jersey was shared between Rik Van Steenbergen, Nello Lauredi and Fiorenzo Magni. He wasn't the slightest bit concerned by the fact that his personal water-carrier, Andréa Carrea, also had a day in yellow – quite the contrary in fact. Having shown his strength by winning the 60-km time trial into Nancy, Coppi looked ahead to the first of the three critical summit finishes on a newly introduced climb up to Alpe d'Huez. When it arrived, the feisty Robic tried to stay with the Italian, but this was Coppi at his very best.

Now in yellow, Coppi produced one of the all-time great performances the next day as he raced towards victory at Sestrières in Italy. He led over the Glandon, Croix de Fer, Galibier and Montgenèvre passes. At the line he was seven minutes clear. His overall lead was 20 minutes.

After Mont Ventoux, where Robic led and Bartali shone, Coppi eased off a touch, but in the Pyrenees he once again showed his best as he led over the Aubisque and Tourmalet before winning in Pau. The gap between Coppi and the rest was now so large that Bartali was happy to give his great rival his wheel when the yellow jersey punctured. Indeed, it reached the point where race director Jacques Goddet doubled the prize money for second place in order to maintain a semblance of suspense behind the untouchable Coppi.

Belgium's Stan Ockers, dubbed a wheel-sucker by Swiss manager Alex Burtin, hung on to that position as Alex Close, Bartali and Robic challenged. The final curtain came down at the third summit finish, that of the Puy-de-Dôme, which was also making its Tour debut. Coppi won again, extending his lead to almost half an hour. The only minor change came when the Spaniard Bernardo Ruiz pinched third place from Robic, who fell to fifth behind 38-year-old Bartali. But this was a race all about one man – the unparalleled Fausto Coppi. Quite simply, he was in a world of his own.

FINAL STANDINGS

1 Fausto Coppi (ITA) Italy 151:57:20
2 Stan Ockers (BEL) Belgium +28:17
3 Bernardo Ruiz (SPA) Spain +34:38
4 Gino Bartali (ITA) Italy +35:25
5 Jean Robic (FRA) France +35:36
6 Fiorenzo Magni (ITA) Italy +38:25
7 Alex Close (BEL) Belgium +38:32
8 Jean Dotto (FRA) France +48:01
9 Andrea Carrea (ITA) Italy +50:20
10 Antonio Gelabert (SPA) Spain +58:16

AVERAGE SPEED (OF WINNER): 31.765 KM/H
TOTAL DISTANCE RACED: 4,827 KM

OPPOSITE Coppi is happy to be doused with the contents of a watering-can as blazing heat descends on the Tour.

OVERLEAF Coppi's fantastic ride on the Bourg d'Oisans–Sestrières stage as depicted in *La Domenica del Corriere*.

BOBET WINS 50TH ANNIVERSARY RACE

The 40th Tour marked the race's 50th anniversary. It was an unusual race for a number of reasons. For a start, none of the previous year's podium finishers lined up. Coppi, Ockers and Ruiz were either injured or too tired by other racing commitments to tackle the Tour. It started in Strasbourg with Bobet, Koblet, Bartali, Magni the big names, plus a team from the West that featured Robic and Jean Malléjac. André Darrigade and Charly Gaul made their debuts, the former for the South-West team, the latter for Luxembourg. The Tour also put a distinctive new jersey up for grabs. A green jersey would be awarded to the most consistently high finisher.

The early action was dominated by Switzerland's Fritz Schär. He took the first two stages and held the yellow jersey until Caen, where Frenchman Roger Hassenforder relieved him of it. Schär retook it in the Pyrenees, where his team leader, Hugo Koblet, crashed and had to abandon. It perhaps didn't help that he had plastered himself with anti-cold patches because it was actually very hot. Second in Cauterets and then first in Luchon, Robic claimed the yellow jersey, but held it for just one day until team-mate François Mahé took it in Albi, only to hand it to another Breton, Malléjac, a day later.

Malléjac kept it for several days, without ever seeming a likely winner. It was clear the Alps would decide the race. The first big climbs proved that. Always up with the main contenders in the Pyrenees, Bobet's time had finally come in his sixth appearance at the Tour. An attack on the Izoard took him clear of the field and he won by more than five minutes in Briançon, taking the lead from Malléjac, who was now second but almost nine minutes down.

The final destination of the title was clear. Finally, it had all come together for Bobet. He sealed the deal in the 70-km time trial between Lyon and Saint-Étienne, taking victory and extending his lead to 14 minutes. The dashing 28-year-old Breton was light years ahead of the rest. As he rode into the Parc des Princes to claim the title, 15 former winners were waiting to congratulate him as part of the 50th anniversary celebrations. The Swiss Schär, who had taken the first two stages, finished sixth and had the honour of being the first winner of the green jersey.

FINAL STANDINGS

1 Louison Bobet (FRA) France 129:23:25
2 Jean Malléjac (FRA) West France +14:18
3 Giancarlo Astrua (ITA) Italy +15:02
4 Alex Close (BEL) Belgium +17:35
5 Wout Wagtmans (NED) Netherlands +18:05
6 Fritz Schär (SWI) Switzerland +18:44
7 Antonin Rolland (FRA) France +23:03
8 Nello Lauredi (FRA) France +26:03
9 Raphaël Geminiani (FRA) France +27:18
10 François Mahé (FRA) West France +28:26

AVERAGE SPEED (OF WINNER): 34.616 KM/H
TOTAL DISTANCE RACED: 4,479 KM

The Breton champion laid the basis for his victory in the Alps, particularly on the Izoard where, as his brother Jean put it: 'He started weaving his yellow jersey.' He is pictured in the Saint-Étienne time trial, where he underlined he was the strong man of the race.

While the riders will worry about the descent off the Col du Tourmalet, the fans are more concerned with the mist and cold that make spectating a chilly experience.

OPPOSITE TOP Louison Bobet replaces his rear wheel after a puncture.

OPPOSITE BOTTOM RIGHT Italian rider Umberto Drei has fallen so heavily that he won't be able to rejoin the race.

OPPOSITE INSET A depiction of Koblet's fall on the Pau–Cauterets stage. The 1951 champion survived the drop but had to abandon the race.

BOBET SEALS SECOND WIN ON IZOARD

For the first time in its 51-year history the Tour started outside France. Amsterdam in the Netherlands received that honour, although the race started without Italy's Coppi and Magni. Had they been judged undesirable due to their involvement with sponsors from outside the sport? The key thing for home fans was defending champion Bobet, leading a very strong French team. They were the favourites, but the Swiss team looked powerful too with Kübler, Koblet, Schär and Clerici. The Belgians had Ockers back, while the Dutch also looked impressive.

Wout Wagtmans underlined the strength of the Dutch when he took the opening stage. He would share the yellow jersey with Bobet as far as the Pyrenees. Bobet took the lead when France came second in a short team time trial in Rouen, where the Swiss showed their potential by winning the test. Kübler's victory in Saint-Brieuc a couple of days later backed that up. However, their hopes were seriously hit when Koblet fell ill and had to abandon the race in the Pyrenees.

Wagtmans regained the lead when he finished second in Angers and he held it until the major Pyrenean stage over the Tourmalet, Aspin and Peyresourde. Little Gilbert Bauvin from the North-East/Centre team ruffled some feathers on the big teams that day, by winning ahead of a Spanish debutant named Federico Bahamontes. Bauvin finally removed the yellow jersey from Wagtmans' shoulders.

Some wondered whether Bauvin, clearly in superb form on the climbs, could hold the lead through the Alps. Sadly for him, it never came to that. An epic break featuring Bobet, Kübler, Ockers, Schär and Wagtmans over lumpy roads on the stage to Millau resulted in Bauvin dropping to second behind Bobet, who was finding his best form just as the race was nearing the Alps. As he had done the previous year, Bobet entered a state of grace on the Izoard, where no one could stay on terms with him. Behind him, the battle was all about second place, which was disputed by Swiss team-mates Schär and Kübler. The latter, the 1950 champion, took it, but only after he had received a taste of his own medicine from Bobet in the Nancy time trial.

In Paris, Bobet the Breton claimed his second consecutive title in a justified blaze of glory, with Swiss riders filling the other steps on the podium, as Kübler came in second and Schär third. The Swiss were delighted that Kübler took the green jersey and the team classification as well, ensuring they left the race with a good bounty. Fourth place went to the highest placed regional rider, Jean Dotto, from the South-East team.

One disappointment was the absence of a photo showing Bahamontes pinching an ice-cream from a spectator on the Col de Romeyère. The Spaniard did feature in plenty of other photos, though, as he claimed the mountains title. But the race was all about Bobet. Could he complete a hat-trick?

FINAL STANDINGS

1   Louison Bobet (FRA) France 140:06:05
2   Ferdi Kübler (SWI) Switzerland +15:49
3   Fritz Schär (SWI) Switzerland +21:46
4   Jean Dotto (FRA) South-East +28:21
5   Jean Malléjac (FRA) West +31:38
6   Stan Ockers (BEL) Belgium +36:02
7   Louis Bergaud (FRA) South-West +37:55
8   Vincent Vitetta (FRA) South-East +41:14
9   Jean Brankart (BEL) Belgium +42:08
10 Gilbert Bauvin (FRA) North-East/Centre +42:21

AVERAGE SPEED (OF WINNER): 33.325 KM/H
TOTAL DISTANCE RACED: 4,669 KM

OPPOSITE A second win for Bobet, who had by now become well established as one of France's great sporting icons.

BOBET COMPLETES A HAT-TRICK

The 1955 race featured 130 riders (20 more than in 1954) in 13 teams, including the first appearance of a complete British team. Louison Bobet was back to defend. His key rivals appeared to be Ferdi Kübler and Jean Robic, but their respective teams, Switzerland and the West, were not as strong as they had been. Still gripped by controversy due to their involvement with 'extra-sportifs' sponsors, the Italians sent a B team that looked very underpowered. If there was to be a concerted threat to the French, it looked likely to come from the Belgians and Dutch.

Spain's Miguel Poblet set things alight by triumphing in Dieppe, becoming the first Iberian to wear the yellow jersey. But the Dutch quickly got their hands on it in a team time trial which put Wout Wagtmans in yellow. His team-mate Wim Van Est also held it for a day, the pair of them sandwiching a short spell in the lead for Frenchman Antonin Rolland.

Rolland regained the lead as the race headed into the Alps. The Alpine action was unusually lacklustre. In the absence of Bahamontes and with Bobet out of sorts, the stand-out performer was little Charly Gaul from Luxembourg, who led over the Vars, Télégraphe and Galibier to finish alone in Briançon. Bobet remained on the defensive when Gaul had attacked, struggling with saddle sores. He might not have carried on had it not been for his brother Jean and a great French team around him, particularly Rolland who relieved some of the

pressure he was under by holding the yellow jersey for so long. Racing in the world champion's rainbow bands helped him too.

The true champion finally emerged on the Ventoux. He flew up and over 'the bald mountain' with a courageous solo attack and held on until Avignon to win by six minutes. In the absence of the Izoard, Bobet had taken control of the race on the Provençal climb. He leapt into second behind his team-mate Rolland, while Gaul slipped back and Kübler lost his grip and abandoned the race. The French, though, lost Jean Malléjac in what were very nearly tragic circumstances. He collapsed on the Ventoux and almost died. Doping was to blame.

Bobet turned the screw in the Pyrenees. Often dancing on the pedals with his good friend Raphaël Geminiani close at hand, he tracked Gaul and Jean Brankart as they upped the pressure. Rolland could not deal with it and ceded the yellow jersey to his team leader in Saint-Gaudens. Exiting the mountains, Bobet once again had the race almost won.

Despite his health problems, he took the title with the fastest average ever and three of his team-mates in the top ten. That gave them the team prize, while Gaul was crowned King of the Mountains and Stan Ockers took the green jersey. Belgium's three-time champion Philippe Thys did a lap of honour with Bobet at the Parc des Princes as the crowd honoured Bobet's achievement with cries of 'Pschitt! Pschitt! Pschitt! Hurrah!' The Frenchman was the face of this French fizzy drink…

FINAL STANDINGS

1 Louison Bobet (FRA) France 130:29:26
2 Jean Brankart (BEL) Belgium +4:53
3 Charly Gaul (LUX) Luxembourg/Mixed +11:30
4 Pasquale Fornara (ITA) Italy +12:44
5 Antonin Rolland (FRA) France +13:18
6 Raphaël Geminiani (FRA) France +15:01
7 Giancarlo Astrua (ITA) Italy +18:13
8 Stan Ockers (BEL) Belgium +27:13
9 Alex Close (BEL) Belgium +31:10
10 François Mahé (FRA) France +36:27

AVERAGE SPEED (OF WINNER): 34.301 KM/H
TOTAL DISTANCE RACED: 4,476 KM

Although affected by dreadful sores, Bobet proved invincible with the rainbow jersey on his back.

WALKOWIAK THE ESCAPE ARTIST

The 43rd Tour started from the champagne capital of Reims, which was fitting as this would be a Tour of huge surprises, a really sparkling race. It was unpredictable from the start because three-time champion Bobet, who would have been the favourite, was convalescing and therefore not on the start line. Consequently, the French had a strong team but no clear leader. Meanwhile, the Swiss were counting on Schär, Spain on Bahamontes and Luxembourg on Gaul. The Dutch and Belgians also looked strong, while there was always the possibility that five regional teams featuring the likes of Dotto, Lauredi, Hassenforder and Walkowiak could add some fizz to this uncertain vintage.

From the start, the race was crazy. Perhaps logically, bouncing Basque André Darrigade had the last word after the peloton had been scattered. He passed the yellow jersey to Belgian Gilbert Desmet, then took it back in the time trial at Rouen, where Gaul, Brankart and Bahamontes showed they were the strongest.

However, although strength is a key factor when it comes to winning the Tour, seeing and seizing an opportunity can also be important, and plenty of riders were attempting to do so. Heading for Caen there were ten riders in the break. The next day to Saint-Malo there were 11. The day after that there were 18. Between Lorient and Angers, 31 riders gave the peloton the slip.

Roger Walkowiak from the North-East/Centre team was in all four attacks and took the yellow jersey after the third of them. On his heels he had Fernand Picot from the West team, but Picot did not pose a real danger. 'Walko' was riding his fourth Tour. He had finished twice and was progressing. He had previously finished second in Paris–Nice and the Dauphiné. He was no mug.

Walkowiak lost his unexpected lead in Bayonne. Gerrit Voorting, Darrigade, Jan Adriaenssens and Wout Wagtmans took turns in the lead on the way to the Alps. There, Walko once again got into the right breakaways, finishing fifth in Turin and also in Grenoble, where he reclaimed the lead. Sixth place in Saint-Étienne boosted his chances even more as he gained ground over most of his rivals apart from France's Gilbert Bauvin. Bauvin, however, was handed a 30-second penalty for receiving pushes. That left 29-year-old Walkowiak more than three minutes ahead, which was enough to ensure his surprise victory in Paris. Bauvin took second but he and his France team-mates were jeered by the crowd.

For Walko, though, there was nothing but praise, particularly from Tour director Jacques Goddet, who considered the 1956 race the best Tour that he had followed, and Walkowiak an ideal winner. Although modest and from an equally modest team, Walko well deserved his victory champagne. After all, he had posted the fastest average in Tour history: 36.268 km/h.

FINAL STANDINGS

1 Roger Walkowiak (FRA) North-East/Centre 124:01:16
2 Gilbert Bauvin (FRA) France +1:25
3 Jan Adriaensens (BEL) Belgium +3:44
4 Federico Bahamontes (SPA) Spain +10:14
5 Nino Defilippis (ITA) Italy +10:25
6 Wout Wagtmans (NED) Netherlands +10:59
7 Nello Lauredi (FRA) South-East +14:01
8 Stan Ockers (BEL) Belgium +16:52
9 René Privat (FRA) France +22:59
10 Antonio Barbosa (POR) Luxembourg/Mixed +26:03

AVERAGE SPEED (OF WINNER): 36.268 KM/H
TOTAL DISTANCE RACED: 4,498 KM

OPPOSITE Walkowiak showed that clever use of tactics can take you a very long way in the Tour.

DEBUTANT ANQUETIL'S MASTERSTROKE

Starting in Nantes, the 44th Tour looked as open as the previous year's. Defending champion Roger Walkowiak returned as part of the France team that was pinning its hopes on a promising debutant, 23-year-old Jacques Anquetil. France's *directeur sportif*, Marcel Bidot, was counting on them to finish with cheers rather than jeers ringing in their ears. Fortunately for Bidot, the race started perfectly: André Darrigade won in Granville and René Privat emulated him in Caen and also took the yellow jersey. Victory in the team time trial followed, then Anquetil claimed victory in his home town of Rouen before taking the lead from Privat in Charleroi.

The race was frenzied until the Alps, but Bidot's men always looked to be in control, even if they did allow Nicolas Barone from the Île de France team to take the yellow jersey for a day. Anquetil won his second stage in Thonon-les-Bains, then moved back into the lead in Briançon, where he finished a minute behind Italy's Gastone Nencini and proved he had the legs to cope with the mountains.

The disappointment of the previous year now all but forgotten, Bidot's riders took two more stages as the race headed south out of the Alps. As Anquetil tightened his grip, his list of potential rivals dwindled considerably. Fifty of the 120 starters failed to get as far as Marseille, including big names such as Clerici, Astrua, Bahamontes, De Bruyne, Wagtmans, Gaul and Close. The danger was now confined to the Spaniard Loroño, Italy's Defilippis and Nencini, the Belgians Janssens and Adriaensens, Dutchman Wim Van Est and the Austrian Adolf Christian riding for Switzerland.

Tragedy hit the race in the Pyrenees when RTL journalist Alex Virot and his motorbike driver René Wagner died when they crashed into a ravine in terrible weather on the road to Ax-les-Thermes. The rain and cold took a toll on the riders too. The field was by now less than half the size it had been at the start, although the French team was largely unaffected, losing only Walkowiak. While the Italians did pose some problems for Anquetil, particularly on the Aubisque, Forestier, Bergaud and Darrigade kept a close watch, waiting for the masterstroke that their leader would surely deliver in the Libourne time trial. He went into the test nine minutes ahead in the standings. Over 66 km, he extended his advantage to 15 minutes over Janssens and Christian.

As Anquetil coasted to victory, France kept on scooping the victory garlands thanks to Darrigade, who finished off the Tour in real style by winning in Tours and the Parc des Princes, where the home fans were delirious. As well as celebrating Forestier's green jersey (he was also fourth overall), Bidot's men had won 13 stages between them, while Jacques Anquetil had been hugely impressive in winning the yellow jersey on his debut. The only major prize to evade their grasp was the mountains title, which went to Nencini.

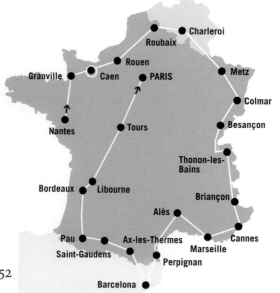

FINAL STANDINGS

1 Jacques Anquetil (FRA) France 135:44:42
2 Marcel Janssens (BEL) Belgium +14:56
3 Adolf Christian (AUT) Switzerland +17:20
4 Jean Forestier (FRA) France +18:02
5 Jesús Loroño (SPA) Spain +20:17
6 Gastone Nencini (ITA) Italy +26:03
7 Nino Defilippis (ITA) Italy +27:57
8 Wim Van Est (NED) Netherlands +28:10
9 Jan Adriaensens (BEL) Belgium +34:07
10 Jean Dotto (FRA) South-East +36:31

AVERAGE SPEED (OF WINNER): 34.365 KM/H
TOTAL DISTANCE RACED: 4,665 KM

OPPOSITE The front page of *Jours de France* shows André Darrigade with his best friend and Tour debutant Jacques Anquetil prior to the start of the race. The pair would take six stage wins between them.

JOURS DE FRANCE

Le Tour de France

Pour la première fois, Jacques Anquetil (à dr.), le coureur français le plus doué de sa génération, prend le départ du Tour de France en compagnie de son meilleur ami André Darrigade.

N° 137 Samedi 29 juin 1957 - Afr. du Nord 60 F. - France 65 F. - 10 F. belges - 90 Cent. suisses - Canada 25 C. - Italie 180

GAUL IMPOSES HIS LAW

The 45th Tour started at the World Exhibition in Brussels. France *directeur sportif* Marcel Bidot had the strongest team on paper, but had to cope with two leaders: defending champion Anquetil and three-time winner Bobet, who had been absent in 1956 and 1957. There was no place for Bobet's right-hand man Raphaël Geminiani. Seething with anger at being passed over, he had found a place on the Centre-Midi team. 'Gem' was determined to complicate the race for his erstwhile team-mates, no doubt assisted by Belgium's Marcel Janssens, Charly Gaul, who was leading a combined Dutch and Luxembourg team, Spain's Federico Bahamontes and Italy's Gastone Nencini.

It quickly became clear the French team was not as united as it had been the year before, which resulted in a strange race. France's André Darrigade won in Brussels, but failed to keep the yellow jersey beyond the next day. That became the norm. No one could stay in yellow for long. Belgium's Jos Hoevanaers, the Dutchmen Wim Van Est and Gerrit Voorting, and Darrigade's team-mate Gilbert Bauvin all had short spells in yellow before Darrigade regained it in Brittany.

Before he did, there were two events of note. On stage seven, Brian Robinson became the first Briton to win a Tour stage in Brest. The following day Charly Gaul beat Anquetil (second) and Bobet (eighth) in the time trial at Châteaulin. Would the French leaders rebound on the Ventoux and in the 74-km time trial at Dijon? Almost everyone suspected they would even though Geminiani, Bahamontes and Italy's Favero dominated the limelight in the Pyrenees. Although Bobet was still well down, it was widely felt that the Ventoux was his turf and that he would impose himself there, just as he had in 1955.

This time, however, Gaul was the man in charge. Only Bahamontes finished within a minute of him. Bobet lost almost four as Geminiani stepped back into the lead. With two minutes on Favero and almost four on Gaul, the 33-year-old leader of the Centre-Midi team allowed himself a spoonful of caviar. It served him well, as the next day through the hills into Gap, Geminiani flew and Gaul struggled, losing 11 minutes. A stage to Briançon over Bobet's favourite Izoard pass followed, but he disappointed and so, once again, did Gaul, as Gem consolidated his lead, with only the mountains of the Chartreuse to cross.

However, these mountains could wreak havoc, especially in bad weather. The rain poured, Gaul was reborn and he put everyone to the sword. In Aix-les-Bains he was 7 minutes ahead of Adriaensens and 14 ahead of Geminiani, whose glorious procession had turned hellish. He called Bobet and Anquetil 'Judas' and cried. Favero had taken the lead and Geminiani was close behind in second, but he knew that Gaul would crucify them both in the final time trial. He wasn't wrong. Dominant on all terrains and in all weathers, Gaul had become the 'angel of the mountains'.

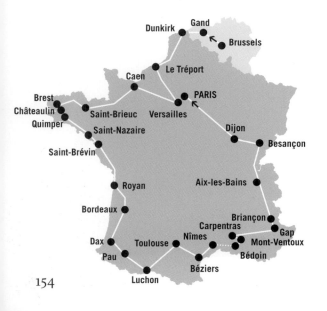

FINAL STANDINGS

1 Charly Gaul (LUX) Netherlands/Luxembourg 116:59:05
2 Vito Favero (ITA) Italy +3:10
3 Raphaël Geminiani (FRA) Centre-Midi +3:41
4 Jan Adriaensens (BEL) Belgium +7:16
5 Gastone Nencini (ITA) Italy +13:33
6 Jozef Planckaert (BEL) Belgium +28:01
7 Louison Bobet (FRA) France +31:39
8 Federico Bahamontes (SPA) Spain +40:44
9 Louis Bergaud (FRA) France +48:33
10 Jos Hoevenaers (BEL) Belgium +58:26

AVERAGE SPEED (OF WINNER): 36.919 KM/H
TOTAL DISTANCE RACED: 4,319 KM

OPPOSITE Gaul is pictured on the cover of *Radar* with his hands on the brake-hoods as he goes on the attack.

OVERLEAF The heat is quite clearly on as members of the peloton gratefully receive a cooling shower from a fireman with a hose.

radar

N° 492 11 JUILLET 1958 70 F. BELGIQUE 12 F. B. SUISSE 1 F. S.

LES TROUPES FRANÇAISES
ÉVACUENT REMADA

LE RUDE MÉTIER DES
GUIDES DE MONTAGNE

Ch. GAUL

TOUTES LES PHOTOS

BAHAMONTES SOARS AS FRENCH CRASH

For this, the 46th Tour, which started in Mulhouse, the French team felt that they had learned a lesson from 1958, when they had failed to contend because they had too many leaders. A pact was made between Anquetil, Bobet, Roger Rivière and Raphaël Geminiani. They agreed to work for one common goal: winning the Tour. However, their task was going to be far from straightforward as the top nine riders from 1958 were on the start line, including Charly Gaul. On top of that, there was a time trial up the Puy-de-Dôme, where anything could happen.

Initially, the French team appeared to have the race under control. André Darrigade won the opening stage and took the yellow jersey. Team-mate Robert Cazala took the lead from Darrigade after winning on day three. French confidence grew in Nantes, where Rivière took a comfortable victory in the 45-km time trial, with Anquetil not too far behind. However, once again, the French were deluding themselves. Cazala lost the jersey in Bayonne to Belgium's Eddy Pauwels. French regional rider Michel Vermeulin took it the next day and crossed the Pyrenees in yellow, before ceding it to another Belgian, Jos Hoevenaers.

The real test came in the 15th stage in that long-awaited time trial up the Puy-de-Dôme. Federico Bahamontes was always likely to perform well, but 'The Eagle of Toledo' produced an outstanding performance on the slopes of the ancient volcano in the Auvergne. Gaul came to life there too, although far too late to be able to retain his title. Going into the Alps, these two supreme climbers blew the race apart. Gaul won in Grenoble with Bahamontes right on his tail. The Spaniard took the lead as the Belgians hung together and the French fell apart. They hit rock bottom in Saint-Vincent. On the road there Bobet threw in the towel. To make matters worse for France's big guns, the riders pushing Bahamontes hardest were both from regional teams. Henry Anglade and François Mahé were now second and third, respectively. There was little consolation for them when Rivière won the final time trial in Dijon ahead of Anquetil, knocked Mahé out of the podium places.

Head and shoulders above the rest, though, was Federico Bahamontes. The first Spanish victory in the Tour was a decisive one. He had also claimed the title of best climber. Second-placed Anglade may have been more of a threat if the French team had not ridden against him, while Anquetil in third consoled himself with the fact that he had finished ahead of Rivière. As they had been in 1956, the French team were greeted with catcalls, which weren't softened by Darrigade's capture of the green jersey. France's apparently invincible armada had been sunk, as Spain, still a very divided country, briefly united to celebrate its great champion.

FINAL STANDINGS

1 Federico Bahamontes (SPA) Spain 123:46:45
2 Henry Anglade (FRA) Centre-Midi +4:01
3 Jacques Anquetil (FRA) France +5:05
4 Roger Rivière (FRA) France +5:17
5 François Mahé (FRA) West/South-West +8:22
6 Ercole Baldini (ITA) Italy +10:18
6 Jan Adriaensens (BEL) Belgium +10:18
8 Jos Hoevenaers (BEL) Belgium +11:02
9 Gérard Saint (FRA) West/South-West +17:40
10 Jean Brankart (BEL) Belgium +20:38

AVERAGE SPEED (OF WINNER): 35.183 KM/H
TOTAL DISTANCE RACED: 4,355 KM

OPPOSITE In the 12.5-km time trial on the Puy-de-Dôme, Bahamontes gained more than a minute on Gaul, three on Anglade, and more than three-and-a-half on Rivière and Anquetil.

NENCINI CRUISES TO VICTORY

The race set off from Lille without Robic, Bobet, Gaul or Geminiani. Anquetil was also absent having just won the Giro d'Italia, while Fausto Coppi was still being mourned after he died due to the effects of malaria. There were, however, still plenty of big names, notably Bahamontes and Roger Rivière, who was leading what was being built up as a more united French team, with Henry Anglade as his very capable right-hand man. The Germans, British, Belgians and Dutch had high hopes too, as did the Italians.

The key players emerged on day one. Rivière romped to victory in the afternoon time trial in Brussels ahead of Gastone Nencini and Anglade. Nencini took the yellow jersey, but was happy to let it pass to French regional rider Joseph Groussard. The Italian may not have been quite so happy to see Anglade take it a day later after he instigated a daring raid with his team-mate Jean Graczyk on the road to Caen.

As in 1956, attacks were coming from all sides. The next day André Darrigade and Graczyk went off, demonstrating France's strength in depth. There was an even more significant break on the following stage to Lorient. Four riders were in it: Rivière, who seemed to have forgotten that Anglade was in the yellow jersey, Nencini, who was happy to outflank Baldini, the Belgian Jan Adriaensens and the German Hans Junkermann. They finished 15 minutes ahead of the peloton, filling the top

four places overall with Adriaensens taking the lead. Being in a similar break in 1956 had helped Roger Walkowiak win that Tour. Would one of this quartet take the title?

That looked increasingly likely in the Pyrenees. Rivière won in Pau, where Nencini regained the yellow jersey. His lead was only 32 seconds over the Frenchman, although Rivière lost a little ground in Luchon, where Bahamontes might have shone if he hadn't quit the race due to injury in Dunkirk. The duel between France's leader and Italy's looked set to continue in the Alps. In between were just a couple of 'transition' stages, where the only climb of note was the 1,028-m Perjuret.

Nencini, who was brilliant on descents, pushed hard up the Perjuret and even harder going down the other side. Rivière rose to his challenge. However, the Frenchman was not blessed with the same ability. He skidded and plunged into a ravine. His team-mate Louis Rostollan saw it happen. Distraught, he yelled: 'Roger has fallen, Roger has fallen.' Rivière lay 20 m below, his back broken, his Tour and career over.

From that point Nencini and his Italian team-mates had complete control. Graziano Battistini moved up into second place thanks to victory in Briançon as Nencini cruised to the finish. It says a good deal that the main incident of note following Rivière's crash was the Tour stopping in Charles de Gaulle's village of Colombey-les-Deux-Églises to salute the president of the republic.

FINAL STANDINGS

1 Gastone Nencini (ITA) Italy 112:08:42
2 Graziano Battistini (ITA) Italy +5:02
3 Jan Adriaensens (BEL) Belgium +10:24
4 Hans Junkermann (FRG) West Germany +11:21
5 Jozef Planckaert (BEL) Belgium +13:02
6 Raymond Mastrotto (FRA) France +16:12
7 Arnaldo Pambianco (ITA) Italy +17:58
8 Henry Anglade (FRA) France +19:17
9 Marcel Rohrbach (FRA) Centre-Midi +20:02
10 Imerio Massignan (ITA) Italy +23:28

AVERAGE SPEED (OF WINNER): 37.21 KM/H
TOTAL DISTANCE RACED: 4,173 KM

Il dramma di un campione. Uno dei più forti corridori del Tour, il francese Roger Rivière, mentre scendeva velocemente per una strada di montagna, perso il controllo della bicicletta, urtò contro il muretto di protezione, lo scavalcò in volo e finì, dopo un salto di 25 metri, in un burrone. Rivière, che solo per un miracolo è uscito vivo dalla paurosa caduta, ha riportato fratture alla colonna vertebrale per cui, quasi certamente, dovrà abbandonare l'attività ciclistica. (Disegno di Walter Molino)

ABOVE LEFT A good deal of artistic licence is evident in this recreation of Rivière's fall, but there is no doubt that this was the race's key moment.

ABOVE RIGHT The Tour's medical staff are being very careful as they assess the extent of Rivière's injuries as he lies in the ravine on the Perjuret.

LEFT Green jersey winner Graczyk and Tour champion Nencini congratulate each other.

ANQUETIL RISES TO HIS OWN CHALLENGE

By 1961, Jacques Anquetil was 27 years old and had reached what tend to be a cyclist's best years. With three Tours under his belt, the blond Norman had already seen it all: a debut victory in 1957, illness causing him to withdraw from the race in 1958, and third place in 1959 as part of a disunited French team. He was, therefore, ready for anything. He had also chosen to ignore the Tour in 1960 in order to focus on the Giro d'Italia and had gained confidence there by beating Gastone Nencini on home ground.

It was suggested the Italian feared Anquetil, principally because he didn't defend his Tour title in 1961. Indeed, the only other previous winner besides Anquetil was Charly Gaul, but the Luxembourger had little chance against a very close-knit French team. Right from the start Anquetil was in great form and could call on Darrigade, Privat, Stablinski, Cazala, Mahé and Mastrotto for support.

As on four previous occasions, Darrigade won the first stage in Versailles and took the yellow jersey. The stage had started in Anquetil's home city of Rouen and, no doubt inspired by that, Anquetil was quickly in the action. He joined Darrigade and a dozen others in the break and gained five minutes on all of the other favourites. In the time trial the same afternoon, he crushed everyone, gaining another three minutes on Gaul, who was eight minutes down already.

Victory in that time trial gave Anquetil the yellow jersey. Many would have been tempted to let some of the lesser lights take it in the days that followed, but Anquetil was determined to keep it. He never looked likely to fail in this goal given his strength and the power of the French team. Gaul did bounce back a bit in the Alps, but he never managed to shake off the after-effects of a crash he suffered on the way to victory in Grenoble. Italy's Guido Carlesi, who was in the first-day breakaway with Anquetil, did his best to put the Frenchman under pressure in the Pyrenees, but he and Gaul were so far behind Anquetil that Tour director Jacques Goddet dubbed them 'the dwarves of the road' in an editorial in *L'Équipe*.

A much more ferocious battle for the green jersey raged between Darrigade and Jean Gainche. As with so much else in this race, the verdict went in France's favour as Darrigade claimed that prize. France also won the team classification and no fewer than nine stages.

According to *L'Équipe*'s Pierre Chany, the race encapsulated Anquetil's 'permanent desire to provoke'. The provocation was directed at himself as much as it was his rivals. He felt he would only progress by pushing himself further than everyone else. Consequently, he had come up with the insane challenge of wearing the yellow jersey from start to finish, which had not been achieved since 1935. Not surprisingly, given his ability and drive, Anquetil managed to do it.

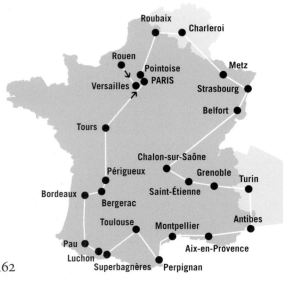

FINAL STANDINGS

1 Jacques Anquetil (FRA) France 122:01:33
2 Guido Carlesi (ITA) Italy +12:14
3 Charly Gaul (LUX) Switzerland/Luxembourg +12:16
4 Imerio Massignan (ITA) Italy +15:59
5 Hans Junkermann (FRG) West Germany +16:09
6 Fernando Manzaneque (SPA) Spain +16:27
7 José Pérez-Francés (SPA) Spain +20:41
8 Jean Dotto (FRA) Centre-Midi +21:44
9 Eddy Pauwels (BEL) Belgium +26:57
10 Jan Adriaensens (BEL) Belgium +28:05

AVERAGE SPEED (OF WINNER): 36.033 KM/H
TOTAL DISTANCE RACED: 4,397 KM

OPPOSITE Heading into the final lap of the final stage on the track at the Parc des Princes, yellow jersey Anquetil sets the pace in front of team-mate Robert Cazala as he prepares to lead him out to win the final sprint.

Darrigade: the whole of the Tour in a sprint

A RIDER WITH all-round ability usually wins the Tour, although on many occasions climbers have taken the title. For sprinters, however, winning the yellow jersey is out of the question, even though André Darrigade could have perhaps done it in 1956 with a bit of luck. In the end, though, Darrigade had consoled himself with winning the Tour in his own way. If you put the 22 stages he won back to back, they do comprise a complete Tour. What is more, he even won a mountain stage in 1959 in Saint-Gaudens.

'The Bounding Basque' reaped this prodigious harvest between 1953 and 1966 over 14 Tours, featuring only one abandon. His first bouquet came in Albi in 1953 during his first Tour. He claimed his last in 1964 in Bordeaux, in his native south-west, where he had always failed to win previously. He won the green jersey twice, in 1959 and 1961, thanks to his eye for a chance, sharp reactions and lightning speed. He also won the opening stage of the Tour five times.

RIGHT In the aftermath of his final stage win in Bordeaux, 'The Blond Arrow' Darrigade climbed onto a stepladder so that the photographers could snap him with the dignitaries in the stadium. Things were done without a great deal of fuss at the Tour back in those days.

NEW FORMAT BUT THE SAME WINNER

In 1962, Jacques Anquetil claimed his third success, equalling Louison Bobet's mark. In an important way, however, this was a very different victory – for the first time since 1929, the cyclists rode for commercial teams rather than in national colours. There was a budding new star on the scene as well, a certain Raymond Poulidor. This 26 year old had been hailed as a potential troublemaker for Anquetil, and the defending champion would make the rider from the Limousin his privileged opponent, an opponent he used in order to push himself harder.

The debutant set off with a broken finger and immediately got his first lesson. Like Gaul the year before, he lost eight minutes on the opening stage and all chance of overall victory, as did Federico Bahamontes. Anquetil, of course, was in the front group and happy to let his team-mates Rudi Altig and Ab Geldermans share spells in the yellow jersey with his old friend Darrigade. The defending champion asserted himself in the 43-km time trial at La Rochelle, then withdrew back into the pack as Belgium's Willy Schroeders led into the Pyrenees.

When the Belgian yielded, the yellow jersey went to a British rider for the first time. Away with the major contenders on a tough stage to Saint-Gaudens, Tom Simpson took the lead, albeit only for a day. When Bahamontes rebounded from his early setback by winning the time trial up to Superbagnères, the Englishman fell back into the pack behind new leader Jozef Planckaert.

Although expected to fade out of contention in the Alps, Planckaert rose to the challenge, maintaining an advantage of just over a minute on Anquetil right through the mountains. As Anquetil waited for the final time trial to come, certain that he would prevail, Poulidor followed the example of Bahamontes by taking a brilliant win in Aix-les-Bains. It promoted him to third place, his final position and a great performance after such a terrible start.

Anquetil's moment had arrived, though. In the 68-km Bourgoin–Lyon time trial, he pulverized the opposition with a graceful but powerful display. Darrigade described him as 'definitely the best rouleur in the world', and it was impossible to argue with that. He was five minutes faster than Planckaert and Poulidor. During the stage, his team manager Antonin Magne saw Anquetil coming up behind and shouted to Poulidor: 'Pull over, Raymond, there is a plane coming by…'

In the Parc des Princes, Anquetil took the top step of the podium for the third time, with Poulidor third after what had been a baptism of fire. A fierce rivalry had been born. Anquetil would use it to 'explode' Tour records, while making few concessions to those attempting to challenge him.

FINAL STANDINGS

1 Jacques Anquetil (FRA) ACBB-Saint Raphaël 114:31:54
2 Jozef Planckaert (BEL) Flandria-Faema +4:59
3 Raymond Poulidor (FRA) Mercier +10:24
4 Gilbert Desmet (BEL) Carpano +13:01
5 Albertus Geldermans (NED) ACBB-Saint Raphaël +14:04
6 Tom Simpson (GBR) VC XII-Leroux +17:09
7 Imerio Massignan (ITA) Legnano +17:50
8 Ercole Baldini (ITA) Ignis +19:00
9 Charly Gaul (LUX) GS Gazzola +19:11
10 Eddy Pauwels (BEL) Wiel's +23:04

AVERAGE SPEED (OF WINNER): 37.317 KM/H
TOTAL DISTANCE RACED: 4,274 KM

ABOVE LEFT 'Anquetil was to cycling what Mozart was to music,' wrote Diario, especially when he was wearing his St Raphaël jersey, which was one of the most attractive ever.

ABOVE RIGHT In the Bourgoin–Lyon time trial, Anquetil overtakes a debutant named Poulidor, beating him by five minutes. He goes on to take the yellow jersey.

BOTTOM RIGHT Anquetil as seen by *L'Équipe* cartoonist Pellos on a promotional postcard from Esso.

ANQUETIL REACHES A NEW LEVEL

The 50th Tour gave Jacques Anquetil the opportunity to become the first rider to win four editions. But it wasn't going to be easy. For a start, the organizers significantly reduced the amount of time trialling, in order to boost the chances of the climbers. On top of that, Anquetil had been troubled by a tapeworm and wasn't completely recovered when the race started. That may explain why Federico Bahamontes stole a march on him on the first day, getting into a four-man break and gaining 90 very handy seconds on the defending champion and his other rivals.

Belgian Eddy Pauwels led the race until the third stage on the cobbles into Roubaix. Anquetil's Irish team-mate Shay Elliott clinched it and took the yellow jersey, which was a first for Ireland on both counts. His spell in the lead lasted until the first time trial in Angers. Anquetil may have been a touch below his best, but he still won it ahead of Raymond Poulidor. Another Belgian, Gilbert Desmet, took the lead and held it impressively as the race went towards and then through the Pyrenees. Bahamontes and Poulidor, both rated better climbers than the defending champion, applied pressure, but both lost time to Anquetil thanks to the bonus minute he earned for victory in Bagnères-de-Bigorre.

As the Alps approached, Bahamontes finally broke free of Anquetil's shackles, winning alone in Grenoble and leapfrogging the Frenchman into second place behind the dogged Desmet, whose resistance finally broke on the road to Val d'Isère the next day. Bahamontes took the lead, but it was a mere three seconds over Anquetil. He needed to gain more time on the stage heading over the Petit Saint-Bernard, the Grand Saint-Bernard, the Forclaz and the Montets, and then into Chamonix. The Spaniard led over all four passes, but it was Poulidor who fell back rather than Anquetil. He may have been struggling but he stuck right on the Spaniard's wheel. It was the Frenchman who took the stage, a minute's bonus and with it the yellow jersey.

With a 54.5-km time trial at Besançon to come, Anquetil looked to have the race won, and he didn't disappoint his fans. Victory there pushed him more than three minutes ahead of Bahamontes, with the much-touted Poulidor eighth, having been dominated by his rival on every terrain. In the Parc des Princes, Anquetil earned himself another Marseillaise, while a disappointed Poulidor watched the ceremony from afar, perhaps reflecting on the fact that, although he was the better climber of the pair, Anquetil had won two of the most beautiful mountain stages.

FINAL STANDINGS

1 Jacques Anquetil (FRA) Saint Raphaël-Geminiani 113:30:05
2 Federico Bahamontes (SPA) Margnat +3:35
3 José Pérez-Francés (SPA) Ferrys +10:14
4 Jean-Claude Lebaube (FRA) Saint Raphaël-Geminiani +11:55
5 Armand Desmet (BEL) Faema-Flandria +15:00
6 Angelino Soler (SPA) Faema-Flandria +15:04
7 Renzo Fontona (ITA) IBAC-Molteni +15:27
8 Raymond Poulidor (FRA) Mercier +16:46
9 Hans Junkermann (FRG) Wiel's +18:53
10 Rik Van Looy (BEL) GBC-Libertas +19:24

AVERAGE SPEED (OF WINNER): 36.448 KM/H
TOTAL DISTANCE RACED: 4,137 KM

OPPOSITE In the 50th Tour de France, Anquetil showed he could overcome his rivals on every terrain if required. Here in the Alps, the defending champion (left) tracks Bahamontes (centre) and Poulidor (right).

THE TOUR THAT SPLIT FRANCE

The third duel between Jacques Anquetil and Raymond Poulidor promised a great deal as Anquetil had just won the Giro and Poulidor the Vuelta. The French fans were split between the two. Half had taken Poulidor, the plucky challenger into their hearts, the other half believed Anquetil was invincible and at the top of his game. As well as the prospect of taking on Poulidor and winning a fifth Tour, Anquetil knew that he could become only the second man after Fausto Coppi to complete the Giro/Tour double.

For the first half the two Frenchmen watched each other closely. Poulidor gained 50 seconds on Anquetil when he punctured in the Alps. The balance tipped back when Anquetil won on the cinder track in Monaco, taking a one-minute bonus, as Poulidor sprinted a lap too early. The Mercier leader slipped back a few seconds more when Anquetil beat him in a time trial at Toulon. Heading into the Pyrenees, Anquetil was second, just over a minute down on Pelforth's Georges Groussard. Poulidor was third, 31 seconds further back.

Renowned bon viveur Anquetil joined in the rest-day festivities in Andorra with relish, devouring much of a whole lamb at a barbecue. The next stage started up the lofty Envalira pass and Bahamontes, Julio Jiménez and Poulidor were right away on the attack. Anquetil couldn't respond; he could barely pedal. Helped by pushes from team-mate Louis Rostollan and perhaps by some champagne handed to him by team director

Raphaël Geminiani to soothe his indigestion, Anquetil finally got going but was five minutes behind when he reached the summit. The road was cloaked in fog, but Anquetil didn't hesitate. Using car lights as a guide, he plummeted down the other side. Incredibly, he caught the group ahead.

If that wasn't bad enough for Poulidor, he hit a pothole, punctured and ended two minutes down on a day when he seemed to have the race won. Rather than ponder his fate, Poulidor responded with a victory in Luchon, showing his class and resilience. Anquetil's advantage was trimmed to nine seconds. Fortune swung the other way in the time trial at Bayonne. Anquetil won it and the yellow jersey. Poulidor was second, but would probably have won if he hadn't punctured and then received a disastrously slow wheel change. Reduced to tears at the finish, Poulidor was now 56 seconds down.

The stage to the summit of the Puy-de-Dôme held the key to the contest. Poulidor had not done any reconnaissance of the climb and paid for it. Anquetil clung to him like a leech until just inside the final kilometre, the two of them famously riding elbow-to-elbow. He gained 42 seconds but had attacked too late. Anquetil, who now led by 14 seconds, admitted to his team manager Geminiani: 'If I had lost the jersey I would have given up.' Anquetil duly won the final 27.5-km time trial into Paris to boost his lead to 55 seconds, the smallest winning margin ever recorded.

FINAL STANDINGS

1　Jacques Anquetil (FRA) Saint Raphaël 127:09:44
2　Raymond Poulidor (FRA) Mercier +0:55
3　Federico Bahamontes (SPA) Margnat +4:44
4　Henry Anglade (FRA) Pelforth +6:42
5　Georges Groussard (FRA) Pelforth +10:34
6　André Foucher (FRA) Pelforth +10:36
7　Julio Jiménez (SPA) Kas +12:13
8　Gilbert Desmet (BEL) Wiel's +12:17
9　Hans Junkermann (FRG) Wiel's +14:02
10　Vittorio Adorni (ITA) Salvarani +14:19

AVERAGE SPEED (OF WINNER): 35.419 KM/H
TOTAL DISTANCE RACED: 4,504 KM

OPPOSITE Anquetil (left) and Poulidor (right) spent most of the race watching each other intently. In the mountains they stuck close together, with Poulidor usually just ahead and Anquetil tracking his every move.

Sunday, 12 July 1964. Poulidor plays his last card on the Puy-de-Dôme. French historian Michel Winock writes: 'The two adversaries appear to be linked to one another like two thistles.' Tour director Jacques Goddet, at the heart of the battle on his motorbike, goes further: 'Their breath, their sweat and the wool from their jerseys intermingles…'

Poulidor: the eternal second

RAYMOND POULIDOR NEVER finished first on the Tour and never wore the yellow jersey, or at least that is what is generally believed. In fact, he did get a yellow jersey on at least three occasions. During the 1974 Tour, after he dominated Eddy Merckx on the climb up Saint-Lary-Soulan, Merckx offered him a yellow jersey out of respect. The second occasion was during an evening at Jacques Anquetil's home when he put one on. The third instance happened when he made a commercial for the department store La Samaritaine – their tag line was 'You find everything in La Samaritaine' – and he managed to find one there.

In the race itself, he narrowly missed out on victory in two prologues (1967, 1973). In addition, it mustn't be forgotten that in 1968 and in 1973 he would almost certainly have taken the jersey if he hadn't fallen.

RIGHT TOP Having failed to take advantage in the late 1960s when Anquetil stepped away from racing, Poulidor then found himself one of many left in Eddy Merckx's slipstream.

RIGHT BOTTOM A huge favourite among French fans, Poulidor was the nearly man who regularly looked like providing a fairytale flourish at the Tour, but his hopes were always undone.

OPPOSITE TOP Poulidor plays draughts with arch-rival Jacques Anquetil in a *Paris Match* picture that plays up the strategic rivalry between the pair. Anquetil, undoubtedly, always had the better of this match-up.

OPPOSITE BOTTOM In 1976, at the age of 40, Poulidor made his final Tour appearance and recorded his eighth podium, finishing third behind Lucien Van Impe. Here Poulidor (second left) is seen relaxing with yellow jersey Van Impe, Raymond Delisle (left) and Joop Zoetemelk.

DEBUTANT GIMONDI STUNS POULIDOR

The 1965 and 1966 Tours had much in common. They were won by Felice Gimondi and Lucien Aimar, respectively. Both were friends of Jacques Anquetil and both had shone in the 1964 edition Tour de l'Avenir. In both cases, the man who lost out was Anquetil's heir apparent, Raymond Poulidor.

In 1965, Anquetil didn't start. Having savoured his difficult and historic victory the previous year, he set himself the target of winning the Dauphiné and Bordeaux–Paris. As Anquetil targeted and achieved that objective, Poulidor looked destined to carry off the Tour crown, but a series of unexpected occurrences ensured that he missed out once again.

At the very last moment, the Italian Salvarani team brought in Gimondi to replace Bruno Fantinato, who had finished 48th in the 1964 Tour. Approaching his 23rd birthday, Gimondi wasn't quite an unknown package as he had dominated Aimar in winning the Tour de l'Avenir, and it was clear that he was ambitious. He proved that from the start, joining the winning breakaway on the second stage to Roubaix, then winning the next day in Rouen to claim his first yellow jersey. That evening he was invited to dine in Anquetil's Rouen home. The defending champion told the Italian he had everything he needed to win and as a bonus, beat 'Poupou', Anquetil's great rival.

Poulidor showed strength and form to win the Châteaulin

time trial, with Gimondi just seconds behind him. But some wondered if the Frenchman hadn't given too much leeway to the debutant, who had a cushion of more than three minutes on Poulidor heading into the Pyrenees. On the first stage in the mountains Gimondi regained the yellow jersey from Belgium's Raymond van de Kerckhove. More significantly, Poulidor gained no time on him.

That changed as the riders headed to the summit finish on Mont Ventoux. Poulidor was majestic, while Gimondi appeared weary, perhaps feeling the effort of finishing third at the Giro just weeks before. His lead was cut to 34 seconds. France looked on expectantly as the Tour moved into the Alps, but Gimondi stood firm. The Alpine stages concluded with a time trial to the top of Mont Revard. As had been the case with the Puy-de-Dôme in 1964, Poulidor had not previewed the climb. The result? He lost 23 seconds to the victorious Gimondi.

The Frenchman's fans were worried but still had confidence that he could wipe out Gimondi's 1-12 lead in the final Versailles–Paris time trial. However, 'Poupou' lost almost exactly that amount as Gimondi triumphed again. Like Anquetil in 1957, the Italian had won the Tour on his first attempt, as Poulidor finished second once again. Gossips said that Anquetil cracked open the champagne that day, all the while thinking about his return in the 1966 Tour.

FINAL STANDINGS

1 Felice Gimondi (ITA) Salvarani 116:42:06
2 Raymond Poulidor (FRA) Mercier +2:40
3 Gianni Motta (ITA) Molteni +9:18
4 Henry Anglade (FRA) Pelforth +12:43
5 Jean-Claude Lebaube (FRA) Ford +12:56
6 José Pérez-Francés (SPA) Ferrys +13:15
7 Guido De Rosso (ITA) Molteni +14:48
8 Frans Brands (BEL) Flandria +17:36
9 Jan Janssen (NED) Pelforth +17:52
10 Francisco Gabica (SPA) Kas +19:11

AVERAGE SPEED (OF WINNER): 35.792 KM/H
TOTAL DISTANCE RACED: 4,177 KM

FELICE GIMONDI
G. S. SALVARANI

TOP LEFT Gimondi powered to victory in 1965, on his first attempt at the Tour.

TOP RIGHT Last-minute replacement Felice Gimondi, regarded as a class act following his victory in the 1964 Tour de l'Avenir, surprised Poulidor.

BOTTOM LEFT As they completed a lap of honour at the Parc des Princes, Poulidor (left) received whistles from the crowd. They seem to be affecting Gimondi (right) as well.

UNHERALDED AIMAR FOILS POULIDOR

Jacques Anquetil was back at the Tour, although he did seem to be in decline. As a five-time champion, Anquetil believed he could win a sixth title, but he covered his options by bringing in young Lucien Aimar and, more notably, Spanish climber Julio Jiménez, winner on the Puy-de-Dôme in 1964. Anquetil found Poulidor stronger and more motivated than ever, even if the German Rudi Altig took the first stage and wore the yellow jersey for ten days. The major event during that period occurred in Bordeaux, where the first-ever anti-doping testing was carried out. The riders were surprised, Poulidor in particular as he was selected to take part. The peloton briefly went on strike the next day in protest, dismounting from their bikes and arguing with race officials.

Attention switched back to the race the following day. A large group escaped, Aimar among them. As he made his move, Poulidor had been caught in behind Anquetil. Italy's Tommaso De Pra won the day in Pau, while Aimar gained seven minutes on all of the likely contenders. The status quo returned as the Tour headed east towards the Alps. Frenchman Jean-Claude Lebaube and West Germany's Karl-Heinz Kunde had spells in yellow, leading up to a 20-km time trial in Val-les-Bains. Poulidor won it to edge ahead of Anquetil, but both were still five minutes behind Aimar, who was closing in on Kunde's lead.

Poulidor clawed some more crucial seconds back on the descent of the Col d'Ornon heading into Bourg-d'Oisans, but he could not escape the grip that Anquetil and Jiménez imposed over the Croix de Fer, Télégraphe and Galibier and into Briançon, where Jan Janssen took yellow with Aimar just 27 seconds behind. Realizing victory was beyond him and very possible for his young team-mate Aimar, Anquetil became the ultimate *super-domestique*. Seeing his team-mate dropped by Poulidor on the Coletta pass, Anquetil paced him back up the group, then signalled for Aimar to follow on the descent as he attacked. No one else responded. Aimar ended the stage in yellow, Poulidor five minutes down in eighth.

As he had done in the past, Poulidor responded with a brave ride into Chamonix, but his deficit was still more than four minutes when a sickening Anquetil abandoned near Saint-Étienne. He had fulfilled his part of the deal. Now it was up to Aimar to complete his. The decision came down to the final 51-km time trial into Paris. As had been the case in equivalent tests in 1964 and 1965, Poulidor finished third, while Aimar was 18th. However, he was still two minutes clear of Poulidor, who missed out on second place to Janssen.

Could Poulidor have done any better? Late on in the race, he broke away on one stage only to see Anquetil's former team-mate Rudi Altig pacing Aimar back up to him. André Darrigade deplored the collusion 'of at least six teams'. Yet his friend Anquetil would still be able to crack open the champagne.

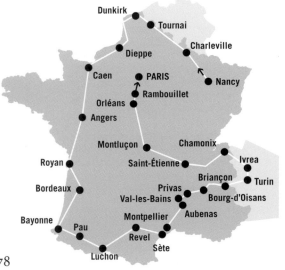

FINAL STANDINGS

1 Lucien Aimar (FRA) Ford-Hutchinson 117:34:21
2 Jan Janssen (NED) Pelforth +1:07
3 Raymond Poulidor (FRA) Mercier +2:02
4 José Antonio Momene (SPA) Kas +5:19
5 Marcello Mugnaini (ITA) Filotex +5:27
6 Herman Van Springel (BEL) Mann +5:44
7 Francisco Gabica (SPA) Kas +6:25
8 Roger Pingeon (FRA) Peugeot +8:22
9 Karl-Heinz Kunde (FRG) Peugeot +9:06
10 Martin Vandenbossche (BEL) Smith's +9:57

AVERAGE SPEED (OF WINNER): 36.76 KM/H
TOTAL DISTANCE RACED: 4,322 KM

OPPOSITE TOP 25-year-old Aimar, seen conferring with Ford *directeur sportif* Raphaël Geminiani, won the Tour without winning a single stage. Gossips said that the Tour's epilogue took place several weeks later at the World Championships in Nurburgring, when Aimar led the struggling Altig back up to touch with Anquetil and Poulidor, returning the favour the German had paid him at the Tour.

OPPOSITE BOTTOM Squeezed in between Julio Jiménez, Jacques Anquetil and some of their allies, Poulidor has let the third man on the Ford team, Lucien Aimar, slip away.

PINGEON TRIUMPHS THANKS TO POULIDOR

Riders prefer the clarity of trade teams, but spectators and organizers often lean towards national teams. So it was that the Tour's organizers decided upon what would be a brief return to the national team format. The adventure only lasted two years, which were difficult ones as the commercial sponsors had by now gained such power that serious problems quickly arose. For example, Jacques Anquetil later admitted that his Ford team-mates Lucien Aimar, Anatole Novak and Jean Stablinski had agreed over lunch one day to let Peugeot's Roger Pingeon win the race after they had almost come to blows.

Raymond Poulidor was, of course, part of the French team that included Pingeon and those three Ford riders, one of whom was the defending champion. Poulidor was still the popular favourite and this time there was no Anquetil lying in ambush, no Gimondi waiting to spring a surprise, and he now knew all about Aimar. Instead, ill-fortune awaited him in the shape of a crash on the Ballon d'Alsace. Forced to change to another bike that didn't fit him, Poulidor dropped right out of overall contention and focused on being a loyal team-mate to Pingeon, France's best-placed rider at that point.

The Tour had started well for Poulidor, who looked like he might win the race's inaugural prologue time trial in Angers, but was pipped by Spain's José-Maria Errandonea. The lead changed hands each day as it headed east into Belgium, where Pingeon seized the yellow jersey thanks to an audacious 60-km solo break over the cobbled climb into Jambes. The French team, with Poulidor as a marvellous road captain, locked down the race so well that they won six stages and never released their hold on the yellow jersey. It slipped onto the shoulders of Raymond Riotte for a day, Pingeon regaining it as Aimar won the stage over the Ballon.

The fiercest competition came from the Italian Gimondi, the Spaniard Jiménez and the Dutchman Janssen, but Pingeon always had either Poulidor or Aimar at his side and often both of them to see him through tough assignments on the Galibier, the Ventoux and the Puy-de-Dôme. The result was an impressive victory for Pingeon when the race finished for the final time in the Parc des Princes velodrome. Poulidor made it a point of honour to win the time trial into the Parc as he came home ninth overall but delighted to have been part of a united French team that had knit well around Pingeon.

However, a very dark shadow hung over the race. Great Britain's Tom Simpson had died on the slopes of Ventoux. Was it sunstroke? Doping? Alcohol? A mix of all three? The debate about that would last for years. All that was certain was that the sport had lost one of its greats – a world champion, Britain's first yellow jersey and a gentleman.

FINAL STANDINGS

1 Roger Pingeon (FRA) France 136:53:50
2 Julio Jiménez (SPA) Spain +3:40
3 Franco Balmamion (ITA) Primavera +7:23
4 Désiré Letort (FRA) Bleuets +8:18
5 Jan Janssen (NED) Netherlands +9:47
6 Lucien Aimar (FRA) France +9:47
7 Felice Gimondi (ITA) Italy +10:14
8 Jozef Huysmans (BEL) Belgium +16:45
9 Raymond Poulidor (FRA) France +18:18
10 Fernando Manzaneque (SPA) Esperanza +19:22

AVERAGE SPEED (OF WINNER): 34.756 KM/H
TOTAL DISTANCE RACED: 4,758 KM

AIMAR JANSSEN GIMONDI POULIDOR

JAMBES

ABOVE Between Roubaix and Jambes (which is also the French word for legs) Roger Pingeon cut short the ambitions of Aimar, Janssen, Gimondi and Poulidor, as *L'Équipe* cartoonist Pellos demonstrates in his inimitable fashion.

OPPOSITE Pingeon (right) with Poulidor, his number one team-mate.

181

JANSSEN SHOWS PERFECT TIMING

It was entirely fitting that the 55th Tour set out from Vittel as this was supposed to be 'The Tour of Good Health' following the tragic death of Simpson the year before. However, it would be nothing of the sort. First José Samyn and then Jean Stablinski, both members of the France team, were victims of anti-doping testing and were excluded from the race, the first riders to be excluded in this way.

As had been the case since 1965, the race looked like Raymond Poulidor's for the taking. He bided his time for the first two weeks, when the race was dominated by sprints. France B's Charly Grosskost claimed the yellow jersey in the prologue. Belgium A's victory in the team time trial then put Herman Van Springel into the lead. Another Belgian, Georges Vandenberghe, from their B team led the way into the Pyrenees.

Vandenberghe was expected to crack heading over the Aubisque and Tourmalet to Saint-Gaudens, but he surprised everyone by staying with the pace of the main contenders, although Poulidor had slipped into that day's break and edged up to fifth, four minutes down on the Belgian. None of the four riders ahead of Poulidor were in his class, and as the race made for Albi on stage 15 his moment finally seemed to have come. The stage was a triumph for Pingeon, who rode almost 200 km alone to victory. A dozen kilometres from the finish, a race motorbike was passing the main group when it had to swerve to avoid fans in the road. It clipped Poulidor's bars,

sending him crashing to the ground. Face bloodied and nose broken, he abandoned two days later.

Dutch leader Jan Janssen, meanwhile, had been steadily picking his way up the leaderboard despite having lost six of his team-mates before the Pyrenees. Heading through the Chartreuse into Grenoble, he stuck close to Van Springel, who he regarded as his major rival. He repeated the feat the next day over four climbs to Sallanches, where Barry Hoban won the day. From there, the race ran north to Paris. Van Springel's team-mate André Poppe almost produced a sensation two days from the finish when he gained 30 minutes on a break, making him leader on the road by a distance. The Belgians didn't need to chase, the French weren't bothered and Janssen didn't have the numbers. Race director Jacques Goddet intervened, determined to avoid a ridiculous finale.

Going into the 55-km time trial between Melun and Paris, there were eight riders within two-and-a-half minutes of yellow jersey Van Springel, including world record holder Ferdinand Bracke. But it was Janssen, who was only 16 seconds back, who thrived under the intense pressure, winning the stage and with it the race by 38 seconds, the closest margin ever. The first Dutchman to win the Tour, the first winner who wore glasses and the first rider to be crowned in the Vincennes velodrome, he had, like Jean Robic in 1947, won the race without wearing the yellow jersey.

FINAL STANDINGS

1 Jan Janssen (NED) Netherlands 133:49:42
2 Herman Van Springel (BEL) Belgium A +0:38
3 Ferdinand Bracke (BEL) Belgium B +3:03
4 Gregorio San Miguel (SPA) Spain +3:17
5 Roger Pingeon (FRA) France A +3:29
6 Rolf Wolfshohl (FRG) Germany +3:46
7 Lucien Aimar (FRA) France B +4:44
8 Franco Bitossi (ITA) Italy +4:59
9 Andrés Gandarias (SPA) Spain +5:05
10 Ugo Colombo (ITA) Italy +7:55

AVERAGE SPEED (OF WINNER): 33.565 KM/H
TOTAL DISTANCE RACED: 4,492 KM

It was a Tour of firsts thanks to the finish in the Cipale velodrome in the Bois de Vincennes and a victory for the Dutch. Surprise winner Jan Janssen, wearing his distinctive sunglasses, is raised by his team and fans in triumph.

THE ARRIVAL OF MERCKX 'THE CANNIBAL'

Pingeon and Janssen's victories, as commendable and deserved as they were, demonstrated the limits and the declining appeal of the national team format in a sport where 'extra-sportif' sponsors were the rule for the rest of the year. Consequently, the Tour reintroduced trade teams and with them came a young champion the likes of which the peloton had never seen. Belgian Eddy Merckx had already proved himself in the amateur ranks and, since turning pro in April 1965, he had built up a palmarès better than most achieved during a long career of racing.

The Tour was about to enter a new era. At the start in Roubaix there were four former winners in the field: Aimar, Gimondi, Janssen and Pingeon, not to mention Poulidor, Van Impe and Van Looy. Merckx took the lead on the second day thanks to the all-round power of Faema in the team time trial. His team-mate Julien Stevens then held it for three, Frenchman Désiré Letort for one, until the Tour received the first demonstration of Merckx's phenomenal ability. Over three passes in the Vosges, Merckx's rivals steadily fell away until, on the Ballon d'Alsace, the Belgian was on his own, pounding the pedals, relentlessly increasing his advantage.

'Relentless' encapsulated the Belgian perfectly. In Chamonix he was second on Pingeon's wheel, in Briançon second to Van Springel, in Digne first, in Aubagne third.

After these consecutive stages his lead was seven minutes. He sat back until the short time trial at Revel, won that and pushed his advantage to eight. Then he went beyond the extraordinary. On the classic Pyrenean stage over the Peyresourde, Aspin, Tourmalet and Aubisque, he moved to a level never previously seen.

Apparently indignant because team-mate Martin Vandenbossche had told him the night before he would be moving at the end of the season, Merckx attacked high on the Tourmalet when it had seemed Vandenbossche was set to lead the race over the famous summit. He waited on the far side of the pass, but no one appeared. So he pressed on. Crossing the Soulor he led by 4-55. On the Aubisque he was seven minutes ahead. On the long run-in to Mourenx, he began to tire, but his lead still went up. He finished eight minutes clear after 140 km on his own. His overall lead was now more than 16 minutes. He added a minute more in the final time trial. 'Merckxissimo' proclaimed the front page of *L'Équipe* the next morning.

Belgium had been waiting 30 years for a Tour winner since Sylvère Maes in 1939. Merckx had not only won the Tour, he had walked off with the lot: seven stages, the yellow jersey, the green jersey, best climber, team classification, the combined. 'The Cannibal' had arrived.

FINAL STANDINGS

1 Eddy Merckx (BEL) Faema 116:16:02
2 Roger Pingeon (FRA) Peugeot +17:54
3 Raymond Poulidor (FRA) Mercier +22:13
4 Felice Gimondi (ITA) Salvarani +29:24
5 Andrés Gandarias (SPA) Kas +33:04
6 Marinus Wagtmans (NED) Willem II +33:57
7 Pierfranco Vianelli (ITA) Molteni +42:40
8 Joaquim Agostinho (POR) Frimatic +51:24
9 Désiré Letort (FRA) Peugeot +51:41
10 Jan Janssen (NED) Bic +52:56

AVERAGE SPEED (OF WINNER): 35.409 KM/H
TOTAL DISTANCE RACED: 4,117 KM

OPPOSITE In the Pyrenees, Merckx set off alone on a break that lasted 140 km. It resembled Fausto Coppi's deeds so much that Jacques Goddet dubbed it 'Merckxissimo'.

Anquetil had been reproached for never having led over a mountain pass. The debutant Merckx made it a point of honour to dominate the stages featuring the Aubisque, Tourmalet and Galibier, where he is under the watchful eyes of Vianelli (front left), Gimondi (behind Merckx's left shoulder) and Pingeon (far left).

OPPOSITE In this Pellos cartoon, Merckx, sitting on a steamroller, is a 'cannibal' who reigns supreme, who dominates the race in every area, but with a smile and with panache. There's also a nod to his debatable exclusion from the Giro d'Italia just a few weeks previously as a result of a controversial dope test, Pellos suggesting that Italy's national tour had to remain the preserve of the home riders no matter what.

MERCKX REIGNS SUPREME

The 1970 race started in Raymond Poulidor country at Limoges, but few were predicting that 'Poupou' or anyone else in the field could prevent Eddy Merckx adding another Tour title to his extensive trophy collection. As well as Poulidor, there were four future winners on the start line – Joop Zoetemelk, Luis Ocaña, Bernard Thévenet and Lucien Van Impe – but Merckx put all of them firmly in their place right from the very first day.

He won the prologue in Limoges, then rather reluctantly allowed team-mate Italo Zilioli to get into the winning break on stage two, which ended with the Italian taking the stage and the yellow jersey. Merckx may perhaps have been dreaming of wearing the yellow jersey from start to finish, but his team manager Lomme Driessens advised a degree of caution. Merckx wasn't happy with the policy but held back for four days. However, neither he nor his team hesitated when Zilioli punctured late on in stage six to Valenciennes. Seeing the chance to gain time on several of his rivals by finishing in the lead group, Merckx also retook the lead.

Having missed out on the opportunity to join the select few who have led the Tour from start to finish, Merckx soon began to close on another record – the eight stage wins taken by Charles Pélissier in 1930. He took his second success the day after, regaining the yellow jersey, then added another three heading towards and through the Alps.

The evening before stage 14 to the summit of Mont Ventoux, Merckx heard of the death of Vincenzo Giacotto, who had built the Faema team around him. Determined to pay tribute to Giacotto and his former team-mate Tom Simpson, who had died on the race's last visit to 'The Giant of Provence', Merckx dropped his rivals 10 km from the finish and rode on alone past the spot where Simpson had fallen. Perhaps forgetting that he already had a victorious Giro in his legs, he won the stage but soon after talking to journalists at the finish he felt faint and passed out. Rushed to an ambulance, he was given oxygen alongside former team-mate Martin Vandenbossche, who had finished second.

He took this warning seriously and, with a nine-minute lead over Zoetemelk, kept close watch on young wolves such as Ocaña and Thévenet, who showed plenty of promise for the future by winning stages in the Pyrenees. Merckx sealed his second Tour success with time trial victories in Bordeaux and Paris. Victory on the final day gave him eight in total, equalling Pélissier's record. Although he missed out on the green jersey by a handful of points to compatriot Walter Godefroot, 'The Cannibal' also added the mountains prize, the combined jersey and the combativity award to his collection of titles. He had finished almost 13 minutes clear of Zoetemelk, who admitted halfway through the race that Merckx was unbeatable. Could his rivals get any closer to him in 1971?

FINAL STANDINGS

1 Eddy Merckx (BEL) Faema-Faemino 119:31:49
2 Joop Zoetemelk (NED) Flandria +12:41
3 Gösta Pettersson (SWE) Ferretti +15:54
4 Martin Vandenbossche (BEL) Molteni +18:53
5 Marinus Wagtmans (NED) Willem II +19:54
6 Lucien Van Impe (BEL) Sonolor +20:34
7 Raymond Poulidor (FRA) Fagor +20:35
8 Antoon Houbrechts (BEL) Salvarani +21:34
9 Francisco Galdos (SPA) Kas +21:45
10 Georges Pintens (BEL) Mann +23:23

AVERAGE SPEED (OF WINNER): 35.589 KM/H
TOTAL DISTANCE RACED: 4,254 KM

OPPOSITE Merckx takes flight in the Alps, his focus anchored on the road ahead, his rivals disappearing in his wake.

OCAÑA'S ABANDON LEAVES MERCKX IN THE CLEAR

Eddy Merckx's panache and immense appetite for victory resulted in some questions being asked about his prospects going into the 58th Tour. His rivals wondered if his exploits in the Spring Classics, Paris–Nice, the Dauphiné and the Midi Libre had exhausted his reserves. Although he hadn't taken part in the Giro, his season had been extremely busy. Did this give them reason for hope?

Merckx initially banished these thoughts as – in his new Molteni colours – he powered his team to victory in the Mulhouse prologue. He backed this statement up by leading in a group of just 15 riders who finished 8 minutes ahead of the pack in Strasbourg. However, a week into the race, on the slopes of the Puy-de-Dôme, Ocaña and Zoetemelk slipped free of his grasp. They didn't have much of an advantage, but it revealed a chink in the Belgian's armour.

That chink widened on the road to Grenoble two days later. Thévenet, Zoetemelk, Pettersson and Ocaña dropped him on the Col de Porte, Ocaña winning the stage with Zoetemelk moving into yellow for the first time. Merckx was rocking ahead of a tough day to Orcières-Merlette, where Ocaña delivered a hammer blow. Zoetemelk, Van Impe and Agostinho went with the Spaniard's early attack, but none of them were able to follow when Ocaña took off alone on the Col du Noyer. Over the final 60 km the Spaniard handed Merckx some of his own medicine, finishing 8-42 up on the

defending champion. Ocaña had carried out a coup d'état that would never be forgotten.

The next day, the wounded champion attacked from the off, initiating a ferocious 250-km pursuit all the way to Marseille. Merckx picked off another 11 seconds in the Albi time trial that followed. But how could he claw back a deficit of 7-23 to deny Ocaña victory in Paris a week later?

As the Tour ventured into the Pyrenees for a stage to Luchon that Ocaña knew like the back of his hand, the leaden heat that had accompanied the race for several days broke in spectacular fashion. A storm raged, making conditions extremely hazardous. During the deluge, as he chased Merckx down the descent off the relatively small Col de Menté, Ocaña skidded and crashed on a hairpin. As he staggered back to his feet, Zoetemelk careered into him. Semi-conscious, Ocaña was evacuated to hospital as José Manuel Fuente won the stage and Merckx regained the yellow jersey.

Merckx considered abandoning, but wasn't happy leaving the title to Zoetemelk or Van Impe. He continued on but refused to wear the yellow jersey out of respect to Ocaña. Merckx triumphed for the third time, but his joy at winning was only half-hearted. This was not a victory he would look back on with affection. It wasn't complete. Ocaña, meanwhile, dreamed of redemption. But he felt no bitterness towards his rival. If he had, why would he have called his dog Merckx?

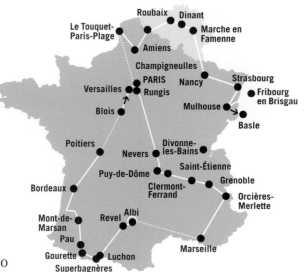

FINAL STANDINGS

1 Eddy Merckx (BEL) Molteni 96:45:14
2 Joop Zoetemelk (NED) Flandria +9:51
3 Lucien Van Impe (BEL) Sonolor +11:06
4 Bernard Thévenet (FRA) Peugeot +14:50
5 Joaquim Agostinho (POR) Hoover +21:00
6 Leif Mortensen (DEN) Bic +21:38
7 Cyrille Guimard (FRA) Fagor +22:58
8 Bernard Labourdette (FRA) Bic +30:07
9 Lucien Aimar (FRA) Sonolor +32:45
10 Vicente López Carril (SPA) Kas +36:00

AVERAGE SPEED (OF WINNER): 37.29 KM/H
TOTAL DISTANCE RACED: 3,608 KM

OPPOSITE A new sponsor for Merckx, but no lessening of his grip on the yellow jersey.

Luis Ocaña makes a solo bid for glory on the Col du Noyer, dropping fellow escapees Zoetemelk, Van Impe and Agostinho. He would finish almost nine minutes up on Merckx.

OPPOSITE TOP LEFT Ocaña receives treatment on the Col de Menté but is unable to continue after holding the yellow jersey for just two days.

OPPOSITE TOP RIGHT Merckx earned the right to wear the yellow jersey but only donned it two days after Ocaña's abandon out of respect for his rival.

OPPOSITE BOTTOM Merckx shares a joke with long-time team-mate Jos Huysmans.

MERCKX BACK TO HIS BEST

As if to erase the doubts that he and many others had about his third Tour success, Eddy Merckx ended the 1971 season with victory in the World Championship, ensuring that he arrived at the 59th Tour in the rainbow jersey. Just weeks before, he had also completed a third victory in the Giro d'Italia. Still only 27, he now had his sights set on a fourth consecutive Tour win. The scene was set for an epic duel with Luis Ocaña, so unfortunate the year before. However, although the duel promised so much, Merckx's main challenge would come from a new and rather unexpected rival.

As usual, Merckx started in the ideal way with an impressive prologue victory in Angers. His hold on the lead lasted just a day, though, as Cyrille Guimard claimed it thanks to bonus time earned as a result of his victory in Saint-Brieuc. Merckx swapped his rainbow jersey for yellow when Molteni won the team time trial, Guimard took it back from him again when he bagged the stage the next day. Merckx reimposed his law in Luchon, taking a decisive lead over Guimard and, more importantly, beating Ocaña in the mountains for the second day in a row. But this wasn't the Ocaña of 1971. Hampered by the effects of a crash on the first Pyrenean stage, his condition worsened and he eventually quit the race with bronchitis in the Alps.

Ocaña had moved into second place when the race finished on Mont Ventoux, where Merckx had once again edged away from him towards the finish. Orcières-Merlette lay ahead, but Merckx wasn't about to be caught out again as the pair finished together. The Belgian nailed the door closed with back-to-back mountain victories in Briançon and Valloire. The latter, a morning stage, was followed by an afternoon run to Aix-les-Bains. Guimard won it with Merckx right on his wheel. Ocaña lost five minutes and, worn down by Merckx, failed to start the next day.

Guimard, two years older than the Belgian, had already spiced up the race with his Gan-Mercier team-mate, 'old' Raymond Poulidor. That continued on the short stage to the top of Mont Revard. Merckx thought he had won it, but Guimard, never noted as a great climber but as dogged as they come, judged the sprint better, confirming his lead in the points competition. Sadly for Guimard and the race, although his head and heart were willing, his knees were not. Tendinitis in his knees became so severe he had to be lifted onto and off his bike. Dropped on the Ballon d'Alsace on stage 17, he abandoned the next day.

Merckx wrapped up his fourth title with a sixth stage win on the final day, which ended with another demonstration of his chivalry. Having inherited the green jersey when Guimard had abandoned, Merckx took his third victory in that competition, but offered the jersey to Guimard, who had come to congratulate him on the finish line at La Cipale.

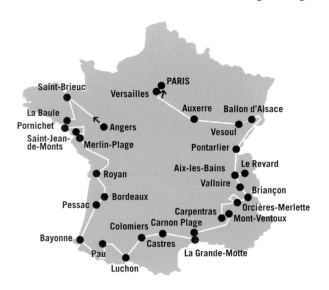

FINAL STANDINGS

1 Eddy Merckx (BEL) Molteni 108:17:18
2 Felice Gimondi (ITA) Salvarani +10:41
3 Raymond Poulidor (FRA) Gan +11:34
4 Lucien Van Impe (BEL) Sonolor +16:45
5 Joop Zoetemelk (NED) Beaulieu +19:09
6 Mariano Martinez (FRA) Magniflex +21:31
7 Yves Hézard (FRA) Sonolor +21:52
8 Joaquim Agostinho (POR) Magniflex +34:16
9 Bernard Thévenet (FRA) Peugeot +37:11
10 Ward Janssens (BEL) Magniflex +42:33

AVERAGE SPEED (OF WINNER): 35.516 KM/H
TOTAL DISTANCE RACED: 3,846 KM

A watchful Merckx, wearing the rainbow jersey as world champion, joins the Michelin man on the podium.

FORTUNE FINALLY FAVOURS OCAÑA

In 1973, Eddy Merckx sat out the Tour having completed a full set of grand tour victories at the Vuelta a España then added a fourth Giro title for good measure. In the Belgian's absence, Luis Ocaña was anointed favourite for the yellow jersey due in part to his supreme, but ultimately doomed performance in 1971, but also to the great form he had shown in winning the Dauphiné. He was supported by a very strong Bic team, which showed its depth on the second day when Frenchman José Catieau took a stage win in Belgium at St Niklaas.

Two days later, Catieau was in the winning break again, earning himself a four-day stint in the yellow jersey. Much more significantly, though, Ocaña was in it too. The break occurred on a section of cobbles 66 km into the Roubaix–Reims stage. One rider instigated, a dozen or so more joined him, including no less than five Bic riders but none of Ocaña's likely rivals, all of whom lost two-and-a-half minutes or more. In Gaillard, Ocaña's solo win gave him the yellow jersey that had been kept warm by his team-mate.

In Merckx's absence, Ocaña then produced a performance the great Belgian would have been proud of. He broke clear on the Galibier with his bitter rival José Manuel Fuente. The pair rode on together towards the Izoard, where Fuente refused to contribute to the pace-making, only moving to the front at the summit to take maximum points in the mountains competition. Riled by this, Ocaña didn't pause when Fuente punctured on the final climb to Les Orres. Victory widened his lead to nine minutes.

Success in the Perpignan time trial stretched Ocaña's advantage even more, but he wasn't anywhere near finished yet. Heading for Luchon over four passes, Ocaña attacked on the last of them, the Portillon, and galloped away with only Zoetemelk for company, although the Dutchman also dropped away before the line, where the Spaniard's lead was now a huge 15 minutes. It had seemed that fortune was favouring him when he had emerged unscathed from a crash after a dog ran into his wheels on stage one. Nothing could surely stop the French-based Spaniard now.

Victorious again on the Puy-de-Dôme and in the final time trial in Versailles, Ocaña had produced a Merckxian performance. Winner by 16 minutes ahead of the ever-improving Bernard Thévenet, Ocaña had taken six stage wins, while Bic had secured the team classification. After two years when his physical and psychological frailty got the better of his innate ability, Ocaña had become only the second Spanish winner of the Tour.

FINAL STANDINGS

1. Luis Ocaña (SPA) Bic 122:25:34
2. Bernard Thévenet (FRA) Peugeot +15:51
3. José Manuel Fuente (SPA) Kas +17:15
4. Joop Zoetemelk (NED) Gitane +26:22
5. Lucien Van Impe (BEL) Sonolor +30:20
6. Herman Van Springel (BEL) Rokado +32:01
7. Michel Périn (FRA) Gan-Mercier +33:02
8. Joaquim Agostinho (POR) Bic +35:51
9. Vicente López Carril (SPA) Kas +36:18
10. Régis Ovion (FRA) Peugeot +36:59

AVERAGE SPEED (OF WINNER): 33.407 KM/H
TOTAL DISTANCE RACED: 4,090 KM

Luis Ocaña leads his bitter rival José Manuel Fuente during their long break over the Galibier and Izoard. Ocaña would finally drop his compatriot on the final ascent up to Les Orres, where his overall lead jumped to more than nine minutes.

TOP José Catieau looks rather overwhelmed as he receives an ovation having taken the yellow jersey.

ABOVE Ocaña acknowledges the ovation from the crowd having secured his victory in Paris.

RIGHT Joop Zoetemelk looks happy to be in the spotlight following his victory in Nancy. The Dutchman would finish fourth overall.

OPPOSITE In the quest for a light bike, Ocaña's Bic team commissioned a state-of-the-art titanium frame complete with drilled brake levers.

MAJESTIC MERCKX EQUALS ANQUETIL

After staying away from the 1973 Tour, Eddy Merckx returned to the race with his sights set on adding a fifth title to the fifth Giro crown he had won just weeks before. This would certainly have marked him out as the favourite, but in truth the opposition was not as strong as it could have been. Defending champion Luis Ocaña was absent having fallen out with the management at his Bic team, while Joop Zoetemelk was battling meningitis in hospital. 1973 runner-up Bernard Thévenet did start, but he was still looking to regain form after a series of crashes at the Vuelta. It said a good deal that Merckx's greatest threat would come from 38-year-old Raymond Poulidor.

The omens were good for Merckx from the start. He won the prologue in Brest, and thereafter the only other riders who had the honour of wearing the yellow jersey were his loyal lieutenant Jos Bruyère and sprinters Gerben Karstens and Patrick Sercu. Bruyère took the lead on the first stage, ensuring that he was in the yellow jersey when the Tour made its first visit to Britain for a stage in Plymouth. Run on a recently opened bypass with none of the Tour's usual hoopla, the stage was a non-event, underlined by the fact that unknown Dutchman Henk Poppe won it. It was his only major pro victory.

Intermediate sprint bonuses decided the destination of the yellow jersey during the opening week of skirmishing. Merckx ended that when he proved quickest of a five-man group at Gaillard. Although dropped by Poulidor on the Col du Chat the following day, Merckx reasserted his control before the finish to secure his fourth stage win with the high Alps and Ventoux looming. Poulidor stalled in the Alps but soared on 'The Bald Mountain', dropping Merckx for a second time, although he failed once again to make anything of it.

In the Pyrenees, the race crossed over to Spain, where it was a target for Basque separatist group ETA. Cars in the Tour convoy were bombed, but the Tour continued on, recrossing the border to finish at Pla d'Adet. Poulidor once again escaped Merckx's clutches, only this time he stayed clear for his first Tour win for nine years. Merckx looked shaky, but each time a rider threatened, he stood firm and they cracked. Poulidor, Spaniard Gonzalo Aja and Italian Wladimiro Panizza got close to Merckx. None of them could sustain their challenge. Spanish climber Vicente López Carril fared better, moving into second at Pla d'Adet, 2-24 down on Merckx. Would he trouble Merckx on the first-ever finish on the summit of the Tourmalet?

Merckx marked the Spaniard tightly, and the pair finished together. In the two time trials on the run-in to Paris, Merckx finished off the contest, equalling Jacques Anquetil's record of five wins. Poulidor finished so strongly he snatched second place from López Carril. Strangely, Anquetil and Merckx both took their historic fifth Tours ahead of Poulidor. Ten years separated the two achievements.

FINAL STANDINGS

1 Eddy Merckx (BEL) Molteni 116:16:58
2 Raymond Poulidor (FRA) Gan-Mercier +8:04
3 Vicente López Carril (SPA) Kas +8:09
4 Wladimiro Panizza (ITA) Brooklyn +10:59
5 Gonzalo Aja (SPA) Kas +11:24
6 Joaquim Agostinho (POR) Bic +14:24
7 Michel Pollentier (BEL) Carpenter-Confortluxe +16:34
8 Mariano Martinez (FRA) Sonolor-Gitane +18:33
9 Alain Santy (FRA) Gan-Mercier +19:55
10 Herman Van Springel (BEL) Mic-De Gribaldy +24:11

AVERAGE SPEED (OF WINNER): 35.241 KM/H
TOTAL DISTANCE RACED: 4,098 KM

OPPOSITE A wet morning in the Tour's first week. Eddy Merckx doesn't seem too concerned, but the battle for the yellow jersey is keeping him warm.

1975
BERNARD THÉVENET
PEUGEOT

THÉVENET ENDS MERCKX'S UNBEATEN RUN

The 1975 Tour stands out as marking the start of a new era for the race. It was the first to finish on the Champs-Élysées. It provided the home nation with its first victory since 1967. Consequently, and more notably, it was also the first Tour Eddy Merckx had participated in and failed to win. There was no record-breaking sixth victory for the Belgian, who finally yielded to Bernard Thévenet.

Merckx started the race well enough, although young Italian Francesco Moser denied him victory in the prologue. The next day, the two riders were again at the forefront, going clear in a small group that gained almost a minute on the main pack. Thanks to this cushion, Moser managed to keep the yellow jersey until the stage six time trial at Merlin Plage, where Merckx claimed the stage and the race lead. The impression that the Belgian winning machine was on course for a sixth title hardened when Merckx won a second time trial in Auch, although his advantage on Thévenet was minimal, partly due to a puncture.

Even when Merckx lost the best part of a minute to Thévenet in the Pyrenees at Saint-Lary-Soulan, it appeared little more than a temporary hiccup. However, the race was about to take a sinister turn on the Puy-de-Dôme. Some cantankerous fans up there made it clear they couldn't stand his domination by waving banners saying that the Tour

needed to be 'de-Merckxified'. One of them got it into his head to do just that by punching the Belgian in the midriff.

After a rest day, the race headed into the Alps, where Merckx appeared to be back to his dominating best. He attacked on the Col d'Allos after resisting six attacks from Thévenet on the Col de Champs. But as he started up the early ramps of the final climb to Pra-Loup, he began to slow. Thévenet passed him, pressing hard to gain as much time as he could and turning a one-minute deficit into a one-minute lead. Merckx blamed the medication he had taken after being punched.

Everyone expected a response at Serre-Chevalier the next day, but it was Thévenet, wearing number 51 like Merckx in 1969 and Ocaña in 1973, who dominated the action, taking a brilliant solo victory and pushing his advantage on Merckx out beyond three minutes. Merckx's hopes of a comeback all but disappeared the next morning when he collided with Ole Ritter on the way to the start and broke his left cheekbone in the resulting crash. Urged to quit by the race doctor, he pressed on to ensure his team-mates got their split of his prize money and to honour Thévenet's superb ride. He continued to fight all the way to the Champs-Élysées, where Thévenet, a good champion who owed a bit to luck and a lot to talent, was crowned. He was also lucky to have, in Eddy Merckx, the greatest and most worthy of runners-up.

FINAL STANDINGS

1 Bernard Thévenet (FRA) Peugeot 114:35:31
2 Eddy Merckx (BEL) Molteni +2:47
3 Lucien Van Impe (BEL) Gitane +5:01
4 Joop Zoetemelk (NED) Gan-Mercier +6:42
5 Vicente López Carril (SPA) Kas +19:29
6 Felice Gimondi (ITA) Bianchi +23:05
7 Francesco Moser (ITA) Filotex +24:13
8 Josef Fuchs (SWI) Filotex +25:51
9 Edouard Janssens (BEL) Molteni +32:01
10 Pedro Torres (SPA) Super Ser +35:36

AVERAGE SPEED (OF WINNER): 34.906 KM/H
TOTAL DISTANCE RACED: 4,000 KM

OPPOSITE Although wearing the yellow jersey, Merckx still tended to attack rather than sit back and wait for his rivals to do so. He wanted to be the first rider to take six victories and to do so with panache. His determination would prove fatal for him.

RIGHT Had he been hit or simply obstructed by a spectator? At the finish it is still unclear, although Merckx is visibly shaken.

BELOW Wounded on the Puy-de-Dôme, hit by a sudden loss of energy at Pra-Loup, Eddy Merckx lost the yellow jersey to Bernard Thévenet and raced in his world champion's rainbow bands. Despite suffering another heavy blow that left him with a fractured cheekbone, he made it a point of honour to attack his successor.

OPPOSITE Wearing the number 51 as Merckx had when he had won the Tour in 1969, Thévenet ups the pressure on Belgium's race leader.

MOUNTAINS KING VAN IMPE REACHES THE SUMMIT

Beaten in 1975, Eddy Merckx was unable to return to make a second challenge for a sixth title because of injury. Nevertheless, Belgium still celebrated another Tour success thanks to elfin climber Lucien Van Impe. Like his compatriot, Van Impe had made his Tour debut in the 1969 race. Although their rivalry was less evident than that between Merckx and Ocaña, it was there due to their shared Belgian background. Certainly, Van Impe often found himself in Merckx's sights, particularly in 1969 and 1970, when 'The Cannibal' shot at anything that moved, including the red polka-dot jersey of the mountains title, which for a long time was the only trophy coveted by Van Impe.

Bernard Thévenet started the race wearing bib number one as the defending champion. In Merckx's absence he was expecting his main rivals to be Gan-Mercier duo Raymond Poulidor and Joop Zoetemelk, Ti-Raleigh's Hennie Kuiper and Gitane's Van Impe, who now had Cyrille Guimard in the team car behind him as *directeur sportif* following his retirement from racing. The race also saw the debut of Belgian powerhouse Freddy Maertens, who would go on to equal Merckx's record for stage victories (eight) and take home the green jersey after wearing the yellow until the ninth stage.

The race really got going in the Alps. Van Impe picked up the baton and the yellow jersey at Alpe d'Huez, where Zoetemelk triumphed. The Dutchman won again at Montgenèvre the next day, when Thévenet finished with the two Lowlanders. However, that was as good as it got for the Frenchman. Increasingly hampered by injury, he slipped down the order, handing over the leadership of the Peugeot team to Raymond Delisle, who pinched the jersey from Van Impe thanks to a courageous victory at Pyrénées 2000.

Perennial mountains champion Van Impe didn't seem overly perturbed by the loss of the yellow jersey, but his *directeur* Guimard felt that his Belgian leader could still claim the title if he was aggressive enough. Guimard urged Van Impe to attack on the Portillon pass as the race made for Saint-Lary-Soulan. Van Impe initially resisted, until directly instructed by Guimard to go on the offensive. Delisle and Zoetemelk didn't respond, as Van Impe scampered across to a group ahead that included Luis Ocaña.

Ocaña drove hard up the Peyresourde, then dropped away as Van Impe continued to press on the final ascent. Thanks to Guimard's tactical vision, the Belgian beat Zoetemelk by more than 3 minutes and Delisle by 12. Back in the yellow jersey, the tiny Belgian increased his advantage in the time trial at Auch and was happy to allow Zoetemelk to take the plaudits on the Puy-de-Dôme as he had the title in the bag. As Van Impe celebrated victory on his eighth attempt, 40-year-old Raymond Poulidor bid the Tour farewell with his eighth podium place, finishing third just as he had on his 1962 debut.

FINAL STANDINGS

1 Lucien Van Impe (BEL) Gitane-Campagnolo 116:22:23
2 Joop Zoetemelk (NED) Gan-Mercier +4:14
3 Raymond Poulidor (FRA) Gan-Mercier +12:08
4 Raymond Delisle (FRA) Peugeot +12:17
5 Walter Riccomi (ITA) Scic-Fiat-Colnago +12:39
6 Francisco Galdos (SPA) Kas-Campagnolo +14:50
7 Michel Pollentier (BEL) Flandria-Velda +14:59
8 Freddy Maertens (BEL) Flandria-Velda +16:09
9 Fausto Bertoglio (ITA) Jollyceramica +16:36
10 Vicente López Carril (SPA) Kas-Campagnolo +19:28

AVERAGE SPEED (OF WINNER): 34.518 KM/H
TOTAL DISTANCE RACED: 4,017 KM

TOP LEFT Van Impe celebrates his coronation as the 1976 champion aboard the Boule d'Or motorbikes.

TOP RIGHT Van Impe holds aloft the Tour-winning pennant on the Champs-Élysées. To his right is runner-up Joop Zoetemelk, to his left are points winner Freddy Maertens, best young rider Enrique Martínez Heredia, third-placed Raymond Poulidor, mountains winner Giancarlo Bellini and fourth-placed Raymond Delisle.

RIGHT Renowned for his desire to innovate, Gitane *directeur sportif* Cyrille Guimard provided Van Impe with a very lightweight carbon-fibre bike for the mountain stages during his Tour-winning ride.

TWO FOR THÉVENET AS MERCKX BOWS OUT

This was in truth a very dull race during its opening two weeks, although that is no comment on the excellent performance of young German Dietrich Thurau, who took the yellow jersey in the prologue and performed miracles to keep it until the race reached the Alps. Thurau's pluck came to the fore on stage two when the race made a very early passage through the Pyrenees. Dropped by defending champion Lucien Van Impe, his predecessor Bernard Thévenet and another favourite, Hennie Kuiper, Thurau joined forces with the returning Eddy Merckx to chase them and save the jersey. Merckx, too, had to yield to the young German in his preferred domain, losing out in the stage five Bordeaux time trial when it seemed certain he would take the lead.

Stalemate followed as the race headed north, turned east, then started south into the Alps, passing through West Germany on the way, where Thurau's heroics drew out huge crowds. The contest only really came alive in the mountain time trial to Avoriaz on stage 15. Zoetemelk won it, but was subsequently handed a ten-minute penalty after testing positive for doping. That didn't alter the fact that Thévenet had finally edged Thurau out of the yellow jersey. The German responded with a stage win in Chamonix, but finally fell out of contention on the climb up to Alpe d'Huez.

The stage up the famous hairpins went to Kuiper. Behind him, Thévenet kept the lead by a margin of eight tiny seconds. Van Impe, who had attacked from a long way out, completely lost his chance when his wheel was clipped by a television car, leaving him stranded until his team car arrived with a new wheel. Some put the blame for this on Henry Anglade, his *directeur sportif*, who didn't have the same tactical acumen as his predecessor, Cyrille Guimard.

As it moved towards its conclusion, this rather odd race was hit by a series of positive drug tests, notably during the 18th stage to Saint-Étienne, where winner Joaquim Agostinho and second-placed Antonio Menéndez both tested positive, as did Luis Ocaña. As with Zoetemelk and two other riders, the product involved was Pemoline.

In the time trial in Dijon, Thévenet gave himself a bit more of a buffer when he won the stage and gained another 28 seconds on Kuiper. He boosted his narrow advantage by another 12 seconds in the final day's time trial on the Champs-Élysées, completing his victory with a 48-second lead over Kuiper, with the unfortunate Van Impe third on a course that didn't suit his strengths. Merckx, who had been dreaming of a sixth Tour win, could only manage sixth place. It was his seventh Tour, but his last. Luis Ocaña also departed the race for good to set himself up as an Armagnac producer.

FINAL STANDINGS

1 Bernard Thévenet (FRA) Peugeot 115:38:30
2 Hennie Kuiper (NED) Raleigh +0:48
3 Lucien Van Impe (BEL) Lejeune +3:32
4 Francisco Galdos (SPA) Kas +7:45
5 Dietrich Thurau (GER) Raleigh +12:24
6 Eddy Merckx (BEL) Fiat +12:38
7 Michel Laurent (FRA) Peugeot +17:42
8 Joop Zoetemelk (NED) Miko +19:22
9 Raymond Delisle (FRA) Miko +21:32
10 Alain Meslet (FRA) Gitane +27:31

AVERAGE SPEED (OF WINNER): 35.419 KM/H
TOTAL DISTANCE RACED: 4,096 KM

LEFT It had to happen. Peugeot's lion cubs finally cracked 'The Cannibal' (above).

THE ARRIVAL OF 'THE BADGER'

Eddy Merckx, Raymond Poulidor and Luis Ocaña had retired, but there were still plenty of potential champions at the start of the 65th Tour in the Dutch town of Leiden. Bernard Thévenet, although out of form, was back to defend his title. Lucien Van Impe was aiming to regain the yellow jersey, while established pillars such as Hennie Kuiper, Joaquim Agostinho, Jos Bruyère and Mariano Martinez also had their backers. However, all would be blown away by a wind that was about to sweep in from Brittany in the west.

Motivated by the start on home soil, the Dutch came out of the traps quickly. Although the judges ruled that Jan Raas's prologue victory would not count towards the overall classification because teeming rain had made the course dangerous, the indignant Dutchman responded in the best way by winning the next day as well. The sprinters then dominated the opening week, Freddy Maertens winning twice and young Irishman Sean Kelly also a victor. The complexion of the race started to change, though, when Tour debutant Bernard Hinault clinched the long time trial at Sainte-Foye-la-Grande.

Leader of the Renault team, French champion Hinault had Van Impe's former *directeur sportif* Cyrille Guimard guiding him. The Breton was also carrying number 51, which in the past had brought luck to Merckx, Ocaña and Thévenet. Dubbed 'The Badger' due to his feisty nature, Hinault spent the first week watching out for trouble and awaiting the time trial. Over 59.3 km, he scattered his far more experienced rivals, although Merckx's former lieutenant Bruyère took the yellow jersey.

The Pyrenees saw Thévenet withdraw as Hinault stepped up into second place, with Zoetemelk on his heels. A growing force on the road, Hinault's reputation increased when he emerged as one of the leaders of a riders' strike in Valence d'Agen. Called to complain about the excessive demands both in terms of time and effort made on riders during days that featured split stages, it led to the annulment of the stage.

The Puy-de-Dôme time trial two days later saw the precocious Hinault drop to third as Zoetemelk stormed to victory, then respond with a bunch sprint win in Saint-Étienne. Alpe d'Huez followed and proved the turning point. Belgian Michel Pollentier, far from the brightest spark in the race, won the stage and took the yellow jersey, only to be disqualified for trying to cheat in a dope control. Kuiper inherited the stage win and Zoetemelk the yellow jersey, but with a slim lead of 14 seconds over Hinault.

Equally matched in the mountains, the contest between 'old' Joop and Hinault was decided in a 72-km time trial between Metz and Nancy. The young gun blitzed his rival, beating him by four minutes as he won the stage. With it came his first yellow jersey and the title, which was confirmed on the Champs-Élysées, where Brittany turned out to celebrate.

FINAL STANDINGS

1 Bernard Hinault (FRA) Renault 107:18:00
2 Joop Zoetemelk (NED) Miko +3:56
3 Joaquim Agostinho (POR) Flandria-Velda +6:54
4 Joseph Bruyère (BEL) C&A +9:04
5 Christian Seznec (FRA) Miko +12:50
6 Paul Wellens (BEL) Raleigh +14:38
7 Francisco Galdos (SPA) Kas +17:08
8 Henk Lubberding (NED) Raleigh +17:26
9 Lucien Van Impe (BEL) C&A +21:01
10 Mariano Martinez (FRA) Jobo +22:58

AVERAGE SPEED (OF WINNER): 36.084 KM/H
TOTAL DISTANCE RACED: 3,908 KM

OPPOSITE The two extremes of the Tour: a debutant called Bernard Hinault (top), a dashing French champion with a steely eye, and Joop Zoetemelk (bottom), a weary 30 year old, who had been collecting places of honour since Merckx's era.

Nicknames

A TREND THAT had started in the pre-war years continued after it. A nickname could spring from anywhere. From a rider's style on the bike, demeanour, origin, hair colour or stature. They emerge from races, from the riders, those close to them, and even from journalists and race announcers. Sometimes they also stem from discussions over a few drinks!

Nicknames remind us of the nature of the Tour and of its champions: of the contact we have with the riders, of the conviviality within the sport. It's a sport where we can get right up close to our idols, and this gives us a chance to have a little fun with them as well.

Djamolidin Abdoujaparov: The Tashkent Express
Robert Alban: Banban
Rudi Altig: Rhine Gold
Henry Anglade: Napoleon
Lance Armstrong: The Boss
Federico Bahamontes: The Eagle of Toledo
Ercole Baldini: The Locomotive
Gino Bartali: The Old Man, Gino the Pious, The Camel
Louis Bergaud: The Flea of Cantal
Roland Berland: The Curate
Paolo Bettini: The Cricket
Franco Bitossi: Crazy Heart
Louison Bobet: The Baker from Saint-Méen. His team-mate Raphaël Geminiani also baptized him Zonzon, but he was the only one allowed to call him that.
Albert Bouvet: The Granite Cutter
Fabian Cancellara: Spartacus

Mark Cavendish: The Man of Man, The Manx Express
Claudio Chiappucci: The Devil
Mario Cipollini: Cipo, The Lion King, SuperMario
Thierry Claveyrolat: The Eagle of Vizille
Régis Clère: Clairon
Alberto Contador: El Pistolero
Fausto Coppi: The Heron, The Albatross
François Coquery: The Mathematician
André Darrigade: The Blond from Les Landes, The Bounding Basque
Roger De Vlaeminck: The Gypsy
Pedro Delgado: Perico
Jean Dotto: The Winemaker of Cabasse
Gilbert Duclos-Lassalle: Gibus
Édouard Fachleitner: The Shepherd of Manosque
Laurent Fignon: The Professor
Chris Froome: Froomedog
Charly Gaul: The Angel of the Mountains, Monsieur Pipi, The Cherub

Left to right: Lily 'The Flea of Cantal' Bergaud, Michel 'Curly' Van Aerde, André 'The Postman' le Dissez and Marcel 'The Red Devil' Queheille.

Rudi 'Rhine Gold' Altig leads Alsatian team-mate André Zimmerman, alias 'Zim-Boumboum'.

Raphaël Geminiani: The Big Gun

André Greipel: The Gorilla

Georges Groussard: The Fougères Cockerel

Roger Hassenforder: Hassen the Pirate

Luis Herrera: Lucho, The Little Gardener of Fusagasuga

Bernard Hinault: The Badger

Miguel Indurain: Big Mig, The Sphinx of Pamplona

Laurent Jalabert: Jaja

Julio Jiménez: The Avila Watchmaker

Hugo Koblet: The Pedaller of Charm

Ferdi Kübler: The Eagle of Adliswil, The Horse

Karl-Heinz Kunde: The Yellow Dwarf

Jacques Marinelli: The Parrot

Raymond Mastrotto: The Bull of Nay

Eddy Merckx: The Cannibal, The Tervueren Ogre

David Millar: Le Dandy

Gastone Nencini: The Lion of Mugello

Vincenzo Nibali: The Shark of the Strait (of Messina)

Luis Ocaña: The Parrot

Marco Pantani: The Pirate, Elefantino

Ronan Pensec: Pinpin

Jean-François Pescheux: Pepêche

Roger Pingeon: Pinpin

Miguel Poblet: The Divine Bald, Sancho Panza

Raymond Poulidor: Poupou

René Privat: The Gaulois, The Chestnut

Michael Rasmussen: Chicken

Ricardo Ricco: The Cobra

Jean Robic: Leatherhead, The Cockerel

Joaquim Rodriguez: Purito

Paolo Savoldelli: The Falcon

Alberic Schotte: Brik

Gerrit Schulte: The Pedalling Fool

Eddy Schutz: The Camel

Tom Simpson: Major Tom

Klaus-Peter Thaler: The Baker

Jan Ullrich: The Ogre of Rostock, Der Kaiser

Lucien Van Impe: The Marmoset

Rik Van Looy: The Emperor of Herentals

Franz Verbeeck: The Milkman of Wilsele

René Vietto: King René, The Groom

Alexandre Vinokourov: Vino

Thomas Voeckler: Ti-Blanc

Bradley Wiggins: Wiggo

Sean Yates: The Animal

Joop Zoetemelk: Zozo

BELOW LEFT Shy Colombian climber Luis Herrera went down in the sport's annals as 'The Little Gardener of Fusagasuga'.

BELOW RIGHT Like 1967 Tour winner Roger Pingeon, Ronan Pensec was dubbed 'Pinpin'.

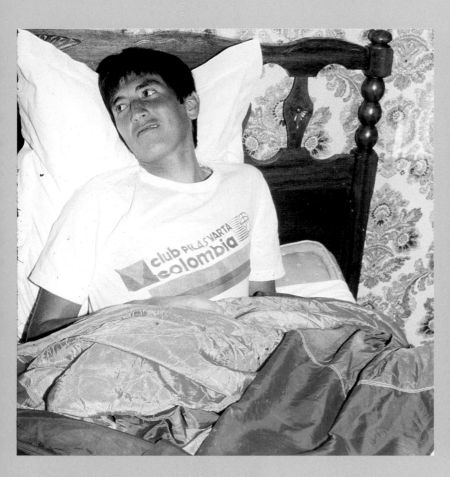

EXCEPTIONAL HINAULT WINS AT A CANTER

Still to prove himself going into the 1978 Tour, Bernard Hinault started the following edition as the hottest of favourites having taken the title. His two toughest opponents were the old stagers Joop Zoetemelk and Joaquim Agostinho, who would both win Alpe d'Huez, but rarely looked likely to deny the Frenchman a second successive crown.

Hinault and Zoetemelk both finished four seconds behind Ti-Raleigh's Gerrie Knetemann in the prologue at Fleurance, from where the race headed straight into the Pyrenees. Hinault's Renault team-mate Jean-René Bernaudeau immediately removed the yellow jersey from Knetemann, then passed it on to his team leader when Hinault won alone at Superbagnères the next day. Leaving the mountains, Ti-Raleigh enlivened the race, winning both of the long team time trials and taking further stage wins thanks to Jan Raas and Leo Van Vliet.

Hinault's serene progress ended on the stage into Roubaix featuring several sections of cobbles from the Paris–Roubaix one-day Classic. Chasing Zoetemelk, who had infiltrated a break, Hinault punctured, got held up by striking miners and lost three minutes and the yellow jersey to his rival. It could have been much worse. Angered by the reaction of his rivals to his travails, Hinault made it clear he would make them pay on the road. He began to do just that by winning a time trial in Brussels. Victory in a long time trial up to Avoriaz four days later put Hinault back in yellow. Only Zoetemelk now remained within 11 minutes of him in the standings.

His rage still firing him, Hinault pulled out more time when finishing second behind Van Impe in Les Ménuires. Zoetemelk struck back with victory in the second of two summit finishes on Alpe d'Huez, but lost his gains and more as Hinault imposed himself once again in the final time trial at Dijon. He had the race in the bag but unlike most Tour winners he did not ease up. He won a bunch sprint in Nogent-sur-Marne, then responded to an unexpected offensive by Zoetemelk on the final stage by counter-attacking.

The Champs-Élysées had never seen anything like it before and hasn't done since. The pair continued on, racing up and down the world's most famous avenue well ahead of the rest of the field, who were nothing more than a sideshow. Hinault, naturally, won the sprint against his Dutch rival, giving him a total of seven stage victories, including sprints, time trials and a mountain top finish. He was truly the complete champion. Zoetemelk was second, and remained so even after he was penalized ten minutes for a positive dope test, such was the gap between the two leaders and the rest.

FINAL STANDINGS

1 Bernard Hinault (FRA) Renault 103:06:50
2 Joop Zoetemelk (NED) Miko +13:07
3 Joaquim Agostinho (POR) Flandria +26:53
4 Hennie Kuiper (NED) Peugeot +28:02
5 Jean-René Bernaudeau (FRA) Renault +32:43
6 Giovanni Battaglin (ITA) Inoxpran +38:12
7 Jo Maas (NED) DAF +38:38
8 Paul Wellens (BEL) Ti-Raleigh +39:06
9 Claude Criquielion (BEL) Kas +40:38
10 Dietrich Thurau (GER) Ijsboerke +44:35

AVERAGE SPEED (OF WINNER): 36.513 KM/H
TOTAL DISTANCE RACED: 3,765 KM

'The Badger' tends to wear yellow, but he would also claim the green jersey in 1979 thanks to his seven stage victories.

Whether taking on Joop Zoetemelk
(above) or trying to get the most
from himself in a time trial (right),
Hinault always gives his best,
right to the end. In both 1978 and
1979, the Dutchman deprived
him for a brief time of the yellow
jersey, before almost inevitably
ending up as runner-up to Hinault.

1980
JOOP ZOETEMELK
TI-RALEIGH

ZOETEMELK RISES AS HINAULT FALLS

The 67th Tour set off from Frankfurt and it was hard to see how anyone could stop Bernard Hinault and his strong personal guard in Renault-Gitane's colours from strolling to a hat-trick. In fact, the race appeared to have been decided in little less than a week as 'The Badger' took the yellow jersey and won three stages. However, Hinault was caught out by two enemies: bad weather and the powerful Ti-Raleigh team that had taken on Joop Zoetemelk as its leader. For the first time Zoetemelk was part of a 100% Dutch team, which was very strong, completely loyal to him, and managed by a pragmatic strategist, Peter Post. To an extent, this Tour offered a final chance to 33-year-old Zoetemelk and a huge opportunity to his team, which had won everything except the Tour.

Hinault was happy to let the yellow jersey go after winning the prologue. Successive wins in the time trial at Spa and in a two-man break with Hennie Kuiper at Lille meant he was almost four minutes to the good on Zoetemelk, but his troubles really began the next day. The weather had already been wet and cold and that continued as the riders tackled several sections of cobbled road heading for Compiègne. A fall and the pounding pace set by Ti-Raleigh left Hinault struggling with tendinitis in his knee. The next day, he was unable to commit himself fully to Renault's effort in the team time trial won by Ti-Raleigh. He continued on

to the mid-race time trial at Laplume and took the yellow jersey. However, he was fifth and well below his best. Zoetemelk, meanwhile, was first and now sat just 21 seconds behind the Frenchman.

In Pau, Hinault was typically bullish. He said he was ready to go on the attack in the Pyrenees. But it soon became clear the tendinitis had made it impossible for him to pedal. Just before 10.30 in the evening, after all the newspapers had gone to press, a rumour started to circulate. Hinault, it was said, had quit the Tour and disappeared into the night. It later turned out he had taken refuge at the Lourdes home of his team-mate Hubert Arbes.

The next day Zoetemelk refused to wear the yellow jersey out of respect for the absent Hinault, just as Ferdi Kübler and Eddy Merckx had previously done. He still had to fight tooth and nail to earn the right to wear yellow that evening in Luchon as Raymond Martin, Mariano Martinez, Sean Kelly, Robert Alban and Kuiper all put him to the test.

Although he wobbled a bit in the Alps, on the key stage at Sept-Laux he regained his composure and stretched his lead to more than five minutes. A final time trial success in Saint-Étienne underlined his superiority. As Zoetemelk completed an unexpected lap of honour on the Champs-Élysées, the Dutch celebrated their second Tour success. French fans, meanwhile, awaited the return of Hinault.

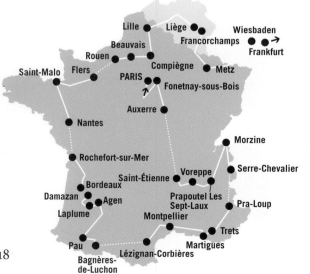

FINAL STANDINGS

1 Joop Zoetemelk (NED) Ti-Raleigh 109:19:14
2 Hennie Kuiper (NED) Peugeot-Michelin +6:55
3 Raymond Martin (FRA) Miko-Mercier +7:56
4 Johan De Muynck (BEL) Splendor +12:24
5 Joaquim Agostinho (POR) Puch-Sem +15:37
6 Christian Seznec (FRA) Miko-Mercier +16:16
7 Sven-Ake Nilsson (SWE) Miko-Mercier +16:33
8 Ludo Peeters (BEL) Ijsboerke-Warncke +20:45
9 Pierre Bazzo (FRA) La Redoute-Motobecane +21:03
10 Henk Lubberding (NED) Ti-Raleigh +21:10

AVERAGE SPEED (OF WINNER): 36.095 KM/H
TOTAL DISTANCE RACED: 3,946 KM

OPPOSITE TOP A good climber and time triallist, the Dutchman Joop Zoetemelk finally won the big prize in 1980. Admittedly, Hinault had to throw in the towel, but Zoetemelk (centre) still had to deal with his compatriot Hennie Kuiper (left) and the Belgian Johan De Muynck (right).

OPPOSITE BOTTOM Zoetemelk had traded the yellow jersey in 1979 with Hinault, who is seen tracking him in the green of points leader. When his French rival quit the 1980 race, Zoetemelk refused to wear yellow until he had earned it on the road out of respect.

RAMPANT HINAULT CRUSHES HIS RIVALS

Bernard Hinault arrived at the 68th Tour as if determined to complete unfinished business following his injury-enforced withdrawal the previous year. He had put that disappointment behind him to an extent by winning what was widely regarded as the toughest World Championship in history at Sallanches. Consequently, he was wearing the rainbow jersey as the Tour set off from Nice. Victory in the prologue meant he immediately swapped his rainbow colours for yellow, although his old sparring partners at Ti-Raleigh relieved him of it when they won the team time trial on day two.

The Dutch squad repeated their success in the second team time trial at Carcassonne, but Hinault wasted no time cutting them down to size. Second place at Pla d'Adet behind Lucien Van Impe vaulted the Frenchman up to second place overall behind a new and very unexpected leader, Peugeot's Phil Anderson, the first Australian to lead the Tour. Hinault pushed Anderson down to second in the time trial that followed and edged away over the next week before consolidating his position with a third time trial victory at Mulhouse.

Two weeks into the race, Hinault's constant pressure finally began to tell on the young Australian in the Alps. At Morzine he lost five minutes, at Alpe d'Huez another 17. When Anderson fell away, the race became a cakewalk for the Frenchman. A close second to Peter Winnen at Alpe d'Huez, he was now almost ten minutes ahead of Van Impe, his closest challenger. Hinault's victory at Le Pleynet the following day extended that to more than 12 minutes. By Paris it was almost a quarter of an hour.

Hinault finished the Tour leaving little doubt about his mastery of his rivals. Like points winner Freddy Maertens, he had won five stages. Van Impe had a fifth success to cheer as well, in his case in the mountains competition. Hinault's third Tour success drew obvious comparisons with Eddy Merckx. However, unlike the Belgian, Hinault had no obvious rivals, although Anderson had shown the potential to become one. Van Impe and Zoetemelk were past their best, while others had a flaw that made it impossible to sustain a challenge to Hinault, who could win a race on any terrain.

FINAL STANDINGS

1 Bernard Hinault (FRA) Renault 96:19:38
2 Lucien Van Impe (BEL) Boston +14:34
3 Robert Alban (FRA) La Redoute +17:04
4 Joop Zoetemelk (NED) Ti-Raleigh +18:21
5 Peter Winnen (NED) Capri Sonne +20:26
6 Jean-René Bernaudeau (FRA) Peugeot +23:02
7 Johan De Muynck (BEL) Splendor +24:25
8 Sven-Ake Nilsson (SWE) Splendor +24:37
9 Claude Criquielion (BEL) Splendor +26:18
10 Phil Anderson (AUS) Peugeot +27:00

AVERAGE SPEED (OF WINNER): 39.002 KM/H
TOTAL DISTANCE RACED: 3,757 KM

OPPOSITE Having been forced to quit the 1980 Tour in the yellow jersey, Bernard Hinault was soon back in it a year later and by the time he was heading for Morzine with Jean-René Bernaudeau (centre) and Fons De Wolf (right) he was close to having the race sewn up.

OVERLEAF Between 1976 and 1981, the king of the finish line was the Belgian Freddy Maertens, who claimed 15 stage wins. That earned him three green jerseys (1976, 1978, 1981) and a spell in the yellow jersey. He also tied the record for number of stage wins in one race, when he took eight in 1976. Here he is seen beating Fons De Wolf on the Champs-Élysées in 1981.

1982
BERNARD HINAULT
RENAULT-ELF-GITANE

HINAULT COMPLETES GIRO–TOUR DOUBLE

The 69th Tour started in Basle and once again pitched France against the Netherlands as Renault-Elf-Gitane faced up to Ti-Raleigh. Bernard Hinault struck the first blow for the French with victory in the prologue. The Dutch responded instantly when Ludo Peeters won the next stage and took the yellow jersey off Hinault's shoulders, although his hold on it proved just as short-lived. Victory on the Ballon d'Alsace the next day put Phil Anderson into yellow jersey for the second year in a row. Much more experienced than he had been in 1981, the Australian wasn't about to let the jersey go as quickly as he had done 12 months earlier.

Anderson wore it for ten days, until Hinault claimed it in the time trial at Valence d'Agen. Unusually, the Frenchman didn't win the test as Ti-Raleigh's Gerrie Knetemann reversed their prologue finishing positions, but from that point his progress towards a fourth title was relatively untroubled. His performances in the Pyrenees lacked the flamboyance and panache of previous years, but that was largely down to the lack of a consistent threat.

Victory in the time trial at Martigues in between the Pyrenees and Alps pushed the champion's lead out to more than five minutes over Anderson, who slipped back even further at Orcières-Merlette. Peugeot gained consolation, however, from a brilliant performance by Pascal Simon, who led over all five passes and clung on to win at the

resort made famous by Luis Ocaña's unforgettable exploit in 1971.

Thanks to his consistency, Joop Zoetemelk once again emerged as Hinault's understudy. Stubborn in his resistance, the Dutchman stuck to Hinault like a limpet. He never looked like threatening the race leader, but could not be shaken, or at least not in the mountains. In the final time trial at Saint-Priest, Hinault emphasized his dominance in that discipline, then produced a final flourish on the Champs-Élysées, beating the sprinters at their own game for his fourth stage win of the race.

This fourth Tour title moved him past Louison Bobet, the other great champion from western France, and placed him one behind Jacques Anquetil and Eddy Merckx. Victory also made Hinault just the fourth rider after Fausto Coppi, Anquetil and Merckx to complete the Giro–Tour double. It was no less than the third time he had beaten Zoetemelk into second place, as Ti-Raleigh's Johan Van der Velde filled the third spot on the podium.

Yet again, though, the gulf between Hinault and the rest had been huge. Anderson had improved, but lacked the climbing ability to stay in contention over three weeks. Simon looked a future contender, but struggled in time trials. In addition, results elsewhere gave no indication that a rider was set to emerge who could challenge 'The Badger'. Barring injury, the odds were already very short on him taking a fifth title in 1983.

FINAL STANDINGS

1 Bernard Hinault (FRA) Renault-Elf-Gitane 92:08:46
2 Joop Zoetemelk (NED) Coop-Mercier +6:21
3 Johan Van der Velde (NED) Ti-Raleigh +8:59
4 Peter Winnen (NED) Capri Sonne-Campagnolo +9:24
5 Phil Anderson (AUS) Peugeot +12:16
6 Beat Breu (SWI) Cilo +13:21
7 Daniel Willems (BEL) Sunair-Colnago +15:33
8 Raymond Martin (FRA) Coop-Mercier +15:35
9 Hennie Kuiper (NED) DAF Trucks +17:01
10 Alberto Fernández (SPA) Teka +17:19

AVERAGE SPEED (OF WINNER): 37.469 KM/H
TOTAL DISTANCE RACED: 3,512 KM

ABOVE Hinault was relatively untroubled on his way to his fourth Tour success. Although once again pressed by Australian Phil Anderson, who is giving his all to stay on the Frenchman's wheel, Hinault looked a champion in need of a serious rival.

RIGHT Anderson (right) held the yellow jersey for 10 days, but Hinault (left) always had the Australian very much in his sights.

The polka-dot jersey

ALTHOUGH THE TOUR has recognized its best climber since 1905 and has had a mountains classification since 1933, when Spaniard Vicente Trueba won the title, it wasn't until 1975 that the prize gained more official status with the introduction of the red polka-dot jersey. The unmistakable design promoted chocolate bars in a polka-dot wrapper produced by Poulain, who initially sponsored the jersey. The design has remained unchanged, even though French supermarket chain Carrefour has sponsored the prize since 1993.

Belgian Lucien Van Impe claimed the first title of King of the Mountains, as the prize has become generally known. It was the third time that Van Impe had been garlanded as the race's best climber. He went on to win the title three more times, tying with his hero, Federico Bahamontes, as the all-time record-holder. However, Frenchman Richard Virenque has since set a new record of seven King of the Mountains titles.

Points are allocated to climbs depending on their category of difficulty. Fourth-category climbs are the easiest and hors-catégorie – literally, above category or super category – are the toughest. Consequently, riders win the most points for being the first to the top of an hors-catégorie climb, which tend to be those in the Alps and Pyrenees.

In 2012, Frenchman Thomas Voeckler won the King of the Mountains title.

Although regarded more as a baroudeur or breakaway specialist than as a pure climber, Voeckler was part of two long breakaways in the mountains, which enabled him to win enough points to capture the title.

ABOVE Wearing the polka-dot jersey, Chris Froome sets the pace for team-mate and race leader Bradley Wiggins in 2012.

OPPOSITE TOP LEFT In 1979 Italy's Giovanni Battaglin was the Tour's King of the Mountains.

OPPOSITE TOP RIGHT Thomas Voeckler cemented his status as France's cycling hero of the moment when he won two mountain stages in 2012, which enabled him to win the polka-dot jersey.

OPPOSITE BOTTOM Anthony Charteau was the surprise french winner of the mountains jersey in 2010.

FRANCE FINDS A NEW STAR

This 1983 Tour mirrored the 1973 race. Hinault, the previous year's winner, did not defend his title, just as Merckx hadn't a decade earlier. Both men had also taken four victories. However, whereas Merckx had opted to focus on other targets, Hinault had had knee trouble since 1980 and needed an operation. In his place, Renault *directeur* Cyrille Guimard reluctantly selected 22-year-old Laurent Fignon, who had already supported Hinault's victorious Vuelta campaign that season. Renault, said Guimard, would target stage wins.

In Hinault's absence the race opened up, as did the organizers' decision to welcome Colombian amateurs from the Varta team in line with their new 'open' format. Alongside these newcomers were Tour heavyweights Van Impe and Zoetemelk, as well as plenty of veterans like Agostinho, Kuiper and Kelly. Victory for Zoetemelk's Coop-Mercier in the team time trial and second place the following day gave Dane Kim Andersen the yellow jersey. He wore it until Pau, where the Irishman Kelly took the lead on the threshold of the Pyrenees.

Heading over the famous quartet of passes into Luchon (the Aubisque, Tourmalet, Aspin and Peyresourde), Peugeot showed their ambition. Scottish climber Robert Millar won ahead of Spanish debutant Pedro Delgado, while Millar's team-mate Pascal Simon took the yellow jersey. The stage took a dreadful toll. Sixteen riders abandoned and many more lost substantial time, notably Kelly and Zoetemelk. The spectacle-wearing Fignon, though, limited his losses and moved into second place, 4-22 down on Simon.

The next day's 11th stage should have been much more straightforward, however, in attempting to avoid a collision with team-mate Bernard Bourreau, Simon fell heavily on his left shoulder. The Renault riders, urged on by Cyrille Guimard, attacked. Peugeot's pursuit of their rivals lasted 40 km. Having been well protected by his team-mates, Simon maintained his substantial advantage, but his pain and his team's doubts increased. An x-ray confirmed a fracture of his shoulder blade.

Simon now had to cross the rollercoaster terrain of the Massif Central. The slightest hump caused him to grimace. Incredibly, over the next three days, Simon only let eight seconds of his lead slip away, but in the Puy-de-Dôme time trial he cracked. He finished five minutes behind Spaniards Arroyo and Delgado, who had done a night-time reconnaissance of the climb. Fignon was now only 52 seconds behind. It was almost all over for Simon. Heading towards Alpe d'Huez, he climbed off on the La Table climb. Fignon, fifth at Alpe d'Huez behind Dutch imp Peter Winnen, took his first yellow jersey. He consolidated his grip on it with victory in the time trial at Dijon and headed on towards the Champs-Élysées to celebrate a debut victory, just as Coppi, Koblet, Anquetil, Merckx and Hinault had done.

FINAL STANDINGS

1   Laurent Fignon (FRA) Renault-Elf-Gitane 105:07:52
2   Angel Arroyo (SPA) Reynolds +4:04
3   Peter Winnen (NED) Ti-Raleigh +4:09
4   Lucien Van Impe (BEL) Metaurobili-Pinarello +4:16
5   Robert Alban (FRA) La Redoute +7:53
6   Jean-René Bernaudeau (FRA) Wolber +8:59
7   Sean Kelly (IRL) Sem-Mavic +12:09
8   Marc Madiot (FRA) Renault-Elf-Gitane +14:55
9   Phil Anderson (AUS) Peugeot +16:56
10 Henk Lubberding (NED) Ti-Raleigh +18:55

AVERAGE SPEED (OF WINNER): 35.914 KM/H
TOTAL DISTANCE RACED: 3,862 KM

OPPOSITE Laurent Fignon celebrates victory on the Champs-Élysées at the end of his debut appearance in the Tour.

1984
LAURENT FIGNON
RENAULT-ELF

FIGNON CRUSHES THE RETURNING HINAULT

Even though he was wearing the French champion's jersey and fronting the Renault team, Laurent Fignon had a very difficult task ahead of him if he aimed to defend his Tour title. Bernard Hinault and Pascal Simon were ready to take him on having recovered from injury, the Colombian amateurs had beefed up their team, Ireland's Roche and Kelly were surely set to progress, as were the Spaniards Arroyo and Delgado. Could Fignon and Guimard's Renault team hold out against a Peugeot team seeking revenge and La Vie Claire – Bernard Tapie and Hinault's new team? What was certain was that there had never been so many riders at the start: 170 starting in 17 teams.

'The Badger' let everyone know he was back right at the very start when he took the first yellow jersey in Noisy-le-Sec, beating Fignon by a whisker in the prologue. However, it would turn out to be the only time he led the race. Renault set a fast pace right from the start. Victory on stage two for Marc Madiot was followed by an impressive team time trial win in Valenciennes. Vincent Barteau then took the yellow jersey on stage five as one of a break that finished 17 minutes clear. Guimard's team combined speed and tactical mastery.

At the time trial in Le Mans, Fignon handed a first lesson to Hinault. Pascal Jules continued Renault's charge in Nantes. In the Pyrenees, as Britain's Robert Millar took the day's honours at Guzet-Neige, Fignon edged closer to Barteau, knowing the

Alps would decide the race. Before that there were further Renault wins for Poisson in Blagnac and Menthéour in Rodez, and another time trial triumph for Fignon at La Ruchère.

Hinault's last hope lay in the Alps, but Fignon, 'The Professor', dismissed it. Heading for Alpe d'Huez, the Colombians came to life. Luis Herrera took an historic victory and Fignon was second across the line. The yellow jersey that had been kept warm for 12 days by his team-mate Barteau was now on Fignon's shoulders. The next day he rode everyone off his wheel to win at La Plagne, then completed a second summit victory at Crans-Montana two days later. Although Hinault was not on top form, he kept battling, but Fignon was in a state of grace. Leaving the Alps, the Parisian handed the Breton one more beating in the Beaujolais time trial, which stretched the gap between them to more than ten minutes.

By showing panache and attacking in the Alps, Hinault had enhanced Fignon's victory just as Merckx had done when he lost out to Thévenet in 1975. Although well beaten into second place, Hinault's popularity mushroomed – the Tour had a new rivalry. On his coat-tails were a number of other potential champions, including his American team-mate Greg LeMond, who had finished third, and Pascal Simon, who was seventh. The Colombians had also added some spice to the race, but no one could do anything to stop Renault. Strong in their heads and legs, they had triumphed.

FINAL STANDINGS

1 Laurent Fignon (FRA) Renault-Elf 112:03:40
2 Bernard Hinault (FRA) La Vie Claire +10:32
3 Greg LeMond (USA) Renault-Elf +11:46
4 Robert Millar (GBR) Peugeot +14:42
5 Sean Kelly (IRL) Skil-Sem +16:35
6 Angel Arroyo (SPA) Reynolds +19:22
7 Pascal Simon (FRA) Peugeot +21:17
8 Pedro Muñoz (SPA) Teka +26:17
9 Claude Criquielion (BEL) Splendor +29:12
10 Phil Anderson (AUS) Panasonic-Raleigh +29:16

AVERAGE SPEED (OF WINNER): 35.882 KM/H
TOTAL DISTANCE RACED: 4,021 KM

OPPOSITE TOP Laurent Fignon's second Tour confirms him and his Renault team as the race's undoubted champions. With his omnipresent bandana, Fignon flies through the mountains and glides along the flat in the time trials. It is Hinault, returning after a knee operation, who bears the brunt of his state of grace.

OPPOSITE BOTTOM The Renault team acknowledge fans after their success in the team time trial at Valenciennes. Next to Fignon in the red jersey of sprints leader is Greg LeMond, who would go on to finish third overall and best young rider on his Tour debut.

HINAULT JOINS ANQUETIL AND MERCKX

By now 31, Bernard Hinault had rebuilt his physical fitness and confidence under the influence of Paul Koechli, a very methodical Swiss *directeur sportif*, who had also recruited Laurent Fignon's former team-mate, Greg LeMond. Wearing their Mondrian-like jerseys, La Vie Claire had the allure of a 'dream team'. As well as riding talent, the team funded by French entrepreneur Bernard Tapie had also invested in disc wheels, Cinelli helmets and Look clipless pedals. Hinault's boys were transformed into high-speed guinea pigs, reviving the tradition of the Tour as a testing ground.

In the absence of the injured Fignon, it quickly became clear that the strongest of Hinault's rivals was his lieutenant LeMond. After Hinault had won his fifth prologue and La Vie Claire took the team time trial, the two team-mates moved into first and second overall following the individual time trial in Strasbourg, where Hinault cantered to victory. He confirmed his return to peak form in the Alps, finishing second behind Luis Herrera at Avoriaz, then second again to Eric Vanderaerden in the time trial at Villard-de-Lans. That pushed his lead to more than five minutes.

Ahead lay Saint-Étienne, the former capital of the sport. As if to avenge so many technical advances that had left her redundant, the old city cast a spell on Hinault. Angered by LeMond infiltrating a break, Hinault, sprinting for all he was worth, tangled with another rider in the final straight and fell.

He lost two minutes to the American and finished with his face bloodied and nose broken. In the Pyrenees, LeMond turned the tables. 'The Badger', who was having trouble breathing, suffered and began to see his lead evaporating.

If Tapie hadn't stepped in to negotiate between his two champions, promising LeMond that Hinault would assist him in 1986 if the American didn't put the Frenchman's fifth title in jeopardy, who knows what might have happened. LeMond might have been tempted to try his luck. As it was, the younger man contented himself with victory in the final time trial at Lac de Vassivière, where he reduced Hinault's advantage to less than two minutes.

However, equalling the record of five Tour victories was as important to La Vie Claire as it was to Hinault, so reason prevailed, a bit like it had done in 1925 when Ottavio Bottecchia had won a Tour that seemed destined for Lucien Buysse. That is how racing goes sometimes. LeMond consoled himself with the combined jersey. However, the question remains: would Hinault have been able to respond to an all-out attack from the pretender to his crown? It is hard to say, although backing a wounded champion into a corner could have had fearsome results. What is certain is that the Breton joined Anquetil and Merckx as a five-time champion. The question LeMond would have liked a firm answer to was whether Hinault would stick to their agreement in 1986.

FINAL STANDINGS

1 Bernard Hinault (FRA) La Vie Claire 113:24:23
2 Greg LeMond (USA) La Vie Claire +1:42
3 Stephen Roche (IRL) La Redoute +4:29
4 Sean Kelly (IRL) Skil-Sem +6:26
5 Phil Anderson (AUS) Panasonic +7:44
6 Pedro Delgado (SPA) Orbea +11:53
7 Luis Herrera (COL) Café de Colombia +12:53
8 Fabio Parra (COL) Café de Colombia +13:35
9 Eduardo Chozas (SPA) Reynolds +13:56
10 Steve Bauer (CAN) La Vie Claire +14:57

AVERAGE SPEED (OF WINNER): 36.391 KM/H
TOTAL DISTANCE RACED: 4,127 KM

Thanks to opponents such as Herrera, Pollentier, Agostinho, Zoetemelk and Fignon, Hinault produced some of the most legendary performances in the history of the Tour. He spent 78 days in yellow, won 28 stages, abandoned the race once when in the yellow jersey, and on his seven other appearances finished first five times and second twice. In each of his eight Tours, he wore the yellow jersey for at least a day and won at least one stage.

OPPOSITE Although the relationship between LeMond, wearing what were then state-of-the-art glasses, and Hinault appears to be good, based on the relaxed nature of this picture, the pair were well aware that they were each other's greatest rival.

TOP Hinault leads the riders challenging for his yellow jersey over the top of a climb in the Alps.

BOTTOM LeMond, Hinault and green jersey winner Sean Kelly take a breather before the final presentation ceremony gets under way in Paris.

LeMOND TRIUMPHANT DESPITE UNEASY ALLIANCE

In 1984 there were plans for a Hollywood movie based around the Tour. *The Yellow Jersey* was set to feature Dustin Hoffman, who followed several stages of that year's race for research purposes. Although the film never got off the ground, the Americans may have missed an opportunity as that year one of their compatriots, a Californian, made his Tour debut in Laurent Fignon's team.

Gregory James LeMond was 23 years old and already wearing the world champion's rainbow jersey. So, he was no bit part player. Indeed, Fignon's understudy was so good that he finished his first Tour in third place behind Fignon and Bernard Hinault. This daring young cyclist was now set to star in a sporting drama worthy of a Hollywood blockbuster. It could have been written by one of cinema's great scriptwriters, but was sketched out by the Tour, the French landscape and, initially at least, by two champions with strong but very different characters.

Following the intervention of La Vie Claire boss Bernard Tapie, LeMond had reined in his own legitimate pretensions to the 1985 Tour in exchange for a promise that the favour would be returned in 1986. However, it quickly became apparent when the race got under way that Hinault was going to find it difficult to accept finishing second when there was a chance of a record-breaking sixth Tour win. When the race entered the Pyrenees Hinault's attacking nature got the upper hand. He went clear with Pedro Delgado heading for Pau,

where LeMond and the rest of the field found themselves five minutes behind the defending champion. Intoxicated by the yellow jersey, the Breton attacked again the next day, à la Merckx. Majestic on the descent of the Tourmalet, he skipped over the Aspin, but imploded on the climb towards Superbagnères, where his American team-mate swept by on his way to victory. LeMond's deficit was now just 40 seconds.

The Alps would prove decisive. At Serre-Chevalier on the Col de Granon, LeMond finally claimed the yellow jersey. However, Hinault wasn't finished yet. The next day he attacked so hard on the descent of the Croix de Fer that it seemed his brake cables had been caught. His aim was to finish off La Vie Claire's only remaining danger, the Swiss Urs Zimmermann. Having succeeded in that objective, Hinault and LeMond climbed up through tens of thousands of fans packed onto Alpe d'Huez and crossed the line hand in hand. The stage went to the Breton, the Tour to the American.

Despite some predictions of disaster, Tapie had managed to stick the different pieces of his team back together. The Breton stuck to his new role of first lieutenant and, therefore, kept his promise. However, the joy that the first American winner of the Tour felt was tarnished by the fact that he had 'apparently won thanks to Hinault'. Such was his disappointment that he allegedly said to his team-mate Vincent Barteau, 'Is that what winning the Tour is all about?'

FINAL STANDINGS

1 Greg LeMond (USA) La Vie Claire 110:35:19
2 Bernard Hinault (FRA) La Vie Claire +3:10
3 Urs Zimmermann (SWI) Carrera +10:54
4 Andrew Hampsten (USA) La Vie Claire +18:44
5 Claude Criquielion (BEL) Hitachi +24:36
6 Ronan Pensec (FRA) Peugeot +25:59
7 Niki Rüttimann (SWI) La Vie Claire +30:52
8 Alvaro Pino (SPA) Zor-BH +33:00
9 Steven Rooks (NED) PDM +33:22
10 Yvon Madiot (FRA) Système U +33:27

AVERAGE SPEED (OF WINNER): 36.92 KM/H
TOTAL DISTANCE RACED: 4,083 KM

OPPOSITE TOP Hinault dreamed of a sixth Tour win, but he had a promise to keep. The Frenchman would show plenty of panache but would eventually stick to his word as an American took the title for the first time.

OPPOSITE BOTTOM The Tour began in 1903, the same year of the first Hollywood Western, but it had to wait 83 years for a cowboy to lasso it. La Vie Claire team-mates Hinault and LeMond head for the finish at Alpe d'Huez. Having been helped by LeMond to win his fifth Tour in 1985, Hinault returns the favour, or at least he does in the Alps. In the Pyrenees he had put on a show of his own.

ROCHE COMPLETES A GLORIOUS DOUBLE

Ireland's Stephen Roche was 48th in 1986, which was the worst Tour finish of his career. His employer, Carrera Jeans, put this bad performance down to the difficulties associated with joining a new team. But Roche had also struggled with a bad knee injury. In 1987, with his knee pain-free and the Giro d'Italia title recently claimed, Carrera had high hopes for their leader, particularly as Bernard Hinault, now retired, and Greg LeMond, recovering from a shooting accident, were absent. But all knew that the Giro–Tour double is seldom achieved.

In addition, Roche had plenty of rivals to consider in a very open race. Laurent Fignon, Pedro Delgado, Jean-François Bernard, Sean Kelly and Luis Herrera were among those who felt they were in with a good chance as well. Initially, though, everyone was more concerned with the Tour's most distant start point in the shadow of the infamous Berlin Wall. Hosting the Tour was part of the celebrations for the city's 750th anniversary.

After Jelle Nijdam took the prologue and Lech Piasecki became the first Pole to wear yellow, Carrera made clear they were fully united behind Roche by winning the team time trial. The lead continued to change hands regularly up to the long time trial at Futuroscope, where Roche won the day and Fignon's team-mate Charly Mottet the yellow jersey. The Pyrenees saw Bernard, Hinault's heir apparent, climb into contention. Mottet remained in command, although

his grip was wavering. Bernard finally loosened it when he climbed Mont Ventoux like a jet plane, beating all records and scattering his rivals. Wearing yellow for the first time, Bernard had a lead of more than two minutes on Roche and Mottet.

Luck counts for a lot on the Tour, and even more so when you're crossing the Vercors massif, which is conducive to ambushes. In the confusion of a feed zone, the yellow jersey punctured, and his rivals accelerated away. At the finish in Villard-de-Lans, where Delgado triumphed ahead of Roche, Bernard conceded more than four minutes. The race had turned on its head. Roche now led Delgado by 40 seconds, but next on the agenda was Alpe d'Huez.

The Spaniard, always very comfortable in the Alps, pinched the jersey and looked likely to wrap up the Tour when he dropped the Irishman on the climb to La Plagne the next day. His hopes apparently gone, Roche responded with an effort which resulted in him collapsing just beyond the line. Instead of leaving the Alps minutes behind, the Irishman was a mere 21 seconds down on Delgado heading into the Dijon time trial, where Roche was very much in his element. Bernard won it, but Roche in second finished a minute up on the Spaniard and went into Paris with a 40-second lead and the yellow jersey on his back. With Giro pink and Tour yellow already in the bag, he went on to take the rainbow jersey to complete 'the triple crown', a feat only otherwise achieved by Eddy Merckx.

FINAL STANDINGS

1 Stephen Roche (IRL) Carrera 115:27:42
2 Pedro Delgado (SPA) PDM +0:40
3 Jean-François Bernard (FRA) Toshiba-Look-La Vie Claire +2:13
4 Charly Mottet (FRA) Système U +6:40
5 Luis Herrera (COL) Café de Colombia +9:32
6 Fabio Parra (COL) Café de Colombia +16:53
7 Laurent Fignon (FRA) Système U +18:24
8 Anselmo Fuerte (SPA) BH +18:33
9 Raúl Alcalá (MEX) 7-Eleven +21:49
10 Marino Lejarreta (SPA) Caja Rural-Orbea +26:13

AVERAGE SPEED (OF WINNER): 34.981 KM/H
TOTAL DISTANCE RACED: 4,039 KM

It is Roche's year. After capturing
the Giro title, he proves irresistible
in the Tour de France, where hellish
roads and opponents like Jean-
François Bernard fail to derail him.
Later, he adds the final cherry on the
cake by winning the rainbow jersey.

The Tour peloton heads towards the Victory Column during the opening day in West Berlin.

The wall of shame

TO CELEBRATE THE 750th anniversary of the founding of Berlin, the 74th edition of the Tour set out from what had been the German capital. The Tour had never started so far away. Not surprisingly, with hundreds of members of the media on a race that is all about bringing peoples and countries together, fingers were pointed at the Berlin Wall, which was doing exactly the opposite.

The riders passed in front of its grey slabs, which had been covered with graffiti and stained with blood, in order to underline the absurdity of it. This

rather daring setting for a Grand Départ had been the idea of Bernard Creff, director of Ibis Hotels in Germany. Tour directors Félix Lévitan and Jean-François Naquet-Radiguet were really taken with it and handed over the project to Xavier Louy, who had the strongest political background among the Tour's hierarchy and was the only one who spoke German. He oversaw the project, which required a passage through East Germany and the support of the authorities on both sides of the Iron Curtain. It was a real success –

and not only on a symbolic level, as some believe that the Tour's weight had played a part in the wall tumbling down for good in 1989.

ABOVE Fagor's François Lemarchand (left), Robert Forest (centre) and Eric Caritoux (right) pose in front of the Berlin Wall before the start of the race.

241

DELGADO WINS ON AND OFF THE ROAD

Having narrowly missed out in 1987 in the colours of Dutch team PDM, Pedro Delgado returned to Spain as leader of the Reynolds team, where he could count on the support of Angel Arroyo and the fast-emerging Miguel Indurain. The race started in Henri Petit-Breton's home town of Pornichet-La Baule, but didn't get going until Alpe d'Huez. Early on, Canadian Steve Bauer and Dutchman Jelle Nijdam both wore the yellow jersey, as the favourites awaited the Alps.

At Alpe d'Huez, Steven Rooks and Gert-Jan Theunisse extended the Dutch love affair with this famous climb, but just behind them and just in front of the Colombians Parra and Herrera, Delgado slipped in to reclaim the yellow jersey he had held in the Alps a year earlier. The stage was not such a happy one for two-time champion Laurent Fignon and eight others who abandoned. The following day's time trial finished in Villard-de-Lans, where Delgado had taken a famous stage win in 1987 just ahead of Stephen Roche, who was absent with injury this time. He repeated that success and approached the Pyrenees with a lead of almost three minutes over Rooks.

Without a Tour win since 1973, Spanish fans poured over the border to urge on 'Perico'. He edged further away from Rooks at Guzet-Neige, where Robert Millar was sent the wrong way at the finish and missed the stage win. Delgado gained a few more seconds at Luz-Ardiden. Thanks to another impressive climbing performance on the Puy-de-Dôme

(19th stage), he moved even closer to emulating Federico Bahamontes and Luis Ocaña, Spain's previous champions.

However, shocking news emerged that put Delgado's hopes in doubt. It leaked out that the yellow jersey had tested positive for probenecid, a product that masked anabolic steroids. The race continued amid confusion. The leader and his team would say nothing. In Spain, there was consternation. Deliverance arrived the evening before the final time trial in the form of a communiqué from the UCI. Although the incriminating product appeared on the International Olympic Committee's list of banned substances, it was not yet on the UCI's. Delgado could continue.

In spite of the pressure and scrutiny he had been under, Delgado managed to remain focused on the race. Fourth place in the final time trial at Santenay moved him seven minutes clear of Rooks and he duly became the first Spaniard to ride onto the Champs-Élysées in the yellow jersey. At a post-race reception, as dancers performed in Delgado's honour, a light-fingered admirer pinched his yellow jersey. But what did it matter to him? The UCI had confirmed he hadn't stolen the yellow jersey and back home in Segovia he was hailed as a hero.

He went on to join the likes of Gino Bartali and Felice Gimondi as one of the few riders to have finished 18 grand tours in the top ten. He contributed to the renaissance in Spanish cycling and future Tour success for his compatriots.

FINAL STANDINGS

1 Pedro Delgado (SPA) Reynolds 84:27:53
2 Steven Rooks (NED) PDM +7:13
3 Fabio Parra (COL) Kelme +9:58
4 Steve Bauer (CAN) Weinmann-La Suisse +12:15
5 Eric Boyer (FRA) Système U +14:04
6 Luis Herrera (COL) Café de Colombia +14:36
7 Ronan Pensec (FRA) Z-Peugeot +16:52
8 Alvaro Pino (SPA) BH +18:36
9 Peter Winnen (NED) Panasonic +19:12
10 Denis Roux (FRA) Z-Peugeot +20:08

AVERAGE SPEED (OF WINNER): 38.856 KM/H
TOTAL DISTANCE RACED: 3,282 KM

ABOVE Delgado (also pictured left) leads the race onto the Champs-Élysées just days after he seemed he might be denied the title after a positive drugs test.

LeMOND'S FAIRYTALE FINALE

When Greg LeMond finally returned to the sport following a shooting accident while out hunting in 1987, few had any confidence in him reaching his previous level. He had, many said, achieved a miracle by making it back to the Tour at all, as leader of the small-budget Belgian ADR team. Although Bernard Hinault was no longer around, LeMond didn't figure among the favourites, who were Fignon, Delgado and Roche. However, during the latter part of those two years of enforced absence, LeMond had trained outstandingly hard, as was immediately evident in the Luxembourg prologue. His performance was overshadowed, though, by Delgado, who missed his start time by more than two minutes.

Although Fignon's Super U team steamed to victory the next afternoon, LeMond drove ADR to finish fifth. He underlined his strength by winning the long time trial in Rennes using triathlon handlebars that improved his aerodynamic efficiency. LeMond now led, initiating a duel that revived memories of the Anquetil–Poulidor battles of yesteryear. Winning time trials was one thing, but could the American stay with the pace in the mountains? Crossing three passes and then climbing to Cauterets, he finished on Fignon's wheel. The next day at Superbagnères he lost 12 seconds to Fignon, who took the yellow jersey.

The pair matched each other as the Tour crossed southern France, making for the Alps, where the first test was a time trial up to Orcières-Merlette. LeMond only finished fifth, but gained 47 seconds on Fignon to lead the race once again. In Briançon, the American consolidated his lead, which was now 53 seconds over the Frenchman. LeMond seemed to have momentum with him, but lost it at Alpe d'Huez the next day. Fignon dropped him and took the yellow jersey with a lead of 26 seconds.

Now the Frenchman was in charge. At Villard-de-Lans he won again, pushing his advantage up to 50 seconds, although it could have been more. LeMond responded by winning the next day in Aix-les-Bains, but gained no time as the yellow jersey was right on his wheel. Indeed, the margin between the pair remained unchanged until the final-day time trial between Versailles and Paris.

The advantage was with Fignon. The time trial was 24.5 km – so not too lengthy, the Frenchman held the yellow jersey and would therefore set off last, and he was also using tri-bars. However, he wasn't as used to them as his rival, he already had a Giro win in his legs and he was suffering badly with saddle sores. LeMond, meanwhile, was fresher and, thanks to his bars, could push a monumental gear of 54 x 12. Fignon rode out of his skin but it wasn't quite enough. LeMond had won by a mere eight seconds, which represented 82 m of the Champs-Élysées – the smallest winning margin ever. LeMond, who had set the fastest average ever for a time trial of 54.545 km/h, collapsed on the road in disbelief.

FINAL STANDINGS

1 Greg LeMond (USA) ADR-Agrigel-Bottecchia 87:38:35
2 Laurent Fignon (FRA) Super U +0:08
3 Pedro Delgado (SPA) Reynolds-Banesto +3:34
4 Gert-Jan Theunisse (NED) PDM +7:30
5 Marino Lejarreta (SPA) Paternina +9:39
6 Charly Mottet (FRA) RMO-Mavic +10:06
7 Steven Rooks (NED) PDM +11:10
8 Raúl Alcalá (MEX) PDM +14:21
9 Sean Kelly (IRL) PDM +18:25
10 Robert Millar (GBR) Z +18:46

AVERAGE SPEED (OF WINNER): 37.481 KM/H
TOTAL DISTANCE RACED: 3,285 KM

OPPOSITE LeMond wasn't expected to figure on his return to the Tour with the unrated ADR team. However, the American used new technology well, notably triathlon handlebars, which helped him win two time trials.

ABOVE The Tour has rarely seen such a duel for the yellow jersey, which passed back and forth between Frenchman Laurent Fignon (in yellow) and American Greg LeMond (left). LeMond took it in the Rennes time trial, Fignon pinched it at Superbagnères. The American got it back at Orcières-Merlette, only to lose it to Fignon again on Alpe d'Huez, before pinching it back at the very last gasp in Paris.

OPPOSITE It was the greatest drama in the history of the Tour, even more thrilling than the commotion on the last day of the 1947 Tour when Jean Robic took the title or of the 1968 race seized by Jan Janssen at the last moment. Someone is just telling LeMond that he has won the Tour as well as the final time trial (top), while the disconsolate Fignon has clearly heard the news (bottom).

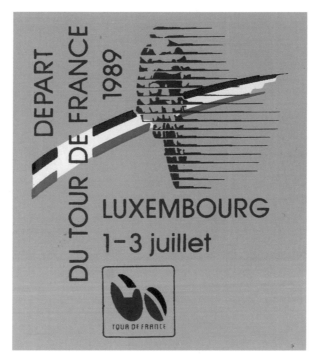

DEPART DU TOUR DE FRANCE 1989

LUXEMBOURG
1-3 juillet

TOUR DE FRANCE

TOUR DE FRANCE 89
AVEC R.M.O

R.M.O

LeMOND FOILS EARLY UPSTARTS

After winning the Tour with a divided team in 1986, then practically all alone in 1989, Greg LeMond was in demand going into the 1990 season and plumped for a team that would be able to do his bidding both on the road and off it. The French Z team was a solid unit, featuring seasoned performers such as Robert Millar, Gilbert Duclos-Lassalle and Eric Boyer. Once again, Laurent Fignon looked the biggest danger, but he lasted only five days before quitting with his morale shattered. However, this didn't make a third victory for LeMond a formality.

The race started in straightforward enough fashion. Fignon's Castorama team-mate Thierry Marie won the prologue at the Futuroscope theme park, with LeMond second. But the script changed on the first road stage, when four riders went clear early on. They looked inoffensive enough, as they made a long-range bid for glory and built up a lead of more than ten minutes. Of the quartet, the least threatening was Dutchman Frans Maassen, who was happy to take the stage win. However, the other three – LeMond's team-mate Ronan Pensec, Claudio Chiappucci and Steve Bauer – had good reason to be more ambitious when the bunch rolled in more than ten minutes behind them.

Bauer took the yellow jersey and kept it for more than a week. The stage seven time trial at Épinal didn't change much. The first big stage in the Alps saw the jersey move from Bauer's shoulders to Pensec's. The Frenchman performed heroically to keep it on Alpe d'Huez, where LeMond finished right on stage-winner Gianni Bugno's wheel and moved into third place, leading the pack now chasing Pensec and Chiappucci.

Pensec lost the lead to the Italian in the time trial at Villard-de-Lans the next day, when LeMond was only fifth. The American now trailed Chiappucci by more than seven minutes. The Italian had shown, though, that he was a strong climber. Could LeMond, or indeed anyone else, overhaul him in the Pyrenees? Perhaps, but it would not be easy. Realizing they needed to act quickly and put the Italian under pressure, LeMond and several other contenders for the title combined their resources on the road to Saint-Étienne following the rest day. Chiappucci lost almost five minutes of his lead.

The race swung away from the Italian on the tough climb up to Luz-Ardiden. LeMond did all the hard work, only to see Miguel Indurain jump past him to win it. Crucially, though, he cut Chiappucci's lead to just five seconds with a long time trial still to come. After Dmitri Konyshev had become the first Russian to win a Tour stage, LeMond finally caught his quarry at Lac de Vassivière, where he gained more than two minutes on the Italian, who had come close to an unbelievable upset. Although he had failed to win a stage, LeMond, resplendent in the world champion's rainbow jersey, had joined Louison Bobet and Philippe Thys as a three-time Tour winner.

FINAL STANDINGS

1 Greg LeMond (USA) Z 90:43:20
2 Claudio Chiappucci (ITA) Carrera +2:16
3 Erik Breukink (NED) PDM +2:29
4 Pedro Delgado (SPA) Banesto +5:01
5 Marino Lejarreta (SPA) ONCE +5:05
6 Eduardo Chozas (SPA) ONCE +9:14
7 Gianni Bugno (ITA) Château d'Ax +9:39
8 Raúl Alcalá (MEX) PDM +11:14
9 Claude Criquielion (BEL) Lotto +12:04
10 Miguel Indurain (SPA) Banesto +12:47

AVERAGE SPEED (OF WINNER): 37.521 KM/H
TOTAL DISTANCE RACED: 3,404 KM

OPPOSITE TOP Flanked by German points champion Olaf Ludwig (left) and French King of the Mountains Thierry Claveyrolat, Greg LeMond receives the acclaim of the crowd on the Champs-Élysées after securing his third Tour title.

OPPOSITE BOTTOM Tracking Dutch rider Erik Breukink on the upper slopes of Alpe d'Huez, world champion Greg LeMond begins to make inroads into the advantage of Pensec and Chiappucci. On the American's wheel are eventual stage-winner Gianni Bugno and King of the Mountains Thierry Claveyrolat.

INDURAIN: THE SPHINX OF PAMPLONA

The 1990 Tour indicated the impending arrival of a new generation of Tour contenders, led by Claudio Chiappucci, Gianni Bugno and Miguel Indurain. However, as the 78th Tour got under way in Lyon it seemed that Greg LeMond was still very much in command. As was the case the previous year, the American finished close behind prologue winner Thierry Marie. Unlike 1990, though, LeMond was part of the small break that finished clear of the bunch on the first road stage, providing him with a handy buffer on most of his rivals.

That coup put the American in the yellow jersey briefly. The team time trial, won by Ariostea, promoted Rolf Sorensen into the lead. Unfortunately for the Dane, a crash on stage five into Valenciennes left him with a broken collar-bone and with no option but to quit. What was already shaping up as an unpredictable Tour became even more so when Marie regained the yellow jersey the next day in Le Havre at the end of a 234-km solo break, the second longest in the race's history.

Normality appeared to have returned when LeMond finished eight seconds behind Indurain in the 73-km time trial to Alençon, which put the defending champion back in yellow, more than a minute clear of Erik Breukink and more than two ahead of the Spaniard. Apparently comfortable as the race headed into the Pyrenees, LeMond had little reason to be concerned when France's Luc Leblanc took the lead as the race crossed over into Spain to Jaca. However, that turned out to be the final time the American led the Tour.

Returning to France for a mighty stage featuring five climbs, LeMond slipped off the back of the lead group just before the top of the Tourmalet. Descending like a stone, he caught the group on the other side of the pass, only to find that Indurain and Chiappucci had already attacked. The pair pressed on hard over the Aspin and then up the final climb to Val Louron, where Indurain was happy to let Chiappucci take the stage while he donned the yellow jersey for the first time. With a three-minute lead on Charly Mottet and LeMond five minutes back in fifth, the lofty Spaniard looked close to invincible, and even more so when he finished second on Alpe d'Huez, just behind Bugno. Victory in the final time trial at Mâcon emphasized Indurain's supremacy.

The topsy-turvy nature of the race was underlined coming into the finish on the Champs-Élysées when green jersey leader Djamolidin Abdoujaparov clipped the foot of a barrier and somersaulted along the final straight. It was that kind of Tour – a race where the unexpected became almost routine.

FINAL STANDINGS

1 Miguel Indurain (SPA) Banesto 101:01:20
2 Gianni Bugno (ITA) Gatorade-Château d'Ax +3:36
3 Claudio Chiappucci (ITA) Carrera +5:56
4 Charly Mottet (FRA) RMO +7:37
5 Luc Leblanc (FRA) Castorama +10:10
6 Laurent Fignon (FRA) Castorama +11:27
7 Greg LeMond (USA) Z +13:13
8 Andy Hampsten (USA) Motorola +13:40
9 Pedro Delgado (SPA) Banesto +20:10
10 Gérard Rué (FRA) Helvetia +20:13

AVERAGE SPEED (OF WINNER): 38.743 KM/H
TOTAL DISTANCE RACED: 3,914 KM

Having broken clear of race leader
Greg LeMond just before crossing
the summit of the Tourmalet, Miguel
Indurain and Claudio Chiappucci head
for the finish at Val Louron, where the
Spaniard will take the yellow jersey
and the Italian the stage victory.

INDURAIN IS 'EXTRATERRESTRIAL'

To celebrate the signing of the Maastricht Treaty that created the European Union, the 79th Tour passed through seven countries. Although LeMond returned to attempt to win a fourth title, it was perhaps fitting that the big favourites for the crown were all European, headed by defending champion Miguel Indurain. Having won the Giro d'Italia just a month before, the Spaniard started quickly, winning the prologue time trial on home ground at San Sebastián, although the yellow jersey passed to two fast-emerging names over the next two days: Alex Zülle and Richard Virenque. The race had its fourth leader in as many days when Virenque's RMO team-mate Pascal Lino took it in Bordeaux.

As the race headed towards the first major time trial, it was apparent that Claudio Chiappucci and his Carrera team were determined to take any opportunity to attack Indurain. The Italian sneaked into a break also featuring LeMond that gained time in Brussels. Stephen Roche did the same at Valkenburg, but Indurain responded with a magnificent performance against the clock in Luxembourg. Bugno, LeMond and Roche lost four minutes, Chiappucci five and a half. Indurain had imposed himself, although Lino still clung to the lead.

Carrera's sniping attacks continued, however. Roche pulled two minutes back at Saint-Gervais before the rest day. The day after it, Chiappucci put on a show that stretched the bounds of credibility. The Italian got into the break early on and, with more than 200 km to the finish, seemed to be focused on picking up points for the King of the Mountains jersey. However, once he shed his breakaway companions with 125 km still remaining to the line, it became clear that his goal was nothing less than Indurain's yellow jersey. On the final climb up to Sestrières, Chiappucci rode through a seething mass of crazed Italian fans. Further down the climb, Indurain responded with everything he had. Indeed, his effort was so huge that he ran out of gas before the finish and lost some of the ground he had gained. Chiappucci won the day, but Indurain kept the lead. The rest were out of it.

The Spaniard refused to allow Chiappucci any leeway after that. The plucky Italian tried his luck at Alpe d'Huez (where Andy Hampsten took a famous win for Motorola), and at La Bourboule summit finish, but the yellow jersey shadowed him. Indurain ended the final time trial nearly on Chiappucci's wheel again having started three minutes behind him. Indurain rode into Paris victorious, his final advantage almost five minutes on Chiappucci, while 1991 runner-up Gianni Bugno was more than ten minutes adrift in third.

Branded 'extraterrestrial' by *L'Équipe* following his astonishing time trial performance in Luxembourg, Indurain did appear to be on another planet compared to his rivals. Could they get any closer in 1993?

FINAL STANDINGS

1 Miguel Indurain (SPA) Banesto 100:49:30
2 Claudio Chiappucci (ITA) Carrera +4:35
3 Gianni Bugno (ITA) Gatorade +10:49
4 Andy Hampsten (USA) Motorola +13:40
5 Pascal Lino (FRA) RMO +14:37
6 Pedro Delgado (SPA) Banesto +15:16
7 Erik Breukink (NED) PDM +18:51
8 Giancarlo Perini (ITA) Carrera +19:16
9 Stephen Roche (IRL) Carrera +20:23
10 Jens Heppner (GER) Telekom +25:30

AVERAGE SPEED (OF WINNER): 39.504 KM/H
TOTAL DISTANCE RACED: 3,983 KM

OPPOSITE In time trials, his discipline of choice, Miguel Indurain would unleash himself and build the essential foundations for his victories. On those days he was free of all restraints and his exploits speak for him. With his aero helmet, tri-bars and low-profile frame, Miguel would push everything he had through his machine, creating big gaps on his rivals and even passing them. On three occasions, he averaged more than 50 km/h over distances above 60 km and even reached the mark of 52 km at Blois in 1992.

INDURAIN COMPLETES HIS HAT-TRICK

Having taken the Giro–Tour double the previous year, Miguel Indurain returned to the 1993 race with the goal of becoming the first rider in history to complete that double in consecutive seasons. Most of his potential rivals were familiar, but he faced a new threat in the shape of Vuelta a España champion Tony Rominger, leader of a rival Spanish team, Clas. The Swiss had not ridden the Tour since 1990, but on the back of consecutive Vuelta successes appeared to have the weapons to challenge Indurain on every terrain.

The Spaniard started fast, winning the prologue at Le Puy-du- Fou, although the sprinters dominated proceedings for the rest of the first week. The availability of time bonuses suited the likes of Wilfried Nelissen and Mario Cipollini. Each won a stage and had two spells in the yellow jersey. Their game of jersey ping-pong ended in Châlons-sur-Marne, where Johan Museeuw took the lead and kept it the following day when the race's youngest participant, American Lance Armstrong, won in Verdun.

Next up was a 59-km time trial at Lac de Madine. Everyone expected Indurain to cruise to victory and, while his winning margin wasn't quite as large as it had been in the equivalent test in Luxembourg 12 months earlier, it was still impressive. He jumped from way back in the pack into the yellow jersey, with Dutchman Erik Breukink his nearest challenger at 1-35. Rominger, well down the standings due to a poor performance by Clas in the team time trial, came fifth having gone off early in the worst of the wet conditions. Given a later start, the Swiss would certainly have been closer to Indurain's time.

That assessment is supported by his performance on the first two stages in the high mountains, which followed the rest day. Victorious at both Serre-Chevalier and Isola 2000, Rominger jumped up to fourth and took a firm grip on the mountains jersey. On each occasion, though, Indurain was right with him. Crushing his rivals wasn't his thing. He made a habit of using his intelligence at summit finishes, allowing his rivals their moment of glory, knowing that he could call in favours at some future point if required. *L'Équipe*'s Philippe Brunel described his style very nicely as 'laidback panache'. The place where he showed that he was the boss, where he really let rip, was in the time trials, in 'the race of truth', the test that pits the rider against himself, the road, time and even history.

Indurain stuck to his philosophy in the Pyrenees, watching Rominger and surprise package Zenon Jaskula very closely and waiting for that final time trial to come. However, when it arrived, Rominger upset every prediction by winning it. Indurain was already so far ahead it made little difference to the final result, but it suggested that the Swiss had the potential to beat the now three-time champion. Indurain's aura of invincibility had taken a significant knock.

FINAL STANDINGS

1 Miguel Indurain (SPA) Banesto 95:57:09
2 Tony Rominger (SWI) Clas-Cajastur +4:59
3 Zenon Jaskula (POL) GB:MG +5:48
4 Alvaro Mejía (COL) Motorola +7:29
5 Bjarne Riis (DEN) Ariostea +16:26
6 Claudio Chiappucci (ITA) Carrera +17:18
7 Johan Bruyneel (BEL) ONCE +18:04
8 Andy Hampsten (USA) Motorola +20:14
9 Pedro Delgado (SPA) Banesto +23:57
10 Vladimir Poulnikov (RUS) Carrera +25:29

AVERAGE SPEED (OF WINNER): 38.706 KM/H
TOTAL DISTANCE RACED: 3,714 KM

OPPOSITE Having won the Giro for the second year in succession, Indurain looks unruffled as he climbs towards a third consecutive Tour victory. Leading the way in yellow, he has Alvaro Mejía on his left shoulder, Tony Rominger to his right and Pole Zenon Jaskula trailing behind.

ABOVE In the mountains his power would enable Miguel to be on equal terms with the best climbers: Tony Rominger (pictured with the Spaniard), Marco Pantani and Richard Virenque. His objective was the yellow jersey, not the polka-dot version.

RIGHT The moment when Greg LeMond's Tour crown starts to slip in 1991 as he drops off the back of the lead group together with yellow jersey Luc Leblanc.

OPPOSITE For the Tour's 90th anniversary, the caricaturist Pierre Charles, alias Pic, decorates a genealogical tree with images of all the winners in the shape of France.

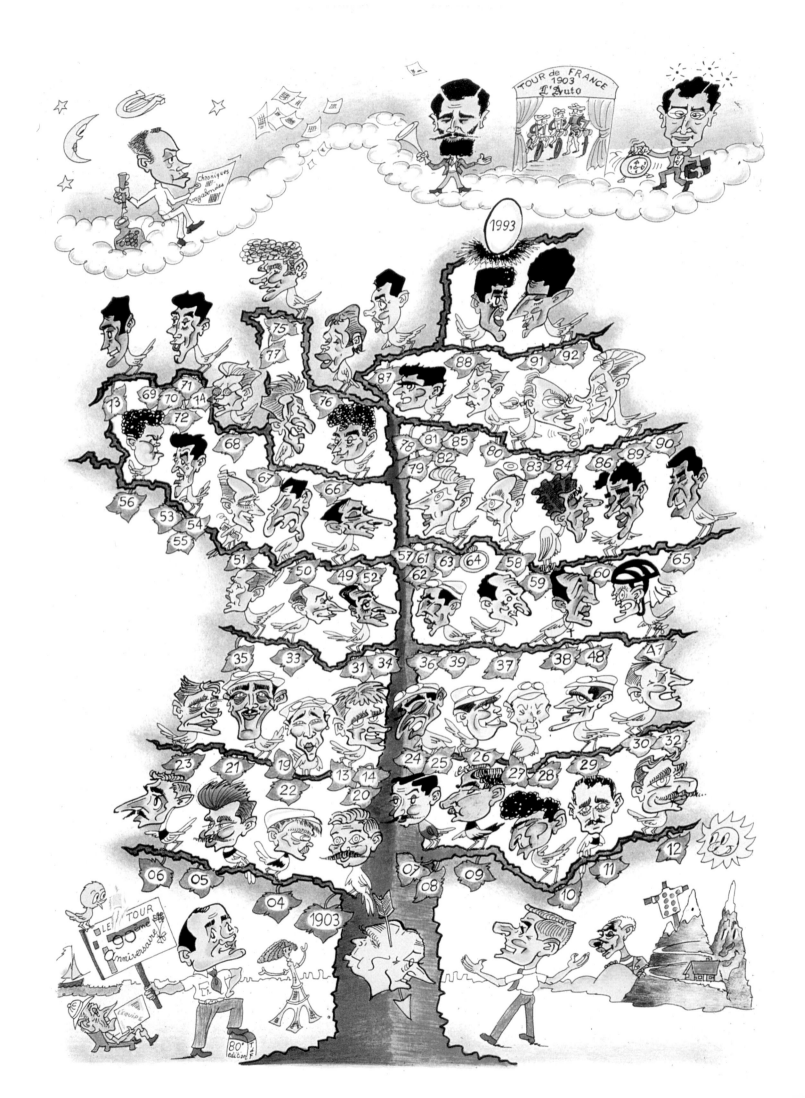

INDURAIN AT HIS IMPERIOUS BEST

The slight indications of fallibility that had been apparent as Miguel Indurain secured his third title had become more obvious in the approach to the 81st Tour. Yet again, the Spaniard had opted to prepare for July by riding the Giro in May. However, he had come up short, losing out to Russia's Evgeni Berzin, while no one had been able to follow new Italian climbing sensation Marco Pantani in the mountains. With Tony Rominger looking more threatening than ever after completing a hat-trick of Vuelta a España victories, Indurain was by no means as strong a favourite as he had been the two previous years.

As usual, the Spaniard imposed himself on his rivals in the Lille prologue, but even 'Big Mig' looked sluggish compared to Tour debutant Chris Boardman. The Briton zipped around the course 15 seconds faster than Indurain. The first road stage ended with another shocking event, this time unwanted. As the bunch hurtled into Armentières, Laurent Jalabert careered into a policeman who had stepped out from the barriers to take a picture. Several other riders went down too, with Wilfried Nelissen the most badly injured. Like Jalabert, the Belgian was unable to continue.

Boardman's hold on the lead ended in the team time trial, but he was back at the centre of attention when the Tour slipped under the Channel for two stages in southern England. Immense crowds lined the roads between Dover and Brighton and on into Portsmouth. When the Tour returned to France, another Briton seized the yellow jersey, this time veteran Sean Yates, who kept it for a day.

The phoney war of the first week ended with the Bergerac time trial. Indurain powered through its 64 km two minutes faster than Rominger and more than five quicker than his other key rivals. Two days on, Indurain stomped away on the first big mountain stage, disappearing into the mist that had settled on Hautacam above Lourdes. Luc Leblanc somehow managed to stick with him and nipped by to win the stage. But what did Indurain care? Rominger was now five minutes back, the other favourites more than eight. Following another heavy defeat at Luz-Ardiden, the ailing Swiss quit the race.

Indurain had beaten three different riders into second place previously, and the only question now was who would end up as best of the rest in Paris. Festina's Richard Virenque looked most likely when he won at Luz-Ardiden, but neither he, nor even Indurain, could match Latvia's Piotr Ugrumov in the final week. Tactically outwitted by Colombian Nelson Rodríguez at Val Thorens, the balding Latvian won back-to-back at Cluses and in the mountain time trial to Avoriaz to sweep past the fading Frenchman, who fell back to fifth behind best young rider Pantani and Hautacam winner Leblanc. In truth, the race had been over since that misty mountain, when Indurain put his fourth win almost beyond question.

FINAL STANDINGS

1 Miguel Indurain (SPA) Banesto 103:38:38
2 Piotr Ugrumov (LAT) Gewiss-Ballan +5:39
3 Marco Pantani (ITA) Carrera +7:19
4 Luc Leblanc (FRA) Festina +10:03
5 Richard Virenque (FRA) Festina +10:10
6 Roberto Conti (ITA) Lampre-Panaria +12:29
7 Alberto Elli (ITA) GB-MG +20:17
8 Alex Zülle (SWI) ONCE +20:35
9 Udo Bölts (GER) Telekom +25:19
10 Vladimir Poulnikov (UKR) Carrera +25:28

AVERAGE SPEED (OF WINNER): 38.381 KM/H
TOTAL DISTANCE RACED: 3,978 KM

OPPOSITE Setting the pace on the first big mountain stage to Hautacam above Lourdes, Indurain is not concerned by Luc Leblanc (right) and Marco Pantani (left), who are tagging along as he hammers out a fierce rhythm. At the summit, the Spaniard would be almost five minutes clear overall and would have the race all but won.

INDURAIN JOINS THE ALL-TIME GREATS

The 82nd Tour started with just one question requiring an answer. Could anyone prevent Miguel Indurain becoming the first rider in history to win five consecutive Tour titles? The Spaniard had altered his route into the Tour, opting to ride the Midi Libre and Dauphiné Libéré instead of the Giro. He had won both races as Rominger claimed the Giro title, setting the scene for another duel between the pair, with the Swiss now backed by the might of the Mapei-GB team.

The sprinters dominated the opening week as the race swept across northern France and into Belgium for three days. Indurain caught his rivals out with an uncharacteristic attack on a long drag heading into Liège. Only Johan Bruyneel managed to go with him. The Belgian described sitting behind Indurain as like 'riding behind a motorbike', but in the closing metres he claimed the stage and yellow jersey.

Had Indurain shown too much too soon? That seemed to be the case when he won the Seraing time trial, but only narrowly, finishing 12 seconds ahead of Bjarne Riis. The pair stood in that order at the top of the standings. A rest day followed and Indurain came out of it determined to take advantage of the first summit finish, just as he had in 1994. Alex Zülle won impressively at La Plagne, with Indurain next over the line and well clear of his rivals scattered down the mountain. Having identified his most likely opponent, Indurain kept Zülle tightly in check, the two of them

finishing together on Alpe d'Huez behind Marco Pantani.

As Indurain stayed close to the bespectacled Swiss, Zülle's team-mates orchestrated a coup that came close to toppling the Spaniard. It started when Laurent Jalabert went clear. Several other ONCE riders attempted to join him, only to be chased down by Banesto and even Indurain himself. Persistence paid off, though, for Melchor Mauri and Neil Stephens, who joined Jalabert. As they went all out to seize the yellow jersey, Indurain called in favours in order to retain it. He held on as Jalabert won the stage, but his team looked ragged.

On the first day in the Pyrenees, Pantani scampered clear to win at Guzet-Neige. The next stage to Cauterets featured six climbs, commencing with the Portet d'Aspet. Soon after the bunch passed over the top, several riders crashed. Frenchman Dante Rezze went off the road and into a ravine. The most seriously hurt, though, was Olympic road champion Fabio Casartelli. Tragically, despite prompt treatment, the Tour's medical team could not save him. The following day's stage was neutralized, Casartelli's Motorola team-mates rolling over the line in Pau first. Two days on, Motorola's Lance Armstrong took an emotional win in Limoges.

Indurain closed out the race with victory in the time trial at Lac de Vassivière, joining Anquetil, Merckx and Hinault as a five-time winner. 'I never compare myself to my idols,' he said humbly. With a sixth Tour win he could yet surpass them…

FINAL STANDINGS

1 Miguel Indurain (SPA) Banesto 92:44:59
2 Alex Zülle (SWI) ONCE +4:35
3 Bjarne Riis (DEN) Gewiss +6:47
4 Laurent Jalabert (FRA) ONCE +8:24
5 Ivan Gotti (ITA) Gewiss +11:33
6 Melchor Mauri (SPA) ONCE +15:20
7 Fernando Escartín (SPA) Mapei +15:49
8 Tony Rominger (SWI) Mapei +16:46
9 Richard Virenque (FRA) Festina +17:31
10 Hernán Buenahora (COL) Kelme +18:50

AVERAGE SPEED (OF WINNER): 39.191 KM/H
TOTAL DISTANCE RACED: 3,635 KM

OPPOSITE TOP Indurain's hold on the yellow jersey was put under severe threat when the ONCE team pulled off a strategic coupon the road to Mende. Melchor Mauri and Neil Stephens are setting the pace in the breakaway group for their team leader Jalabert, who is wearing the green jersey just behind Motorola's Andrea Peron.

OPPOSITE BOTTOM LEFT Although Jalabert failed to knock Indurain off top spot, he could not have timed his victory better as the stage into Mende took place on Bastille Day.

OPPOSITE BOTTOM RIGHT Victory in the final time trial ensures Indurain's promotion into the five-time winners' club.

The effort is showing on Indurain's face as he's urged on towards yet another time trial victory by fans at the roadside.

Indurain: the Tour's greatest time triallist?

ALTHOUGH OCCASIONALLY BEATEN in prologues and mountain time trials, Miguel Indurain only lost one long time trial during his Tour reign, to Tony Rominger in 1993 at Montlhéry, a defeat bracketed by nine winning performances during his conquests of the yellow jersey. These were very high-class performances that ranked him among the best rouleurs in the Tour's history.

In 1991, at Mâcon, on a course measuring 57 km, he won at an average speed of 47.665 km/h. From that point on and up to his defeat in his quest for a sixth yellow jersey he would continue to improve. At Luxembourg in 1992, he was staggering over 65 km: he averaged more than 49 km/h and finished six minutes quicker than Laurent Fignon, who he overtook. At Blois, at the finale of that same Tour, he crossed another barrier by averaging an explosive 52 km/h over 64 km.

In 1993, over 59 km at Lac de Madine, he averaged more than 48.6 km/h. In 1994, between Périgueux and Bergerac, he once again averaged better than 50 km/h over 64 km. And in 1995, he was even more dazzling: after an impressive attack with Bruyneel in the Ardennes, he still managed to average close to 50.5 km/h between Huy and Seraing. He was very much in control in that 1995 Tour as he claimed a second great victory in the time trial at Lac de Vassivière.

His reign was both impressive and flawless. Sometimes he wore the aero helmet of a modern-day knight and on other occasions he didn't. Sometimes he used disc wheels, on others he used spoked wheels. He reigned in the same way as Jacques Anquetil, doing what he needed to do to win his last three yellow jerseys after initially starting out with fantastic escapades. His first two successes, in 1991 and 1992, were sewn up with raids in the Pyrenees and Alps, where he shared centre stage with Claudio Chiappucci.

The fact that Miguel was the best is underlined by the fact that each year a different rider finished second to him: in between Gianni Bugno in 1991 and Alex Zülle in 1995 were Claudio Chiappucci, Tony Rominger and Piotr Ugrumov. Cycling was advancing but Miguel remained in charge as former winners Fignon, LeMond, Delgado and Roche bid farewell to the sport. It should also be pointed out that, despite being reproached for his overwhelming focus on the Tour, he also won the Giro in 1992 and 1993, completing a famous double in those years just as Coppi, Anquetil, Merckx and Hinault had done before him, and that's without mentioning his Olympic title, his hour record and his other successes.

LEFT In much the same way as Jacques Anquetil, Indurain took full advantage of his supreme ability in time trials, leaving his rivals with far too much ground to make up in the mountains, especially as he was rarely distanced on the climbs.

OPPOSITE In spite of being discreet and even shy, Banesto's champion left an indelible mark on the history of the Tour: his five consecutive wins were completed ahead of five different riders, which had never been seen before.

RIIS DOWNS INDURAIN BUT ADMITS DOPING

Winning a sixth consecutive Tour was never going to be an easy proposition for Miguel Indurain, especially as he had another very powerful team to worry about. Team Telekom had signed Bjarne Riis and brought through young German Jan Ullrich. The slender, balding, 32-year-old Dane had finished third in 1995. To say that he had improved since he had turned pro was putting it mildly. As for 22-year-old Ullrich, he had already been an amateur world champion.

The Spaniard's hopes weren't helped when he arrived at the Tour a touch overweight. Usually, he would shed a few kilos before the serious action started. Unfortunately for him, it was cold, wet and there were lots of crashes. Indurain had to stay on the defensive, which left him two kilos above his ideal fighting weight.

The first stage in the Alps took the race to Les Arcs. French hope Laurent Jalabert was dropped on the Madeleine, yellow jersey Stéphane Heulot abandoned in tears due to tendinitis, and Alex Zülle and Johan Bruyneel crashed on the sodden mountain roads. It seemed Indurain had avoided the worst when, just 3.5 km from the finish, he cracked. Luc Leblanc flew off to claim the stage victory, while Indurain lost three minutes on Riis.

It was a big step back and it was only the start. His lack of form was confirmed in the time trial the next day, then again the day after at Sestrières at the end of a stage shortened due to high winds, snow and intense cold. Riis thumbed his nose at the peloton and rode off to take the yellow jersey, his second, after having already worn it in 1995. Indurain lost another 28 seconds, but how much would he have lost if the Iseran and Galibier had not been removed from the itinerary?

The answer came in the Pyrenees at Hautacam, where Riis claimed his second stage win and Indurain lost another 2-28. A response was expected on the following day's stage, which finished in Indurain's home city of Pamplona. But it never came. Indurain rode past his family and fans eight minutes down on the main contenders. He staged a gallant last stand at Saint-Émilion, where only Ullrich could beat him in the time trial, then trailed into Paris in 11th place. Riis finished ahead of his team-mate and the pretender to his crown, Ullrich, while France's Richard Virenque was third having also picked up a third mountains title.

Riis was not a popular winner, largely due to rumours circulating about his artificially elevated haematocrit level. In 2007 he finally admitted he had cheated by using the blood-booster EPO. Disqualified in June 2007, his name returned to the race's palmarès in July 2008, but with a mention of his admission. Indurain may not have won a sixth victory, but the race had certainly been distorted. Riis's yellow jersey is now gathering mould at the bottom of a box in his garage.

FINAL STANDINGS

1 Bjarne Riis (DEN) Telekom 95:57:16
2 Jan Ullrich (GER) Telekom +1:41
3 Richard Virenque (FRA) Festina +4:37
4 Laurent Dufaux (SWI) Festina +5:53
5 Peter Luttenberger (AUT) Carrera +7:07
6 Luc Leblanc (FRA) Polti +10:03
7 Piotr Ugrumov (LAT) Roslotto-ZG Mobili +10:04
8 Fernando Escartín (SPA) Kelme +10:26
9 Abraham Olano (SPA) Mapei +11:00
10 Tony Rominger (SWI) Mapei +11:53

AVERAGE SPEED (OF WINNER): 39.237 KM/H
TOTAL DISTANCE RACED: 3,765 KM

OPPOSITE Already in the yellow jersey, Bjarne Riis casts an almost dismissive look at defending champion Miguel Indurain before accelerating away to victory at the summit finish of Hautacam.

ULLRICH UNVEILS HIS INNER OGRE

In 1997, the cycling world was still unaware of the scandals that would engulf Bjarne Riis and many of his former team-mates at Team Telekom a decade later. The powerful German squad lined up in Rouen with the aim of adding a second consecutive title. Miguel Indurain was there but no longer in a competitive role. He had joined the civilian ranks and appeared alongside Eddy Merckx and Bernard Hinault and others to pay homage to Jacques Anquetil, the first five-time winner who was from Rouen.

The previous Tour had shown very clearly that Riis's strongest rival was likely to be the young German in his own team. Could he keep Jan Ullrich at bay? The answer came at Andorra-Arcalis in the Pyrenees, where Ullrich revealed the extent of his power on the final climb and in doing so became 'The Ogre of Rostock'. Marco Pantani and Richard Virenque lost more than a minute, Riis more than three. Like several great riders before him, Ullrich donned his first yellow jersey at the age of 23.

Ullrich demonstrated this show of force was no one-off in the 51-km time trial at Saint-Étienne. He finished three minutes ahead of Riis and overtook Virenque to gain another three minutes on the Frenchman. The race's hierarchy had been established, which enabled Pantani and Virenque to take centre stage in the Alps. While they made hay, the German in the yellow jersey was never far behind. Once out of the mountains, Ullrich increased the gaps he had established on fellow podium finishers Virenque and Pantani during the final time trial at EuroDisney, stretching his advantage to 9 minutes on the Frenchman and more than 14 on the Italian, before being crowned on the Champs-Élysées.

Ullrich's victory was so impressive that it was widely predicted he would harvest many titles. We now know that his success ended there, although he did finish second five times, on three occasions behind Lance Armstrong. In that same year of 1997, his compatriot Erik Zabel added to Telekom's success by winning the green jersey and three stages. The squad also won the team prize. However, in 2006 the Puerto inquiry, which was set up in Spain to investigate EPO use and blood doping, and overseen by the doctor Eufemiano Fuentes, snared Ullrich and also led to confessions from his fellow team-mates Zabel and Rolf Aldag.

This cast a dark shadow over this golden age for Germany's champions as, unfortunately, it was also revealed to be the age of EPO and growth hormone. Ullrich's 1997 victory was never formally challenged but, in the wake of the Puerto affair, he was not allowed to start the 2006 Tour and his career ended at the age of 33. Today he is involved in humanitarian work. He speaks when he judges the moment is right, at one point saying: 'The problem isn't Ullrich, it's doping in cycling.' The drama that would later surround Pantani underlined that.

FINAL STANDINGS

1 Jan Ullrich (GER) Telekom 100:30:35
2 Richard Virenque (FRA) Festina +9:09
3 Marco Pantani (ITA) Mercatone Uno +14:03
4 Abraham Olano (SPA) Banesto +15:55
5 Fernando Escartín (SPA) Kelme +20:32
6 Francesco Casagrande (ITA) Saeco +22:47
7 Bjarne Riis (DEN) Telekom +26:34
8 José María Jiménez (SPA) Banesto +31:17
9 Laurent Dufaux (SWI) Festina +31:55
10 Roberto Conti (ITA) Mercatone Uno +32:26

AVERAGE SPEED (OF WINNER): 39.239 KM/H
TOTAL DISTANCE RACED: 3,944 KM

OPPOSITE Between Bourg-d'Oisans and Courchevel, Richard Virenque and Festina put on a show. The Frenchman didn't take the yellow jersey from Jan Ullrich, but consoled himself with the stage win and escalating 'Virenquemania'. Behind them it was carnage.

The green jersey

INTRODUCED IN 1953 on the occasion of the Tour's 50th anniversary, the green jersey has marked out, using a points system, the most consistently high finisher each day.

The title has tended to be dominated by the sprinters, as more points are available on flat stages than in the mountains or time trials. Masters of every type of skill, these riders have pure speed, the ability to weave through tight gaps and no fear of going elbow to elbow with their rivals; they can accelerate once and then again, know which is the best wheel to follow and how to find shelter. Explosive and kamikaze in their approach, they are well aware that the risk of high-speed crashes is ever-present. As sprints start to unwind,

the green jersey contenders are invisible, but on the line the best of them are in everyone's photos.

The king of the points champions is Germany's Erik Zabel, who won six consecutive green jerseys between 1996 and 2001. Despite winning 23 stages over the past five years, Britain's Mark Cavendish has only won the green jersey once, in 2011, underlining that the fastest sprinter is not necessarily the man who rides off in green.

Since 1975 the most prestigious rendez-vous for the green jersey contenders has been the final stage finish on the Champs-Élysées. Cavendish has a phenomenal record there, winning this stage for the past four years.

ABOVE Mark Cavendish claimed the green jersey in 2011, when he won on the Champs-Élysées for the third year in succession, a streak he extended in 2012.

OPPOSITE TOP 2002 – A gesture of peace between Erik Zabel, in green, and Robbie McEwen, his eventual successor.

OPPOSITE BOTTOM LEFT 2002, 2004, 2006 – Nothing is yielded as Spain's Oscar Freire goes shoulder to shoulder with Australia's Robbie McEwen. The Spaniard wins the stage, the Australian the jersey.

OPPOSITE BOTTOM RIGHT Cyrille Guimard never won the points title, but is closely associated with this prize. In 1971, he wore green but eventually finished second in the standings to Eddy Merckx. A year later, he pushed Merckx almost all the way to Paris in the battle for the yellow jersey, but was forced to retire two days from the finish. As a tribute to his courage, Merckx presented him with the green jersey on the final podium.

PANTANI EMERGES FROM THE STORM

Due to the fact his ears stuck out, Italian climber Marco Pantani was nicknamed 'Elefantino', the Italian name for Dumbo. His bandana, earring and tattoo earned him a moniker he liked a lot more, 'The Pirate'… He was third in 1997, but this year the elephant would take flight and the pirate would become a king of the seas. Why was that? Simply because in 1998 the Tour was hit by a storm the likes of which it had never seen during its 95-year existence, and because the divine Marco, bald head and all, played his part in saving it.

The dark clouds began to form three days before the start of the race in Ireland, the home of Seamus Elliott, Sean Kelly and Stephen Roche. The start was later than usual to avoid a clash with the World Cup. France had hosted it for the second time and the home team had clinched the trophy, resulting in national euphoria. Sadly for the Tour, it quickly began to produce very different feelings, which were initiated by talk of drug trafficking.

On 8 July, Festina soigneur Willy Voet was stopped at the French–Belgian border. Police searched his car and found it was full of EPO and other doping products. As Voet himself revealed, organized drug use was taking place, as Festina *directeur sportif* Bruno Roussel and the team doctor later admitted. The judiciary and the courts went to work, acting with dignity and respect. Just because the affair implicated 'the giants of the road' was no reason

to take sweeping action and at the same time forget the riders' most basic rights.

But the storm was terrible. Fortunately, in the face of it, the Tour had two strong commanders, a double-headed leadership you could say: on the one hand, there was Jean-Marie Leblanc, the race director and leader on the ground, and on the other there was Jean-Claude Killy, the president of ASO, the company within the Amaury group that has specialized in organizing sporting events since 1993. They were both ex-competitors. Killy was a famous triple Olympic skiing champion from the Grenoble Games of 1968, while Leblanc was a former 'giant of the road'. Before becoming a brilliant journalist specializing in cycling and boxing, he had finished two Tours, in 1968 and 1970.

The riders knew that he was one of them, which was absolutely essential considering the difficult conversations that had to be had with them on several occasions, first of all during the strike at Tarascon-sur-Ariège, then at Aix-les-Bains, when they felt they were being given a rough ride by their critics and were contemplating stopping altogether. The conversation that Leblanc had with Bjarne Riis, Laurent Jalabert and Luc Leblanc kept the race going. He put everything into perspective, calmed things down and called for common sense on both sides, as he also asked the judicial authorities and the police to show more respect and dignity.

FINAL STANDINGS

1 Marco Pantani (ITA) Mercatone Uno 92:49:46
2 Jan Ullrich (GER) Telekom +3:21
3 Bobby Julich (USA) Cofidis +4:08
4 Christophe Rinero (FRA) Cofidis +9:16
5 Michael Boogerd (NED) Rabobank +11:26
6 Jean-Cyril Robin (FRA) US Postal Service +14:57
7 Roland Meier (SWI) Cofidis +15:13
8 Daniele Nardello (ITA) Mapei +16:07
9 Giuseppe Di Grande (ITA) Mapei +17:35
10 Axel Merckx (BEL) Polti +17:39

AVERAGE SPEED (OF WINNER): 39.983 KM/H
TOTAL DISTANCE RACED: 3,875 KM

OPPOSITE Following a police raid on the TVM team's hotel, the Tour peloton came to a halt soon after the start of the stage leaving Albertville. The riders, including eventual champion Marco Pantani, removed their race numbers in order to protest at what they perceived as ill-treatment over the previous fortnight.

Maintaining reason and human perspective were the two pillars that Leblanc clung to in order to keep the Tour on track during all this tumult. His defence of the race was heroic despite the furore that was swirling around him. It never swayed his resolve. Instead, Leblanc showed himself to be 'Captain Courageous' by saving the race and getting it to Paris.

At Brive, the Festina team had to be ejected from the race when it was revealed that there was organized doping within the squad, even though Richard Virenque continued to deny it. The King of the Mountains had been third in 1996, second in 1997, and had been thinking he could win in 1998. But the rug was pulled from under his feet, leaving lots of Frenchmen who had been seduced by his fiery nature and panache crying foul. Recovering from this was almost mission impossible. However, Leblanc never let go of the helm and, thanks largely to Pantani, the race stayed off the rocks and reached a safe harbour.

The race needed a gifted climber to get it back on track. Pantani answered the call and climbed into the clouds and into legend, first in the Pyrenees at Plateau de Beille, where he loosened Jan Ullrich's grip on the yellow jersey, and then at Les Deux-Alpes, where he took hold of it for good having

destroyed 'The Ogre of Rostock', who finished nine minutes down in 25th place. The German tried to recoup his losses the next day at Albertville, but 'The Pirate' kept a close eye on him.

In Aix-les-Bains, where the stage ended up being neutralized, several other teams jumped ship for a variety of reasons, but the race continued the next day to Neuchâtel, where Tom Steels led in a peloton that had also lost King of the Mountains Rodolfo Massi, who had been detained by the police at Chambéry. Ullrich nibbled away a bit of his substantial deficit between Montceau-les-Mines and Le Creusot, where mine-worker Louis Gauthier, who would go on to become a 'giant of the road', would write the stage results in chalk on the side of wagons for his friends who worked down in the mine.

All that remained was for the Tour, the caravan, the 96 survivors of the racing and Jean-Marie Leblanc to reach Paris, where they received a rapturous welcome. Both fans and race followers knew that La Grande Boucle had come back from the very edge. After France's victory in the World Cup Final, this was another beautiful victory, and principally it was down to Pantani's defeat of Ullrich.

THE RISE AND FALL OF AN AMERICAN HERO

The 3rd July, 1999, the date of the Grand Départ of the 86th Tour de France, wasn't an ordinary day in the history of the race. There were several reasons for this: it was the first time the race had started in the Vendée, at the Puy-du-Fou to be precise; the race saw the return of two personalities who had been viewed as undesirable by the race organization, Richard Virenque and ONCE team manager Manolo Saiz; it also saw the return following a two-year absence due to long-term treatment for testicular cancer of the American Lance Armstrong.

After abandoning his first two Tours in 1993 and 1994, he finished 36th in 1995 and had abandoned again in 1996. This was his fifth Tour and he was riding it as leader of the American US Postal team, which was totally devoted to his needs. He was getting on for 28 and his former team-mates Andreu and Hincapie could see that he had metamorphosed: he had thinned down, boosted his muscle bulk and his pedal cadence had changed, particularly in the mountains, as he had shown in finishing fourth in the 1998 Vuelta.

Previously regarded as a one-day race specialist, Armstrong did have some decent stage race results on his record, but was about to step up to an entirely new level. More than a decade down the line, when the US Anti-Doping Agency published its dossier into the systematic doping practices employed by the US Postal team, it became clear that Armstrong was not only

doping himself but was at the centre of that wider programme. However, as the race dubbed 'The Tour of Renewal' got under way, the American was set to become its figurehead thanks to one of the most incredible stories ever seen in world sport.

Other elements contributed to making this a rather extraordinary Tour: Marco Pantani, the defending champion, was absent following his exclusion from the Giro as a result of an elevated red blood cell count; 1996 winner Bjarne Riis had retired; and Jan Ullrich, his successor in 1997, was absent due to injury. In short, the Tour had rarely been so open, and this impression was only underlined when, in the 6.8-km prologue, Armstrong Mark II triumphed by seven seconds from bespectacled Swiss Alex Zülle, one of the Festina riders who had been ejected from the previous year's race.

Armstrong only got a brief glimpse of his first yellow jersey because on stage two, which crossed the Passage du Gois, Estonia's Jaan Kirsipuu snaffled it from him, thanks to the bonus seconds he gained at the finish. That stage turned out to be very important as about 100 of the 178 starters lost significant time as a result of a mass pile-up on the Gois, a coastal causeway that sat below water level at high tide. Zülle lost more than six minutes in the incident and ended up seven minutes down on the American.

The sprinters made hay as far as Metz, particularly the showy Mario Cipollini, who started a run of four consecutive

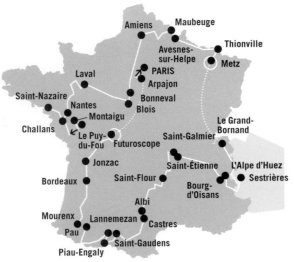

FINAL STANDINGS

1 No winner *
2 Alex Zülle (SWI) Banesto +7:37
3 Fernando Escartín (SPA) Kelme +10:26
4 Laurent Dufaux (SWI) Saeco +14:43
5 Angel Casero (SPA) Vitalicio Seguros +15:11
6 Abraham Olano (SPA) ONCE +16:47
7 Daniele Nardello (ITA) Mapei +17:02
8 Richard Virenque (FRA) Polti +17:28
9 Wladimir Belli (ITA) Festina +17:37
10 Andrea Peron (ITA) ONCE +23:10

AVERAGE SPEED (OF WINNER): 40.276 KM/H
TOTAL DISTANCE RACED: 3,870 KM
* Lance Armstrong was stripped of the title by the UCI in October 2012

OPPOSITE The Armstrong of 1999 was very different to the rider who had quit the 1996 Tour due to illness, not suspecting that he had testicular cancer. Previously best known for his achievements in one-day races, he re-emerged as an invincible champion, who was equally at home in time trials and in the mountains.

stage wins in Blois, where the average speed for the day was an astonishing 50.355 km/h. In Metz, Armstrong nailed up his colours by crushing his rivals in the 56.4-km time trial, and then he gave a repeat performance on the road to Sestrières, where he took a definitive grip on the yellow jersey. Between the Alps and the Pyrenees, a number of riders challenged Armstrong, but they all remained six or seven minutes back. Fernando Escartín stood out in particular, but even he couldn't close the gap.

Indeed, the biggest concern for the American was constant questioning by French newspaper *Le Monde* about the presence of a corticosteroid that had been detected in his urine following stage one of the race. Armstrong initially denied he had taken anything and also that he had a medical exemption certificate that enabled him to take a skin cream to treat a saddle sore. In the final week of the race he admitted that

he didn't have an exemption certificate and that he had made a mistake when saying he hadn't used any medication.

Back on the road, the final time trial at Futuroscope allowed Armstrong to confirm his supremacy: Zülle ended up seven minutes back and Escartín ten. On the Champs-Élysées, Armstrong posed on the podium with Erik Zabel, who had taken the green jersey for a fourth time, and Virenque, who had finished in polka dots for a fifth. Despite a few doping stories, the Tour seemed to have got back on track after the chaos of 1998. A few of the dope control samples were stored away to enable further analysis when testing methods had improved, and these would provide further reason for doubt about Armstrong's achievements. However, for the moment, the overriding feeling was one of joy. For those people stricken by cancer, the American became an incredible symbol of what could be achieved.

TOP RIGHT AND OPPOSITE Seven is the figure that links climber Richard Virenque and American Lance Armstrong. The Frenchman won seven polka-dot jerseys, while the American, whose bars look like some kind of claw designed by NASA, won seven consecutive yellow jerseys. Armstrong, though, would be stripped of his seven titles in 2012.

TOP LEFT Lance Armstrong wins at Sestrières.

RIGHT A series of crashes on the Passage du Gois and the mechanical problems that were the result of them ensured that some of the outsiders such as Switzerland's Alex Zülle lost almost all hope of victory.

ARMSTRONG'S SECOND TOUR BRINGS MORE QUESTIONS

The 2000 Tour, which Lance Armstrong and his teammates prepared for in typically American fashion by undertaking meticulous reconnaissance of the key sections, started once again in Futuroscope, near Poitiers, where 'The Boss' had confirmed his victory the year before. This seemed a positive omen, even though Marco Pantani and Jan Ullrich were back in the field.

Armstrong took the yellow jersey (denied him by David Millar and a mere two seconds in the prologue) as things began to get really serious in the Pyrenees at Hautacam, where the American was right on the heels of stage-winner Javier Otxoa. That set up a second consecutive victory, even though Pantani confirmed his return to form by teasing him on the Ventoux and at Courchevel, and Virenque and Ullrich teamed up to put him under pressure at Morzine.

The American had already created some leeway for himself and still had time for a final crushing whirl of the pedals at Mulhouse, where he stretched his final advantage: runner-up Jan Ullrich finished six minutes back, while diminutive Spanish climber Joseba Beloki, who was riding for Festina, was more than ten. Erik Zabel took the green jersey for the fifth time and Colombia's Santiago Botero from the Kelme team denied Richard Virenque a sixth King of the Mountains title. The Frenchman gained some consolation by finishing sixth overall.

Once again, though, US Postal had to fend off allegations of doping impropriety. During the race, French TV journalists followed a car driven by a member of the team's staff, who stopped and put a rubbish bag in a roadside bin. The TV crew retrieved the bag and found quantities of medical products, including Actovegin, a product derived from calves' blood used to treat diabetes and considered by some to have blood-boosting effects. The team claimed that no riders used Actovegin, while one of the staff needed it for diabetes. A French investigation into the incident closed two years later without any charges being laid against the team.

FINAL STANDINGS

1 No winner *
2 Jan Ullrich (GER) Telekom +6:02
3 Joseba Beloki (SPA) Festina +10:04
4 Christophe Moreau (FRA) Festina +10:34
5 Roberto Heras (SPA) Kelme +11:50
6 Richard Virenque (FRA) Polti +13:26
7 Santiago Botero (COL) Kelme +14:18
8 Fernando Escartín (SPA) Kelme +17:21
9 Francisco Mancebo (SPA) Banesto +18:09
10 Daniele Nardello (ITA) Mapei +18:25

AVERAGE SPEED (OF WINNER): 39.569 KM/H
TOTAL DISTANCE RACED: 3,662 KM
* Lance Armstrong was stripped of the title by the UCI in October 2012

OPPOSITE TOP Before a stage start, a summit meeting takes place between the holders of the yellow and green jerseys, the American Lance Armstrong and the German Erik Zabel.

OPPOSITE BOTTOM Reconnaissance of the route, methodical organization and a team designed to be able to deal with any situation – all of that was only possible because Lance Armstrong devoted himself 'body and soul' to the Tour and ensured that he kept a close eye on and controlled everyone.

ARMSTRONG CLAWS BACK THE GREAT ESCAPE

Would the 2001 Tour, the 88th edition, which started in Dunkirk, enable Armstrong to emulate his compatriot Greg LeMond, who had taken his third win in 1990, becoming the first American to achieve that honour? Lance was determined to do so, as it meant he went a step closer to bettering the achievement of his compatriot, with whom he had a very testy relationship.

This race was extremely unpredictable in its nature even before the riders had reached the first key tests. A rampant Laurent Jalabert won twice, notably on 14 July at Verdun, while on the stage to Pontarlier, in terrible conditions, a 14-man break came together and ended up more than half an hour clear. Were we going to get a shock result à la Walkowiak in 1956?

Some may have hoped so, but Armstrong had a date with history, and his return to the forefront of affairs came both quickly and with impressive power in the Alps at Alpe d'Huez and Chamrousse, where the American claimed two victories. But there was also a touching side story: François Simon, who had been in the great escape, took the yellow jersey in almost the same place where his brother Pascal had lost it when he had been forced to abandon in 1983.

Thanks to these two shows of force, Armstrong moved into a podium position, although he was still 13 minutes down on little Simon. He would only need two more stages and then a tightening of the screw at Pla d'Adet, where he swept everyone away, to earn his first yellow jersey of the 2001 event, and in so doing move four minutes ahead of the previous holder. The next day at Luz-Ardiden, Jan Ullrich tried to attack but couldn't shake off his rival, although he did move into second place overall.

In the Saint-Amand-Montrond time trial, Armstrong boosted his advantage even more, leaving Ullrich almost seven minutes down, while Beloki once again claimed the third step on the podium, which ended up the same as the previous year's. However, Laurent Jalabert was perhaps the happiest man on the Champs-Élysées having secured the polka-dot jersey.

FINAL STANDINGS

1 No winner *
2 Jan Ullrich (GER) Telekom +6:44
3 Joseba Beloki (SPA) ONCE +9:05
4 Andrei Kivilev (KAZ) Cofidis +9:53
5 Igor González de Galdeano (SPA) ONCE +13:28
6 François Simon (FRA) Bonjour +17:22
7 Oscar Sevilla (SPA) Kelme +18:30
8 Santiago Botero (COL) Kelme +20:55
9 Marcos Serrano (SPA) ONCE +21:45
10 Michael Boogerd (NED) Rabobank +22:38

AVERAGE SPEED (OF WINNER): 40.07 KM/H
TOTAL DISTANCE RACED: 3,458 KM

* Lance Armstrong was stripped of the title by the UCI in October 2012

OPPOSITE TOP With the peloton dithering in the appalling weather, the breakaway riders combine their efforts on the road to Pontarlier. On the right is François Simon, who was one of the escapees who capitalized on this unexpected development. He moved into the yellow jersey a few days later, emulating brother Pascal's achievement in 1983.

OPPOSITE BOTTOM Armstrong's legend continued to grow as he completed a hat-trick of Tour victories. His popularity soared in the USA, where cycling had previously been very much a niche sport.

The white jersey

INTRODUCED IN 1975, the first year
that the Tour de France finished on
the Champs-Élysées, the white jersey
for the best young rider was intended
to encourage and highlight young
talents on the race. It fulfilled that
role immediately, as Tour debutant
Francesco Moser shocked Eddy Merckx
by winning the prologue in that year,
taking the yellow jersey initially before
riding into Paris in white having
finished seventh overall.

At that point, there was no age limit
on those eligible for entry into the Tour.
Instead, the rule stated that racers
competing for the right to wear white
should have been professionals for no
more than three seasons. In 1983, the rule
changed again so that only first-year pros
were eligible to compete. In 1987, entry

was adjusted once again so that only
riders who were less than 26 on 1 January
following the Tour were eligible.

Only three riders have won the best
young rider competition on multiple
occasions: Marco Pantani (1994–5),
Jan Ullrich (1996–8) and Andy Schleck
(2008–10). However, only Schleck has
worn the white into Paris more than
once as the jersey was not presented
between 1989 and 1999. Although the
competition was still recognized, the
presentation of the white jersey was
removed in order to reduce the length
of the post-stage protocol ceremony.

Only four riders have won the best
young rider title and the yellow jersey in
the same Tour: Laurent Fignon (1983),
Jan Ullrich (1997), Alberto Contador
(2007) and Andy Schleck (2010).

ABOVE Francesco Moser was the first rider to
win the white jersey of best young rider. He led
the competition from start to finish thanks to his
victory in the prologue, finishing seventh overall,
a place behind compatriot Felice Gimondi,
who is tracking him here.

OPPOSITE TOP Dietrich Thurau looked like he
might wear the yellow jersey from start to finish
on his Tour debut in 1977, but the German
faded in the final week, finishing fifth in the
white jersey, a place ahead of Eddy Merckx,
who is on Thurau's wheel.

OPPOSITE BOTTOM LEFT Phil Anderson (right)
presented the only consistent threat to Bernard
Hinault (left) in 1981. The Australian led the
race for a day and held second place until the
final week, when fatigue caught up with him
and resulted in him losing the white jersey
to Peter Winnen.

OPPOSITE BOTTOM RIGHT Like Jan Ullrich,
Luxembourg's Andy Schleck won the white
jersey on three consecutive occasions.

RUMSAS AFFAIR TAINTS ARMSTRONG'S FOURTH TITLE

In 2002 the Tour started in Luxembourg for the second time and Charly Gaul, winner of the 1958 Tour, was there to get it under way. Back then, who would have believed that Americans, Australians, Colombians, Estonians and Latvians would one day play the key roles in the race? In little more than 30 years, the Tour had modernized and become a race with a worldwide perspective, leaving Gaul somewhat lost within the global village where Armstrong was competing for a fourth title and showed his intent right from the prologue.

With an overweight Jan Ullrich absent, Joseba Beloki presented the biggest challenge to the American, although Colombian Santiago Botero caused a stir when he beat Armstrong in the 52-km time trial at Lorient.

However, the Tour really got going in the Pyrenees. As usual, Armstrong imposed himself in these very first key tests, delivering two blows. He had already done this in 1999 and in 2001, and he repeated the treatment at La Mongie and Plateau de Beille.

Beloki tried to hang on to his coat-tails with ONCE team-mate Igor González de Galdeano, who had held the yellow jersey going into the Pyrenees. But the American increased his advantage on the Ventoux – where he was right on the heels of a resurgent Virenque – and at La Plagne and finally in the Mâcon time trial. Beloki confirmed that he was the best of the rest by taking second on the podium, where he and Armstrong were joined by Lithuania's Raimondas Rumsas, who reminded us that doping remained the Tour's worst enemy after his wife was arrested at a border crossing having been found with banned products. Winner of a second King of the the Mountains title Laurent Jalabert, alias 'Jaja', bowed out of the sport in true style.

Following Levi Leipheimer's admission in October 2012 that he had doped prior to 2008, the UCI stripped him of his eighth place finish. A former team-mate of Armstrong's at US Postal, Leipheimer was at that time riding for the Dutch Rabobank team.

FINAL STANDINGS

1 No winner *
2 Joseba Beloki (SPA) ONCE +7:17
3 Raimondas Rumsas (LIT) Lampre +8:17
4 Santiago Botero (COL) Kelme +13:10
5 Igor González de Galdeano (SPA) ONCE +13:54
6 José Azevedo (POR) ONCE +15:44
7 Francisco Mancebo (SPA) ibanesto.com +16:05
8 **
9 Roberto Heras (SPA) US Postal Service +17:12
10 Carlos Sastre (SPA) CSC +19:05

AVERAGE SPEED (OF WINNER): 39.92 KM/H
TOTAL DISTANCE RACED: 3,278 KM
 * Lance Armstrong was stripped of the title by the UCI in October 2012
 ** Levi Leipheimer was stripped of eighth place after he confessed
    to doping prior to 2008

In 2002 Armstrong faced barely a single threat to his dominance and coasted to his fourth victory, which as with his other tour titles was later stripped for doping offences.

SPECTACLE THROUGHOUT CENTENARY TOUR

For its centenary in 2003, the Tour began with a prologue in Paris and then headed out from Montgeron, where it had first started life on 1 July 1903. If Lance Armstrong could complete a fifth win he would join four of the Tour's greats: Anquetil, Merckx, Hinault and Indurain. This provided him with a real challenge. The fact that the Tour was set to feature the five cities that staged finishes back in 1903 – that is to say Lyon, Marseille, Toulouse, Bordeaux and Nantes – didn't bother the Texan, who knew that the race would be decided at Alpe d'Huez and Luz-Ardiden.

On both occasions, he was in the thick of it. On the first of these summits he was close enough to stage-winner Ibán Mayo to take the yellow jersey from Richard Virenque. On the second he was strong enough to overcome a crash caused when he collided with a spectator on the final climb to gain time on Jan Ullrich, who was once again his most threatening rival. Any detrimental effect of this crash was swept away by the kind of panache and sang-froid he had already shown a few days earlier near Gap, when he had just managed to avoid Joseba Beloki, who had fallen heavily on a bend coming down the Côte de la Rochette. Armstrong rode into and across a field, rejoining the race route on the next bend.

In the Pornic time trial, the day before the race set off from Ville-d'Avray for the Champs and the great centenary procession, he forced his main rival Jan Ullrich to take risks, which led to the German crashing, while David Millar took the stage victory, although he later admitted doping to do so. The German knew the odds were against him, but felt that he had a good hand, because he was just a minute behind and felt that… well, he thought he had a chance but ended up second to Armstrong for the third time.

As for the American, he avoided all of the traps that had been laid for him and became the fifth member of the five-time winners' club. It seemed that he had been anointed by Henri Desgrange, whose initials returned to the yellow jersey that Armstrong wore for 13 stages. The average speed of the race was so rapid that it nearly reached 41 km/h. Once again Virenque provided a French presence among the prize-winners as he rode off with a sixth polka-dot jersey.

Was the American champion going to stop there? He was now close to 32, the age when Hinault hung up his wheels. Of course not. He was fascinated by the prospect of winning six in a row, of achieving something that had been beyond everyone else, of outdoing even Merckx in his persistence.

FINAL STANDINGS

1 No winner *
2 Jan Ullrich (GER) Bianchi +1:01
3 Alexandre Vinokourov (KAZ) Telekom +4:14
4 Tyler Hamilton (USA) CSC +6:17
5 Haimar Zubeldia (SPA) Euskaltel +6:51
6 Ibán Mayo (SPA) Euskaltel +7:06
7 Ivan Basso (ITA) Fassa Bortolo +10:12
8 Christophe Moreau (FRA) Crédit Agricole +12:28
9 Carlos Sastre (SPA) CSC +18:49
10 Francisco Mancebo (SPA) ibanesto.com +19:15

AVERAGE SPEED (OF WINNER): 40.94 KM/H
TOTAL DISTANCE RACED: 3,427 KM
* Lance Armstrong was stripped of the title by the UCI in October 2012

ABOVE Whether it was Joseba
Beloki falling on a mountain bend
or a spectator tangling with his
bars on the climb up to Luz-Ardiden,
Lance reacted instantly. In the first
case he veers off to avoid Beloki and
is forced to cut across a mountain
meadow before leaping a ditch and
rejoining the race.

OVERLEAF There is no chance of
missing the presence of Basque fans
in the Pyrenees, their orange T-shirts
marking out their support of their
heroes on the Euskaltel team.

287

DOPING STORIES INTENSIFY AS ARMSTRONG WINS SIX

The 2004 Tour started in Liège with an extraordinary face-to-face between Lance Armstrong and *Sunday Times* journalist David Walsh, co-author with Pierre Ballester of the book *L.A. Confidentiel: Les Secrets de Lance Armstrong*. Walsh and Ballester had spoken to some of Armstrong's former team-mates and, notably, to former US Postal soigneur Emma O'Reilly and had provided circumstantial evidence of Armstrong having used performance-enhancing drugs.

During his pre-race press conference, where Walsh was sitting in the front row, Armstrong looked directly at the Irish journalist and said: 'Extraordinary allegations require extraordinary evidence.' Although Walsh and Ballester had not been able to provide complete proof of Armstrong's wrongdoing, many of the allegations they made and people they talked to later featured in the 2012 USADA dossier on the US Postal team, which led to Armstrong being stripped of his Tour de France titles.

Once the race got under way, Armstrong set about demolishing his rivals, as if driven on by the anger that was evident that day in Liège. He started in a relatively low-key manner, as Fabian Cancellara took the first yellow jersey in Liège. Armstrong claimed it briefly at Arras following a team time trial that was dominated by his US Postal team, but allowed it to slip away onto the shoulders of little-known Frenchman Thomas Voeckler, who had slipped into a breakaway between Amiens and Chartres and gained 16 minutes.

As long as Voeckler and his Brioches La Boulangère team bore the weight of protecting the yellow jersey, Armstrong could preserve his energy for the decisive moments. While the race was in a kind of limbo, the French riders went to town, led once again by Richard Virenque, who won in Saint-Flour on Bastille Day. The next day David Moncoutié picked up the baton at Figeac.

In the Pyrenees, at Plateau de Beille, Armstrong altered the course of the race with Ivan Basso and Andreas Klöden, but Voeckler managed to hang on to the yellow jersey by a mere 22 seconds, which enabled him to carry it into the Alps. At this point, Armstrong came into his own, winning at Villard-de-Lans, then adding a second success in the time trial up to Alpe d'Huez, then claiming a third success at Le Grand Bornand, where he neutralized Klöden's late attack. For good measure he added a fourth success in just a few days in the Besançon time trial.

FINAL STANDINGS

1 No winner *
2 Andreas Klöden (GER) T-Mobile +6:19
3 Ivan Basso (ITA) CSC +6:40
4 Jan Ullrich (GER) T-Mobile +8:50
5 José Azevedo (POR) US Postal +14:30
6 Francisco Mancebo (SPA) Illes Balears-Banesto +18:01
7 Georg Totschnig (AUT) Gerolsteiner +18:27
8 Carlos Sastre (SPA) CSC +19:51
9 **
10 Oscar Pereiro (SPA) Phonak +22:54

AVERAGE SPEED (OF WINNER): 40.553 KM/H
TOTAL DISTANCE RACED: 3,391 KM

* Lance Armstrong was stripped of the title by the UCI in October 2012
** Levi Leipheimer was stripped of ninth place after he confessed to doping prior to 2008

OPPOSITE Complimenting Thomas Voeckler, who for a good deal of the 2004 Tour managed to keep the yellow jersey out of Armstrong's hands, before the American imposed himself at Alpe d'Huez, where he unleashed his unmatchable power and crushed his rivals on his way to a record-breaking sixth Tour win.

On the 18th stage, the American showed his control extended to more than just winning stages and holding the yellow jersey. When Filippo Simeoni jumped across to a group of breakaway riders, Armstrong responded to his attack and chased across on the Italian's wheel. Simeoni was a long way from being a threat in the race, but had previously accused controversial Italian training consultant Michele Ferrari of providing him with doping products. Ferrari also happened to be Armstrong's coach. With the peloton chasing behind and closing the gap, the yellow jersey made it clear that he would not drop back from the break unless Simeoni did so as well. Simeoni reluctantly agreed and dropped back to the peloton, where he received a good deal of abuse from several of his compatriots.

Armstrong's sixth victory was sealed with the big gaps he'd won in his earlier Tours: he was six minutes clear of runner-up Andreas Klöden, with Italy's Ivan Basso on the third step of the podium. Virenque took his seventh King of the Mountains title, setting a new record. The leading French rider overall was Christophe Moreau in 12th. As for little Thomas Voeckler, who had held the yellow jersey for ten stages, he limited his losses and finished 18th.

USADA dossier leads to Armstrong's disgrace

HAVING STEPPED AWAY from the Tour in 2005, Armstrong could not resist the challenge of returning to the race looking for an eighth title in 2009. However, by that point, the weight of evidence against Armstrong was continuing to grow despite his continued denial of any use of banned products. In 2006, two former US Postal riders, one Armstrong's close friend and key lieutenant Frankie Andreu, admitted to using banned products including EPO during their time on the Tour. Andreu confessed he had started doping in 1995 when he was on the Motorola team with Armstrong, backing up admissions previously made by another Motorola rider, Steven Swart.

In 2010, another former US Postal rider, Floyd Landis, who had also been a close friend and key lieutenant to Armstrong, turned up at the Tour of California and accused US Postal team manager Johan Bruyneel of introducing him to doping in 2002. Landis said he had first used EPO in 2003, and alleged that he had picked up the dose from Armstrong's house. Although widely discredited, having continually stated that he had not doped to win the 2006 Tour or at any other time during his career – only to confess four years later after apparently attempting to blackmail Bruyneel and Armstrong into giving him a place on the Astana team – Landis provided the spark that ultimately led to Armstrong's downfall.

The publicity storm created by his allegations led to the US Food and Drug Administration launching an investigation into claims that his former US Postal team engaged in organized doping practices and that Armstrong was one of the riders to take part. In May 2011, while this investigation was ongoing,

Tyler Hamilton, another former US Postal stalwart who had been very close to Armstrong, appeared on US TV's primetime news show *60 Minutes* and admitted that not only had he used EPO and other banned products himself, but that he had seen Armstrong using them as well. Hamilton also backed up a claim made by Landis that Armstrong had been able to cover up a positive test at the 2001 edition of the Tour of Switzerland.

In February 2012, it was announced that the FDA investigation into the US Postal team was being dropped, news that was welcomed by Armstrong. However, the US Anti-Doping Agency then announced it would be carrying out its own investigation led by the organization's CEO, Travis Tygart. In June 2012, USADA formally charged Armstrong and five associates, including Bruyneen and Ferrari, with doping. Armstrong's legal team launched a suit stating that USADA did not have jurisdiction in the case, but the judge found for USADA.

In the wake of this decision, in August 2012, Armstrong announced that he would not be taking the case to arbitration, as was his right. In a statement, he said: 'There comes a point in every man's life when he has to say, "Enough is enough." For me, that time is now. I have been dealing with claims that I cheated and had an unfair advantage in winning my seven Tours since 1999… The toll this has taken on my family, and my work for our foundation and on me leads me to where I am today – finished with this nonsense.'

On 24 August, USADA handed Armstrong a lifetime ban and also disqualified him from all of his results since 1 August 1998, including his seven

Tour de France titles. A USADA statement said: 'The evidence against Lance Armstrong arose from disclosures made to USADA by more than a dozen witnesses who agreed to testify and provide evidence about their first-hand experience and/or knowledge of the doping activity of those involved in the USPS Conspiracy as well as analytical data. As part of the investigation Mr Armstrong was invited to meet with USADA and be truthful about his time on the USPS team but he refused.

'Numerous witnesses provided evidence to USADA based on personal knowledge acquired, either through direct observation of doping activity by Armstrong, or through Armstrong's admissions of doping to them that Armstrong used EPO, blood transfusions, testosterone and cortisone during the period from before 1998 through 2005, and that he had previously used EPO, testosterone and hGH [human growth hormone] through 1996. Witnesses also provided evidence that Lance Armstrong gave to them, encouraged them to use and administered doping products or methods, including EPO, blood transfusions, testosterone and cortisone during the period from 1999 through 2005. Additionally, scientific data showed Mr Armstrong's use of blood manipulation including EPO or blood transfusions during Mr Armstrong's comeback to cycling in the 2009 Tour de France.'

Armstrong was sanctioned for:
• Use and/or attempted use of prohibited substances and/or methods including EPO, blood transfusions, testosterone, corticosteroids and masking agents.
• Possession of prohibited substances and/or methods including EPO, blood

transfusions and related equipment (such as needles, blood bags, storage containers and other transfusion equipment and blood parameters measuring devices), testosterone, corticosteroids and masking agents.
• Trafficking of EPO, testosterone and corticosteroids.
• Administration and/or attempted administration to others of EPO, testosterone and cortisone.
• Assisting, encouraging, aiding, abetting, covering up and other complicity involving one or more anti-doping rule violations and/or attempted anti-doping rule violations.

On 10 October, USADA released its 'reasoned decision' dossier, detailing evidence it had gathered against

Armstrong and five associates who were behind what it described as 'the most sophisticated, professionalized and successful doping program that sport has ever seen'. The 1,000-page dossier included statements from 26 individuals, including no fewer than 15 riders 'with knowledge of the US Postal Service Team (USPS Team) and its participants' doping activities'. It also included 'direct documentary evidence including financial payments, emails, scientific data and laboratory test results that further prove the use, possession and distribution of performance enhancing drugs by Lance Armstrong'.

On 22 October, following confessions of doping by a series of US Postal riders including George Hincapie, Levi

Leipheimer, Michael Barry, David Zabriskie, Christian Vande Velde and Tom Danielson, the UCI announced that it was confirming the lifetime ban on Armstrong. At a press conference, UCI president Pat McQuaid declared: 'Lance Armstrong has no place in cycling.'

In January 2013, Armstrong admitted to doping to win all of his seven Tour titles during a televised interview by Oprah Winfrey. 'I am flawed, deeply flawed,' he acknowledged.

ABOVE Armstrong returned to the Tour in 2009, finishing third. A year later, allegations made by his former team-mate Floyd Landis led to a USADA investigation that eventually resulted in Armstrong being stripped of his seven Tour titles.

CONTADOR REIGNS AFTER RASMUSSEN'S WITHDRAWAL

In the wake of the previous year's scandal, picking a favourite for the 94th Tour was no easy task. There was no outstanding candidate, although the Kazakh Astana team looked particularly strong with two former podium finishers in their ranks: Alexandre Vinokourov and Andreas Klöden.

For the first time, the race started in Great Britain, with a prologue in central London followed by a road stage to Canterbury. Local hopes for the prologue were pinned on Londoner Bradley Wiggins. However, Swiss powerhouse Fabian Cancellara proved himself a level above his rivals as a crowd estimated to be more than a million-strong lined the route. More than two million fans filled the roadsides the next day, when Robbie McEwen emerged in the final metres to triumph in Canterbury. Thanks partly to another stage victory, Cancellara remained in yellow as far as the Alps. German Linus Gerdemann took the jersey from him, only to lose it the next day at Tignes to Danish climber Michael Rasmussen.

Vinokourov, meanwhile, had almost quit the race after a bad crash in the first week, but rebounded to win the time trial at Albi, then again at Loudenvielle after a daredevil descent off the Peyresourde. In between Alberto Contador took a hugely impressive win at Plateau de Beille ahead of Rasmussen, which lifted the Spaniard into second place behind the Dane. The Tour paused at Pau, where doping once again became the main focus. Vinokourov was ejected from the race after the dope control from Albi revealed he had undergone a blood transfusion.

A storm was also gathering around Rasmussen. Dubbed 'Chicken' because of his emaciated physique, the leader of the Rabobank team came under fire from the media when it was revealed that he had misled the authorities about his whereabouts prior to the Tour and had consequently missed out-of-competition doping controls. Although he never tested positive, fans whistled him when he beat Contador on the Aubisque the day after the rest day. This show of force from the Dane came to nothing when his team forced him to quit the race after the stage, spiriting him away like a thief in the night.

With Rasmussen gone, Contador inherited first place but refused to wear the yellow jersey between Pau and Castelsarrasin, as he wanted to earn it by right. He knew the title would be decided in the 55.5-km time trial between Cognac and Angoulême and had good reason to fear the riders lying just behind him, Cadel Evans and Levi Leipheimer. However, racing in the yellow jersey transformed Contador, who succeeded where Pereiro had failed a year earlier by holding off the Australian and the American, who ended a mere 23 and 31 seconds down on him, respectively. The gaps between podium finishers had never been so tight.

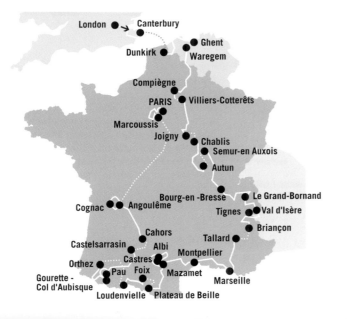

FINAL STANDINGS

1 Alberto Contador (SPA) Discovery Channel 91:00:26
2 Cadel Evans (AUS) Predictor-Lotto +0:23
3 *
4 Carlos Sastre (SPA) CSC +7:08
5 Haimar Zubeldia (SPA) Euskaltel-Euskadi +8:17
6 Alejandro Valverde (SPA) Caisse d'Epargne +11:37
7 Kim Kirchen (LUX) T-Mobile +12:18
8 Yaroslav Popovych (UKR) Discovery Channel +12:25
9 Mikel Astarloza (SPA) Euskaltel-Euskadi +14:14
10 Oscar Pereiro (SPA) Caisse d'Epargne +14:25

AVERAGE SPEED (OF WINNER): 39.23 KM/H
TOTAL DISTANCE RACED: 3,559.5 KM

*In October 2012 Levi Leipheimer admitted doping both before and during the 2007 season and was subsequently stripped of his third-place finish in this race.

ABOVE Michael Rasmussen was starting to look unassailable in the yellow jersey when questions about his whereabouts before the Tour began to grow. The Dane insisted he had been in Mexico, but he had been spotted training in Italy, thereby illicitly avoiding the possibility of undergoing out-of-competition dope controls.

LEFT The only rider who could compete with Rasmussen in the mountains was best young rider Alberto Contador, who is seen delivering his 'El Pistolero' victory salute as he beats the Dane at Plateau de Beille.

VETERAN SASTRE MAKES EXPERIENCE COUNT

The race started without the defending champion Alberto Contador, who was the victim of offences committed by the Astana team during 2007. The Kazakh squad had brought in former US Postal and Discovery Channel boss Johan Bruyneel and most of his riders including Contador with a view to making a clean start, but Tour organizers ASO refused to give Astana a place in the race despite their protestations that the old regime had been swept away.

Two riders dominated the opening half of the race. The first was young British sprinter Mark Cavendish. The 23-year-old Manxman won his first Tour stage in Châteauroux and thereafter was almost unbeatable in the bunch sprints, racking up another three victories before his Columbia-High Road team pulled him out of the race before the Alps. The second was Italian Riccardo Riccò. Winner of two mountain stages in incredible fashion, Riccò subsequently tested positive for the blood-boosting product CERA, leading to the withdrawal of his Saunier Duval team. In October 2008, it was revealed that time trial winner Stefan Schumacher and King of the Mountains Bernhard Kohl had also tested positive for CERA. They were stripped of their results.

The battle for the yellow jersey began to take shape at Hautacam, where Cadel Evans took the lead, a second clear of Fränk Schleck. Evans hung on until the Italian ski resort of Prato Nevoso, where Schleck nipped away to gain nine seconds and the lead. After a thrilling stage up and over the immense Bonette-Restefond pass, the race came down to a tough stage over the Galibier and Croix de Fer passes to Alpe d'Huez. Schleck and Carlos Sastre's CSC team-mates set a fierce pace to the foot of the final ascent, where Sastre made the first move. Schleck couldn't attack behind his team-mate and no one else wanted to or was able to. Sastre pressed on unchallenged up the Alpe's 21 hairpins, putting a dagger through the hopes of his rivals. He took the stage and the yellow jersey. Paris was just four days away and the experienced Sastre knew exactly what was required to win.

The Spaniard, who had finished every Tour since 2001, went into the Saint-Amand-Montrond time trial knowing how to gauge his effort. Riding as aerodynamically as possible and also spurred on by the yellow jersey, Sastre defended the lead he had over Evans (1-34) and Denis Menchov (2-39) tooth and nail. He crossed the line with 58 seconds in hand on the Australian and 1-13 on the Russian. He'd done it. On the Champs-Élysées, the final moment of consecration arrived for this fine champion at the age of 33. His team won that prize as well, while another Spaniard, Oscar Freire, claimed the green jersey. It left no doubt that Spanish cycling had changed since the years when their riders were simply content with taking the King of the Mountains title. Now the descendants of Cepeda and Trueba could boast 11 Tours to their credit.

FINAL STANDINGS

1 Carlos Sastre (SPA) CSC-Saxo Bank 87:52:52
2 Cadel Evans (AUS) Silence-Lotto +0:58
3 *
4 Denis Menchov (RUS) Rabobank +2:10
5 Christian Vande Velde (USA) Garmin +3:05
6 Fränk Schleck (LUX) CSC-Saxo Bank +4:28
7 Samuel Sánchez (SPA) Euskaltel-Euskadi +6:25
8 Kim Kirchen (LUX) Columbia-High Road +6:55
9 Alejandro Valverde (SPA) Caisse d'Epargne +7:12
10 Tadej Valjavec (SLO) Ag2r +9:05

AVERAGE SPEED (OF WINNER): 40.50 KM/H
TOTAL DISTANCE RACED: 3,559.5 KM
* Bernhard Kohl finished third but was stripped of his Tour results in October 2008 after it was announced he had tested positive for CERA.

As his rivals continue to eye each other further down the climb to Alpe d'Huez, Carlos Sastre has just 3 km to go before claiming what will be the biggest win of his career, as it will set him on the path to overall victory.

With the resort of Alpe d'Huez now coming into his sights, Carlos Sastre closes on what would be a Tour-deciding victory on the famous climb.

CONTADOR OVERCOMES SCHLECK AND IN-FIGHTING

After being prevented from defending his title in 2008, Alberto Contador returned at the 96th Tour as co-leader of the Astana team alongside Lance Armstrong, who had come out of retirement at the age of 38 in order to raise the profile of his cancer foundation. Their most likely rivals were the Schleck brothers on the Saxo Bank team, together with 2008 champion Carlos Sastre and two-time runner-up Cadel Evans.

The Schlecks' team-mate Fabian Cancellara won the opening time trial in Monaco and led the race for the first week, when it quickly became clear civil war was brewing in the Astana camp. Armstrong cleverly caught several of his rivals including Contador napping in strong cross-winds in the Camargue, while the Spaniard responded with a late attack on the climb up to Arcalis in Andorra, where he regained most of his losses and Italian Rinaldo Nocentini nudged Cancellara out of the yellow jersey.

The week between the Alps and the Pyrenees saw stalemate between the main contenders, but plenty of action among the sprinters. After bagging two stages in the first week, Mark Cavendish added a further two. The race for yellow came to life again heading for the summit finish at Verbier in Switzerland – this presented Contador with the opportunity to attack and he didn't hesitate. Only Andy Schleck was able to finish within a minute of the Spaniard, who claimed the lead.

Contador all but sealed the title at the end of a controversial stage to Le Grand Bornand. He finished alone with the Schlecks, but immediately came under fire from senior members of his team, who accused him of riding without regard for the podium chances of Armstrong and Klöden. In the wake of this very public and bitter criticism, Contador responded by winning the time trial in Annecy, from where he had a relatively pressure-free ride into Paris. The Schlecks' last chance of upsetting the Spaniard disappeared on the penultimate stage to the summit of Mont Ventoux, where a strong headwind prevented them from making any attacks.

The Tour transferred by train to Paris for the final stage, won by Cavendish by several lengths, which gave him six stage wins, although Thor Hushovd won the points title. As for Contador, he admitted that his 'cohabitation' with Armstrong had exhausted him as much as the battle with the Schlecks, saying 'the tension was greater in the hotel than it was in the race'.

Contador finished more than four minutes ahead of Andy Schleck, with Armstrong initially placed third.* However, in October 2012 the UCI stripped the American of all his results from 1999 onwards following the publication of the US Anti-Doping Agency dossier revealing organized doping within Armstrong's former US Postal team. It also suggested Armstrong had doped during the 2009 Tour. The UCI elevated Britain's Bradley Wiggins to third place.

FINAL STANDINGS

1 Alberto Contador (SPA) Astana 85:48:35
2 Andy Schleck (LUX) Saxo Bank +4:11
3 Bradley Wiggins (GBR) Garmin +6:01
4 Fränk Schleck (LUX) Saxo Bank +6:04
5 Andreas Klöden (GER) Astana +6:42
6 Vincenzo Nibali (ITA) Liquigas +7:35
7 Christian Vande Velde (USA) Garmin +12:04
8 Roman Kreuziger (CZE) Liquigas +14:16
9 Christophe Le Mével (FRA) Française des Jeux +14:25
10 Sandy Casar (FRA) Française des Jeux +17:19

AVERAGE SPEED (OF WINNER): 40.31 KM/H
TOTAL DISTANCE RACED: 3,459.5 KM
* Lance Armstrong and Mikel Astarloza were both stripped of top 10 finishes as the result of doping infringements

ABOVE Andy Schleck leads yellow jersey Alberto Contador (also pictured right) and Lance Armstrong towards the finish on the Ventoux. The young rider from Luxembourg would end up splitting the two rivals from Astana, although Armstrong was subsequently stripped of his third-place finish.

ANDY SCHLECK CAPTURES HIS FIRST YELLOW JERSEY

The 97th Tour looked set to provide another enthralling chapter in the bitter rivalry between defending champion Alberto Contador and seven-time winner Lance Armstrong. However, the contest fizzled out into a non-event on the first stage in the high mountains, when the American's age caught up with him and he faded almost out of sight. Instead, Contador was pushed all the way by Andy Schleck, who ended the race feeling like he could well have won it, only to have the title presented to him almost two years later when the Court of Arbitration for Sport ruled that Contador should be stripped of the title after a positive drugs test for clenbuterol.

There was plenty of controversy on the road too. Prologue king Fabian Cancellara claimed the yellow jersey in Rotterdam, but held it only as far as Spa two days later. The stage featured a number of climbs from Liège-Bastogne-Liège. Light rain and oil on the road rendered the descents of some of these climbs almost unrideable. Dozens of riders crashed, including Andy Schleck. Prompted by Cancellara, the bunch ceased hostilities for the day to allow dropped riders to regain lost ground. There were plenty more crashes the next day as well. It featured several cobbled sections from Paris-Roubaix. Fränk Schleck's hopes ended on one of them when he crashed and broke a collar-bone.

Andy Schleck's drive wasn't dimmed by the loss of his brother. Victory at Avoriaz put him into second place behind new yellow jersey Cadel Evans. Unfortunately, the Australian had cracked his elbow in a crash that day and tearfully yielded the lead to Schleck on the stage that followed. Although the Luxembourger lost vital seconds to Contador on the steep Montée Laurent Jalabert at Mende, he looked to have the measure of the Spaniard. He recognized, though, the need to gain more time in the Pyrenees if he hoped to retain the yellow jersey. Sensing his moment had come on the Port de Balès, Schleck attacked, only for his chain to unship, leaving him pedalling thin air. Contador and several others shot past and the next time the fuming Schleck saw them was after the finish in Luchon, where Contador had seized the yellow jersey.

A critical stage to the summit of the Tourmalet followed a rest day in Pau. Schleck went all out to shake Contador on the misty pass, but failed to do so and Contador remained eight seconds ahead. However, it later became apparent that the rest day had been the more critical of the two days as it was then that Contador tested positive for clenbuterol. The Spaniard managed to edge a few more seconds clear of the Luxembourger in the final time trial through the Bordeaux vineyards and rode into Paris victorious once again, only to have the title taken away when the CAS delivered its judgement in February 2012.

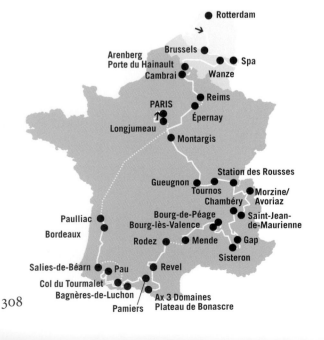

FINAL STANDINGS

1 Andy Schleck (LUX) Saxo Bank 91:59:27
2 Denis Menchov (RUS) Rabobank +1:22
3 Samuel Sánchez (SPA) Euskalt-Euskadi +3:01
4 Jurgen Van Den Broeck (BEL) Omega Pharma-Lotto +6:15
5 Robert Gesink (NED) Rabobank +8:52
6 Ryder Hesjedal (CAN) Garmin +9:36
7 Joaquim Rodríguez (SPA) Katusha +10:58
8 Roman Kreuziger (CZE) Liquigas +11:15
9 Chris Horner (USA) Team Radioshack +11:23
10 Luis León Sánchez (SPA) Caisse d'Epargne +13:42

AVERAGE SPEED (OF WINNER): 39.896 KM/H
TOTAL DISTANCE RACED: 3,642 KM
* Alberto Contador finished 39 seconds ahead of Andy Schleck
  but was stripped of the title after a positive test for clenbuterol.

OPPOSITE TOP Having lost the yellow jersey to Contador in controversial circumstances two stages beforehand, Andy Schleck goes on the attack with the aim of retaking the jersey at the summit finish on the Tourmalet.

OPPOSITE BOTTOM After a process lasting 18 months, Andy Schleck finally did get the yellow jersey back following Contador's disqualification after testing positive for clenbuterol. The Spanish champion maintained that he had ingested the product by eating tainted meat.

THIS PAGE The mountains are a vital component of the Tour's majesty, providing as they do beauty, wildness and a decisive impact on the race. The exploits of the Kings of the Mountains remain the most spectacular of the race, but thanks to a wide range of technical developments, reconnaissance of the route, high-altitude training camps and improvements in training and physical conditioning, the strongest riders are better able to cope with these tests. This truly is the era of titans.

OVERLEAF Viewed from above, a stage start is still a beautiful thing. The crowd, the riders and the mix of colours are fascinating. For fans, this is the best opportunity they get to see the riders close up, all waiting behind the start line for the race director to give them the signal that it is time for them to perform.

DOGGED EVANS TOO STRONG FOR SCHLECK

Cadel Evans's victory in the 98th Tour came about in a rather unheralded manner. He only made his debut in the race at the age of 28, perhaps one of the latest first appearances by an eventual winner in the event's history. He then took the title aged 34, making him one of the oldest Tour winners. At home on every terrain having already had an outstanding career as a mountain biker, Evans was also as dogged as his hero, Miguel Indurain. Like the Spaniard, he won the Tour at his seventh attempt. The Australian's victory came thanks in part to his previous career in mountain biking, as he avoided crashing in a race beset by rain, mass pile-ups, and even a car knocking some of the riders to the ground. Among those affected were canny old foxes Alexandre Vinokourov and Andreas Klöden, and young wolves Bradley Wiggins, Jurgen Van den Broeck and Janez Brajkovic.

Ahead of the riders as they departed from the Vendée were summit finishes at Luz-Ardiden, Plateau de Beille, Alpe d'Huez and, notably, the Galibier, which was set to feature twice in order to celebrate the centenary of its first appearance. The race came to life during the stage through the Auvergne to Saint-Flour. Five riders were in the break when a driver in the race convoy had a moment of madness and drove into two of them. Thankfully, both were able to continue after treatment. The remaining trio persisted with their escapade and the effervescent Thomas Voeckler took the yellow jersey. With

a lead of around four minutes, it was thought he could hold the lead into the Pyrenees. However, once there he raised French hopes by controlling attacks from Samuel Sánchez and the Schlecks.

He was forced to defend the lead every day, but he did so well enough that at the finish of stage 17 in Pinerolo he still had an advantage of 1-18 on Evans and a little more on the Schlecks. He finally came under sustained pressure when Andy Schleck launched an astounding long-range attack on the road to the Galibier. Having gone clear on the Izoard, he turned the race upside down, winning alone on the famous summit. Thanks to Evans's dogged chase behind Schleck, Voeckler held on to the lead by just 15 seconds. The next day, Voeckler finally ran out of juice on the torturous ramps of Alpe d'Huez, where he ceded the lead to Andy Schleck, who now led Evans by 57 seconds going into the following day's time trial in Grenoble.

Evans took full advantage of his time trialling prowess, soon gobbling up Schleck's advantage and establishing a comfortable lead of his own. Moments after Mark Cavendish had confirmed his first green jersey success with his fourth win of the race on the Champs-Élysées, Evans became Australia's first Tour champion. There was some consolation for the Schleck brothers, who claimed the second and third steps of the podium.

FINAL STANDINGS

1 Cadel Evans (AUS) BMC Racing 86:12:22
2 Andy Schleck (LUX) Leopard-Trek +1:34
3 Fränk Schleck (LUX) Leopard-Trek +2:30
4 Thomas Voeckler (FRA) Europcar +3:20
5 Samuel Sánchez (SPA) Euskaltel-Euskadi +4:55
6 Damiano Cunego (ITA) Lampre-ISD +6:05
7 Ivan Basso (ITA) Liquigas-Cannondale +7:23
8 Tom Danielson (USA) Garmin-Cervélo +8:15
9 Jean-Christophe Péraud (FRA) Ag2r-La Mondiale +10:11
10 Pierre Rolland (FRA) Europcar +10:43

AVERAGE SPEED (OF WINNER): 39.79 KM/H
TOTAL DISTANCE RACED: 3,430.5 KM
* Alberto Contador finished fifth but was disqualified following retroactive confirmation of his two-year ban in the wake of his positive test at the 2010 Tour

OPPOSITE TOP The 2011 race's jersey winners: Samuel Sánchez (polka-dot), Mark Cavendish (green), Cadel Evans (yellow) and Pierre Rolland (white).

OPPOSITE BOTTOM Having been left to do all the chasing behind Andy Schleck by Alberto Contador, Fränk Schleck and Thomas Voeckler, Cadel Evans grinds his way towards the summit of the Galibier. At the end of the stage he ended up 57 seconds down on Andy, a gap that he easily managed to overturn in the Grenoble time trial.

WIGGINS CLAIMS A YELLOW JERSEY FOR BRITAIN

The British have waited a long time to win the Tour, but when they finally did achieve that dream they did so in style as Bradley Wiggins topped the podium and his compatriot and team-mate Chris Froome finished second. Wiggins rode with great intelligence and adapted the skills he has gained on the track to the reality of a Tour route that featured 100 km of time trialling, an exercise in which he excels, just like Miguel Indurain, the champion whose pictures adorned his walls when he was a teenager.

His victory was not achieved by chance, as he worked hard to be a complete road rider after being an accomplished track rider. He put in work at altitude, lost weight to become a better climber (9 kg in total), followed a strict dietary regime, looked at the technical aspects of his riding in order to improve his rhythm and performance, using, for example, ovular chainrings, which have been overlooked by many riders but which, according to former champion rider and coach Cyrille Guimard, can produce a gain of up to 10%...

It took Wiggins seven years and six Tours to go from 123rd place to first, to step up from being the little-known pursuiter to the giant who dominated France. His steady progress would perhaps have been even faster if it hadn't been for his abandons in 2007 and 2011, when he was forced to quit on the seventh stage when already among the list of contenders for the title thanks to his performance in 2009

when he finished fourth in a Tour made for climbers like Alberto Contador and Andy Schleck. On this occasion those climbers weren't around, and it probably would not have made any difference if they had been. The large amount of time trialling suited Wiggins perfectly, but he had also worked hard to be a lot more competitive in the mountains. His motivation, humility, clear thinking and a strong team that was built around him did the rest.

All that remained was for Wiggins to negotiate the 3,500 km, 20 passes and 22 stages of the 99th Tour. Some suggested Froome was stronger than Wiggins, and that certainly seemed to be the case towards the end of the Pyrenean stages. But Wiggins was in the yellow jersey, he was the leader of Team Sky, and it was he who opened indisputable gaps in the two long time trials. The fact that Sky kept the race under such tight control concerned some journalists, who forgot that it's often been that way. The Tour is sprinkled with discrepancies of this kind. Nevertheless, Bradley won his two stages – and how many winners have not managed that from Walkowiak to Aimar? – and he wore and defended the yellow jersey very capably for 14 days.

And did you notice that he took the yellow jersey on the seventh stage? The previous year he had to abandon on that very same stage. Coincidence maybe, but perhaps fate had decided Britain's time had finally come.

FINAL STANDINGS

1 Bradley Wiggins (GBR) Team Sky 87:34:47
2 Chris Froome (GBR) Team Sky +3:21
3 Vincenzo Nibali (ITA) Liquigas-Cannondale +6:19
4 Jurgen Van Den Broeck (BEL) Lotto-Belisol +10:15
5 Tejay Van Garderen (USA) BMC Racing +11:04
6 Haimar Zubeldia (SPA) RadioShack-Nissan +15:41
7 Cadel Evans (AUS) BMC Racing +15:49
8 Pierre Rolland (FRA) Europcar +16:26
9 Janez Brajkovic (SLO) Astana +16:33
10 Thibaut Pinot (FRA) FDJ-BigMat +17:17

AVERAGE SPEED (OF WINNER): 34.900 KM/H
TOTAL DISTANCE RACED: 3,488 KM

OPPOSITE With the Arc de Triomphe providing an entirely fitting backdrop, Bradley Wiggins sweeps round a corner on the Champs-Élysées with Sky team-mate Mark Cavendish on his wheel. Wiggins is just minutes away from becoming Britain's first Tour champion.

100TH TOUR MIXES HISTORY AND INNOVATION

There is always a huge amount of conjecture prior to the launch of any year's Tour de France route. However, the rumour mill went into overdrive as everyone awaited race director Christian Prudhomme's announcement of the final details for the 100th edition of La Grande Boucle, which finally came in mid-October last year. By then, Tour organizers ASO had already revealed that the race would make its first-ever visit to Corsica, spending the opening three days on that beautifully rugged Mediterranean island. But what would follow? Rumour had it that the Tour wouldn't finish in Paris, that it would feature summit finishes on several of the race's most celebrated peaks, that it would include a stop in every city that hosted a stage of the inaugural race.

Ultimately, Prudhomme revealed that there was indeed something to the rumours, but rather than opting for a route that is outrageously over the top, he and his organizing team have remained true to the Tour's principles by presenting a balanced course with one or two very unexpected twists.

Although Corsica has not previously featured on the Tour route, the island has a long-standing connection with professional racing, most recently thanks to its hosting in late March of the Criterium International, a two-day race also owned and run by ASO. The three Corsican stages on the Tour offer something for every type of rider. The sprinters should dominate on the first into Bastia. It would be no surprise to see the top climbers on the attack during the following stage across the mountainous centre of the island to Ajaccio. Stage three is hilly and presents breakaway specialists with an opportunity for glory.

The Tour then heads to the French mainland for a short team time trial in Nice. The favourites will be aiming to limit their time losses as much as possible, although the gaps shouldn't be all that significant. The main contenders will have to remain watchful on three nervy stages across the Midi that should suit the sprinters and baroudeurs, breakaway specialists who know they must commit fully when they attack if they are to have any hope of holding off the fast-moving peloton into the finish.

The race reaches the Pyrenees on its second weekend. The summit finish at Ax 3 Domaines is sure to bring some significant changes to the overall standings, especially as it is preceded by the tough ascent of the Col de Pailhères. The shake-up in the battle for the yellow jersey should continue the next day as the riders tackle five passes on the road to Bagnères-de-Bigorre. Everyone will be glad that the first rest day follows that test.

Having transferred a long way north to Saint-Nazaire, the race action recommences with a stage in France's cycling heartland of Brittany. The finish in Saint-Malo should smile on the sprinters. This leads into the first of two individual time trials, covering 33 km between Avranches and Mont Saint-Michel, the spectacular abbey that seems to float on the sea when the tide sweeps in around it. Two more stages follow that will pit sprinters against breakaway specialists.

The Tour's third weekend begins with an unpredictable stage into Lyon, where two short, steep climbs could catch out some of the contenders. Similarly, Sunday's stage may mean any riders having an off day are 'going to pay cash'. It finishes atop Mont Ventoux, 'The Bald Mountain', where the wind and heat can have a huge impact on the desolate upper slopes.

Following the second rest day, the most crucial section of the route commences with a stage through the foothills of the Alps to Gap. This will get the legs nicely warmed up for the second individual time trial. Unlike the first, which is flat and will suit the time trial specialists, this is a hilly test where the climbers could thrive. The mountain goats are sure to dominate stage 18, which for the first time in race history features no less than two ascents of Alpe d'Huez thanks to a newly improved road over the Col de Sarenne.

Another testing mountain stage over five passes follows to Le Grand Bornand, which leads into the first-ever summit finish at the Semnoz resort high above Annecy, where the yellow jersey could change hands right before the final run into Paris. There's innovation too on the final day: the riders will start in the grounds of Louis XIV's palace at Versailles and finish on the Champs-Élysées as night falls. This will show off 'The City of Lights' in stunning fashion, particularly as the finishing circuit takes the riders around the Arc de Triomphe for the first time in the Tour's history.

Mont-Saint-Michel
Avranches **11**
Saint-Malo
Fougères **12**
Versailles
21
PARIS
Champs-Élysées

10
Saint-Gildas-des-Bois
13 Tours
Saint-Nazaire
Loire-Atlantique
Saint-Amand-Montrond
14
Saint-Pourçain-sur-Sioule
Semnoz
Le Grand-Bornand
Lyon
20
Annecy
Givors **15**
Alpe-d'Huez
19
Bourg-
d'Oisans
Chorges
Vaison-la-Romaine
18
17 Embrun
Albi
16
Gap
Vaucluse
Nice
Vauluse
Mont Ventoux
4
8
Aix-en-Provence
5
Castres
7
Cagnes-sur-Mer
Saint-Girons
6
Montpellier
Bagnères-de-Bigorre
9
Marseille
Ax 3 Domaines

KEY
● Stage start
● Stage finish
○ Rest day

Calvi
2 Bastia
3
Ajaccio
1
Porto-Vecchio

STAGE	START AND FINISH	DATE	DISTANCE	STAGE	START AND FINISH	DATE	DISTANCE
1	Porto-Vecchio > Bastia	Saturday, June 29th	212 km	12	Fougères > Tours	Thursday, July 11th	218 km
2	Bastia > Ajaccio	Sunday, June 30th	154 km	13	Tours > Saint-Amand-Montrond	Friday, July 12th	173 km
3	Ajaccio > Calvi	Monday, July 1st	145 km	14	Saint-Pourçain-sur-Sioule > Lyon	Saturday, July 13th	191 km
4	Nice > Nice (Team time-trial)	Tuesday, July 2nd	25 km	15	Givors > Mont Ventoux	Sunday, July 14th	242 km
5	Cagnes-sur-Mer > Marseille	Wednesday, July 3rd	219 km	-	Vaucluse	Monday, July 15th	
6	Aix-en-Provence > Montpellier	Thursday, July 4th	176 km	16	Vaison-la-Romaine > Gap	Tuesday, July 16th	168 km
7	Montpellier > Albi	Friday, July 5th	205 km	17	Embrun > Chorges (Individual time-trial)	Wednesday, July 17th	32 km
8	Castres > Ax 3 Domaines	Saturday, July 6th	194 km	18	Gap > Alpe-d'Huez	Thursday, July 18th	168 km
9	Saint-Girons > Bagnères-de-Bigorre	Sunday, July 7th	165 km	19	Bourg-d'Oisans > Le Grand-Bornand	Friday, July 19th	204 km
-	Saint-Nazaire - Loire-Atlantique (Rest day)	Monday, July 8th		20	Annecy > Annecy – Semnoz	Saturday, July 20th	125 km
10	Saint-Gildas-des-Bois > Saint-Malo	Tuesday, July 9th	193 km	21	Versailles > Paris Champs-Élysées	Sunday, July 21st	118 km
11	Avranches > Mont-Saint-Michel (Individual time-trial)	Wednesday, July 10th	33 km				

319

TOUR CLASSIFICATIONS

Tour	Year		Overall		Points		Mountains		Young Rider
1	1903		Maurice Garin						
2	1904		Henri Cornet						
3	1905		Louis Trousselier						
4	1906		René Pottier						
5	1907		Lucien Petit-Breton						
6	1908		Lucien Petit-Breton						
7	1909		François Faber						
8	1910		Octave Lapize						
9	1911		Gustave Garrigou						
10	1912		Odile Defraye						
11	1913		Philippe Thys						
12	1914		Philippe Thys						
13	1919		Firmin Lambot						
14	1920		Philippe Thys						
15	1921		Léon Scieur						
16	1922		Firmin Lambot						
17	1923		Henri Pélissier						
18	1924		Ottavio Bottecchia						
19	1925		Ottavio Bottecchia						
20	1926		Lucien Buysse						
21	1927		Nicolas Frantz						
22	1928		Nicolas Frantz						
23	1929		Maurice Dewaele						
24	1930		André Leducq						
25	1931		Antonin Magne						
26	1932		André Leducq						
27	1933		Georges Speicher					Vicente Trueba		
28	1934		Antonin Magne					René Vietto		
29	1935		Romain Maes					Félicien Vervaecke		
30	1936		Sylvère Maes					Julián Berrendero		
31	1937		Roger Lapébie					Félicien Vervaecke		
32	1938		Gino Bartali					Gino Bartali		
33	1939		Sylvère Maes					Sylvère Maes		

Tour	Year		Overall		Points		Mountains		Young Rider
34	1947		Jean Robic				Pierre Brambilla		
35	1948		Gino Bartali				Gino Bartali		
36	1949		Fausto Coppi				Fausto Coppi		
37	1950		Ferdinand Kübler				Louison Bobet		
38	1951		Hugo Koblet				Raphaël Geminiani		
39	1952		Fausto Coppi				Fausto Coppi		
40	1953		Louison Bobet		Fritz Schär		Jesús Loroño		
41	1954		Louison Bobet		Ferdinand Kübler		Federico Bahamontes		
42	1955		Louison Bobet		Stan Ockers		Charly Gaul		
43	1956		Roger Walkowiak		Stan Ockers		Charly Gaul		
44	1957		Jacques Anquetil		Jean Forestier		Gastone Nencini		
45	1958		Charly Gaul		Jean Graczyk		Federico Bahamontes		
46	1959		Federico Bahamontes		André Darrigade		Federico Bahamontes		
47	1960		Gastone Nencini		Jean Graczyk		Imerio Massignan		
48	1961		Jacques Anquetil		André Darrigade		Imerio Massignan		
49	1962		Jacques Anquetil		Rudi Altig		Federico Bahamontes		
50	1963		Jacques Anquetil		Rik Van Looy		Federico Bahamontes		
51	1964		Jacques Anquetil		Jan Janssen		Federico Bahamontes		
52	1965		Felice Gimondi		Jan Janssen		Julio Jiménez		
53	1966		Lucien Aimar		Willy Planckaert		Julio Jiménez		
54	1967		Roger Pingeon		Jan Janssen		Julio Jiménez		
55	1968		Jan Janssen		Franco Bitossi		Aurelio González Puente		
56	1969		Eddy Merckx		Eddy Merckx		Eddy Merckx		
57	1970		Eddy Merckx		Walter Godefroot		Eddy Merckx		
58	1971		Eddy Merckx		Eddy Merckx		Lucien Van Impe		
59	1972		Eddy Merckx		Eddy Merckx		Lucien Van Impe		
60	1973		Luis Ocaña		Herman Van Springel		Pedro Torres		
61	1974		Eddy Merckx		Patrick Sercu		Domingo Perurena		
62	1975		Bernard Thévenet		Rik Van Linden		Lucien Van Impe		Francesco Moser
63	1976		Lucien Van Impe		Freddy Maertens		Giancarlo Bellini		Enrique Martínez Heredia
64	1977		Bernard Thévenet		Jacques Esclassan		Lucien Van Impe		Dietrich Thurau
65	1978		Bernard Hinault		Freddy Maertens		Mariano Martínez		Henk Lubberding
66	1979		Bernard Hinault		Bernard Hinault		Giovanni Battaglin		Jean-René Bernaudeau

Tour	Year		Overall		Points		Mountains		Young Rider
67	1980		Joop Zoetemelk		Rudy Pevenage		Raymond Martin		Johan van der Velde
68	1981		Bernard Hinault		Freddy Maertens		Lucien Van Impe		Peter Winnen
69	1982		Bernard Hinault		Sean Kelly		Bernard Vallet		Phil Anderson
70	1983		Laurent Fignon		Sean Kelly		Lucien Van Impe		Laurent Fignon
71	1984		Laurent Fignon		Frank Hoste		Robert Millar		Greg LeMond
72	1985		Bernard Hinault		Sean Kelly		Luis Herrera		Fabio Parra
73	1986		Greg LeMond		Eric Vanderaerden		Bernard Hinault		Andrew Hampsten
74	1987		Stephen Roche		Jean-Paul van Poppel		Luis Herrera		Raúl Alcalá
75	1988		Pedro Delgado		Eddy Planckaert		Steven Rooks		Erik Breukink
76	1989		Greg LeMond		Sean Kelly		Gert-Jan Theunisse		Fabrice Philipot
77	1990		Greg LeMond		Olaf Ludwig		Thierry Claveyrolat		Gilles Delion
78	1991		Miguel Indurain		Djamolidine Abdoujaparov		Claudio Chiappucci		Álvaro Mejía Castrillón
79	1992		Miguel Indurain		Laurent Jalabert		Claudio Chiappucci		Eddy Bouwmans
80	1993		Miguel Indurain		Djamolidine Abdoujaparov		Tony Rominger		Antonio Martín
81	1994		Miguel Indurain		Djamolidine Abdoujaparov		Richard Virenque		Marco Pantani
82	1995		Miguel Indurain		Laurent Jalabert		Richard Virenque		Marco Pantani
83	1996		Bjarne Riis		Erik Zabel		Richard Virenque		Jan Ullrich
84	1997		Jan Ullrich		Erik Zabel		Richard Virenque		Jan Ullrich
85	1998		Marco Pantani		Erik Zabel		Christophe Rinero		Jan Ullrich
86	1999		No winner		Erik Zabel		Richard Virenque		Benoît Salmon
87	2000		No winner		Erik Zabel		Santiago Botero		Francisco Mancebo
88	2001		No winner		Erik Zabel		Laurent Jalabert		Óscar Sevilla
89	2002		No winner		Robbie McEwen		Laurent Jalabert		Ivan Basso
90	2003		No winner		Baden Cooke		Richard Virenque		Denis Menchov
91	2004		No winner		Robbie McEwen		Richard Virenque		Vladimir Karpets
92	2005		No winner		Thor Hushovd		Michael Rasmussen		Yaroslav Popovych
93	2006		Óscar Pereiro		Robbie McEwen		Michael Rasmussen		Damiano Cunego
94	2007		Alberto Contador		Tom Boonen		Mauricio Soler		Alberto Contador
95	2008		Carlos Sastre		Óscar Freire		Vacated		Andy Schleck
96	2009		Alberto Contador		Thor Hushovd		Franco Pellizotti		Andy Schleck
97	2010		Andy Schleck		Alessandro Petacchi		Anthony Charteau		Andy Schleck
98	2011		Cadel Evans		Mark Cavendish		Samuel Sánchez		Pierre Rolland
99	2012		Bradley Wiggins		Peter Sagan		Thomas Voeckler		Tejay van Garderen

BY RIDERS

Rank	Rider	Country		Titles	Year
1	Jacques Anquetil		FRA	5	1957, 1961, 1962, 1963, 1964
	Eddy Merckx		BEL	5	1969, 1970, 1971, 1972, 1974
	Bernard Hinault		FRA	5	1978, 1979, 1981, 1982, 1985
	Miguel Indurain		ESP	5	1991, 1992, 1993, 1994, 1995
5	Louison Bobet		FRA	3	1953, 1954, 1955
	Greg LeMond		USA	3	1986, 1989, 1990
	Philippe Thys		BEL	3	1913, 1914, 1920
8	Gino Bartali		ITA	2	1938, 1948
	Ottavio Bottecchia		ITA	2	1924, 1925
	Alberto Contador		ESP	2	2007, 2009
	Fausto Coppi		ITA	2	1949, 1952
	Laurent Fignon		FRA	2	1983, 1984
	Nicolas Frantz		LUX	2	1927, 1928
	Firmin Lambot		BEL	2	1919, 1922
	André Leducq		FRA	2	1930, 1932
	Sylvère Maes		BEL	2	1936, 1939
	Antonin Magne		FRA	2	1931, 1934
	Lucien Petit-Breton		FRA	2	1907, 1908
	Bernard Thévenet		FRA	2	1975, 1977

BY COUNTRY – OVERALL

Rank	Country		Wins
1		France	36
2		Belgium	18
3		Spain	12
4		Italy	9
5		Luxembourg	5
6		United States	3
7		Netherlands	2
		Switzerland	2
9		Australia	1
		Denmark	1
		Great Britain	1
		Germany	1
		Ireland	1

BY COUNTRY – POINTS

Rank	Country		Wins
1		Belgium	19
2		France	9
3		Germany	8
4		Australia	4
		Ireland	4
		Netherlands	4
7		Uzbekistan	3
8		Switzerland	2
		Norway	2
		Italy	2
11		Spain	1
		Great Britain	1
		Slovakia	1

BY COUNTRY – KING OF THE MOUNTAINS

Rank	Country		Wins
1		France	21
2		Spain	17
3		Italy	12
4		Belgium	11
5		Colombia	4
6		Denmark	2
		Luxembourg	2
		Netherlands	2
9		Switzerland	1
		Great Britain	1

BY COUNTRY – YOUNG RIDER

Rank	Country		Wins
1		France	6
2		Italy	5
		Netherlands	5
		Spain	5
5		Germany	4
6		Luxembourg	3
		United States	3
8		Colombia	2
		Russia	2
10		Australia	1
		Mexico	1
		Ukraine	1

TOUR RECORDS

MULTIPLE WINNERS

Five victories

- Jacques ANQUETIL (1957, 1961–1964)
- Eddy MERCKX (1969–1972, 1974)
- Bernard HINAULT (1978, 1979, 1981, 1982, 1985)
- Miguel INDURAIN (1991–1995)

Three victories

- Philippe THYS (1913, 1914, 1920)
- Louison BOBET (1953–1955)
- Greg LEMOND (1986, 1989, 1990)

Two victories

- Lucien PETIT-BRETON (1907, 1908)
- Firmin LAMBOT (1919, 1922)
- Ottavio BOTTECCHIA (1924, 1925)
- Nicolas FRANTZ (1927, 1928)
- André LEDUCQ (1930, 1932)
- Antonin MAGNE (1931, 1934)
- Sylvère MAES (1936, 1939)
- Gino BARTALI (1938, 1948)
- Fausto COPPI (1949, 1952)
- Bernard THÉVENET (1975, 1977)
- Laurent FIGNON (1983, 1984)
- Alberto CONTADOR (2007, 2009)

SMALLEST GAPS BETWEEN THE WINNER AND RUNNER-UP (SINCE 1947)

Eight seconds (1989) between Greg LEMOND (USA) and Laurent FIGNON (Fra)

23 seconds (2007) between Alberto CONTADOR (Spa) and Cadel EVANS (Aus)

32 seconds (2006) between Oscar PEREIRO (Spa) and Andreas KLÖDEN (Ger)

38 seconds (1968) between Jan JANSSEN (Ned) and Herman VAN SPRINGEL (Bel)

40 seconds (1987) between Stephen ROCHE (Irl) and Pedro DELGADO (Spa)

NB: The eight-second gap which separated LeMond and Fignon in 1989 is the smallest winning margin of all time.

LARGEST GAPS BETWEEN WINNER AND RUNNER-UP (SINCE 1947)

28–17 (1952) between Fausto COPPI (Ita) and Constant OCKERS (Bel)

26–16 (1948) between Gino BARTALI (Ita) and Albéric SCHOTTE (Bel)

22–00 (1951) between Hugo KOBLET (Swi) and Raphaël GEMINIANI (Fra)

17–54 (1969) between Eddy MERCKX (Bel) and Roger PINGEON (Fra)

15–51 (1973) between Luis OCAÑA (Spa) and Bernard THÉVENET (Fra)

NB: The biggest winning margin of all time was 2:59:21 (1903) between Maurice GARIN (Fra) and Lucien POTHIER (Fra)

NUMBER OF WEARERS OF THE YELLOW JERSEY BY NATION

- France: 83
- Belgium: 54
- Italy: 25
- Netherlands: 17
- Germany: 12
- Spain: 12
- Switzerland and Luxembourg: 9
- Denmark: 6
- Australia: 5
- Great Britain: 4
- United States and Ireland: 3
- Canada: 2
- Austria, Poland, Portugal, Russia, Estonia, Colombia, Norway and Ukraine: 1

NUMBER OF DAYS IN YELLOW

■■ Eddy MERCKX (BEL): 111

■■ Bernard HINAULT (FRA): 79

■ Miguel INDURAIN (SPA): 60

■■ Jacques ANQUETIL (FRA): 52

LARGEST NUMBER OF RIDERS TO WEAR THE YELLOW JERSEY DURING ONE TOUR

Eight

In 1958 (Darrigade, Hoevenaars, Van Est, Bauvin, Voorting, Geminiani, Favero, Gaul)

In 1987 (Nijdam, Piasecki, Maechler, Mottet, Gayant, Bernard, Roche, Delgado)

SMALLEST NUMBER OF RIDERS TO WEAR THE YELLOW JERSEY DURING ONE TOUR

One

1924 (Bottecchia)

1928 (Frantz)

1935 (R. Maes)

Two

1920 (Mottiat and Thys)

1921 (Mottiat and Scieur)

1925 (Benoît and Bottecchia)

1934 (Speicher and Magne)

1961 (Darrigade and Anquetil)

1970 (Zilioli and Merckx)

1972 (Guimard and Merckx)

1977 (Thurau and Thévenet)

MOST GREEN JERSEY VICTORIES

Six

▬ Erik ZABEL (Ger) (1996–2001)

Four

■■ Sean KELLY (Irl) (1982, 1983, 1985, 1989)

Three

▬ Jan JANSSEN (Ned) (1964, 1965, 1967)

■■ Eddy MERCKX (Bel) (1969, 1971, 1972)

■■ Freddy MAERTENS (Ned) (1976, 1978, 1981)

▬ Djamolidine ABDOUJAPAROV (Uzb) (1991, 1993, 1994)

▨ Robbie McEWEN (Aus) (2002, 2004, 2006)

GREEN JERSEY WINS BY NATION

■■ Belgium: 19

■■ France: 9

▬ Germany: 7

▬ Netherlands, ■■ Ireland and ▨ Australia: 4

▬ Uzbekistan: 3

✚ Switzerland: 2

■■ Italy, ■ Spain, ▬ Norway and ▨ Great Britain: 1

MOST POLKA-DOT JERSEY WINS

Seven

■■ Richard VIRENQUE (Fra) (1994–1997, 1999, 2003, 2004)

Six

■ Federico BAHAMONTES (Spa) (1954, 1958, 1959, 1962–1964)

■■ Lucien VAN IMPE (Bel) (1971, 1972, 1975, 1977, 1981, 1983)

POLKA-DOT JERSEY WINS BY NATION

■■ France: 21

■ Spain: 16

■■ Italy: 12

■■ Belgium: 11

▬ Colombia: 4

▬ Luxembourg, ▬ Netherlands and ▬ Denmark: 2

▨ Great Britain and ✚ Switzerland: 1

MOST WHITE JERSEY VICTORIES

Three

Jan ULLRICH (Ger) (1996–1998)

Andy SCHLECK (Lux) (2008–10)

Two

Marco PANTANI (Ita) (1994, 1995)

MOST WHITE JERSEY WINS BY NATION

Six

France

Five

Netherlands, Spain and Italy

Four

Germany

Three

Luxembourg

Two

Colombia, United States and Russia

One

Australia, Mexico and Ukraine

HIGHEST AVERAGE SPEED FOR TOUR VICTORIES

40.781kph: Oscar PEREIRO (Spa) in 2006

40.940 km/h: Lance ARMSTRONG (USA) in 2003 (disqualified)

41.654 km/h: Lance ARMSTRONG (USA) in 2005 (disqualified)

FASTEST ROAD STAGES

50.355 km/h: Laval–Blois (191 km) in 1999 by Mario CIPOLLINI (Ita)

49.938 km/h: Bordeaux–Saint Maixent l'Ecole (203.5 km) in 2003 by Pablo LASTRAS (Spa)

49.417 km/h: Evreux–Amiens (158 km) in 1993 by Johan BRUYNEEL (Bel)

FASTEST TIME TRIALS (LONGER THAN 20 KM)

54.545 km/h: Versailles–Paris (24.5 km) in 1989 by Greg LEMOND (USA)

54.361 km/h: Pornic–Nantes (49 km) in 2003 by David MILLAR (GBR)

53.986 km/h: Fribourg en Brisgau–Mulhouse (58.5 km) in 2000 by Lance ARMSTRONG (USA) (disqualified)

NB: In the 2005 Tour, David ZABRISKIE (USA) won the opening Fromentine–Noirmoutier en l'Ile time trial at an average of 54.676 km/h but over a distance of 19 km

FASTEST TEAM TIME TRIALS

57.324 km/h: Tours–Blois (67.5 km) in 2005 by Discovery Channel

54.930 km/h: Mayenne–Alençon (67 km) in 1995 by Gewiss

54.610 km/h: Berlin–Berlin (40 km) in 1987 by Carrera

FASTEST PROLOGUES

55.152 km/h: Lille–Lille (7.2 km) in 1994 by Chris BOARDMAN (GBR)

54.193 km/h: Dublin–Dublin (5.6 km) in 1998 by Chris BOARDMAN (GBR)

53.660 km/h: London–London (7.9 km) in 2007 by Fabian CANCELLARA (Swi)

BIGGEST GAPS BY A STAGE-WINNER (SINCE 1947)

22–50: José Luis VIEJO (Spa) in 1976 (Montgenèvre–Manosque) after breakaway of 160 km

21–48: Pierino BAFFI (Ita) in 1957 (Pau–Bordeaux) after breakaway of 130 km

20–31: Daan DE GROOT (Ned) in 1955 (Millau–Albi) after breakaway of 170 km

NB: In 2001, on the Colmar–Pontarlier stage, a group of breakaway riders finished 35–54 ahead of the peloton.

LONGEST LONE BREAKAWAYS (SINCE 1947)

253 km: Albert BOURLON (Fra) in 1947 (Carcassonne–Luchon). Winning margin: 16–30

234 km: Thierry MARIE (Fra) in 1991 (Arras–Le Havre). Winning margin: 1–54

223 km: José PÉREZ-FRANCÉS (Spa) in 1965 (Ax-les-Thermes–Barcelona). Winning margin: 4–23

MOST STAGE VICTORIES IN ONE TOUR

Eight

Charles PÉLISSIER (Fra) (1930)

Eddy MERCKX (Bel) (1970, 1974)

Freddy MAERTENS (Bel) (1976)

OLDEST TOUR WINNERS

36

🏴🏴 Firmin LAMBCT (Bel) in 1922

34

🏴🏴 Henri PÉLISSIER (Fra) in 1923

🏴🏴 Gino BARTALI (Ita) in 1948

🏴 Cadel EVANS (Aus) in 2011

33

🏴🏴 Firmin LAMBOT (Bel) in 1919

🏴🏴 Léon SCIEUR (Bel) in 1921

🏴🏴 Lucien BUYSSE (Bel) in 1926

🏴 Joop ZOETEMELK (Ned) in 1980

NB: Age at Tour finish.

MOST STAGE VICTORIES (INCLUDING TIME TRIALS)

34

🏴🏴 Eddy MERCKX (Bel)

28

🏴🏴 Bernard HINAULT (Fra)

25

🏴🏴 André LEDUCQ (Fra)

23

🏴 Mark CAVENDISH (GBR)

22

🏴🏴 André DARRIGADE (Fra)

20

🏴 Nicolas FRANTZ (Lux)

19

🏴 François FABER (Lux)

17

🏴🏴 Jean ALAVOINE (Fra)

16

🏴🏴 Charles PÉLISSIER (Fra)

🏴🏴 Jacques ANQUETIL (Fra)

🏴🏴 René LE GRÈVES (Fra)

MOST TIME TRIAL VICTORIES

20

🏴🏴 Bernard HINAULT (Fra), including five prologues

16

🏴🏴 Eddy MERCKX (Bel), including three prologues

11

🏴🏴 Jacques ANQUETIL (Fra)

YOUNGEST TOUR WINNERS

19

🏴🏴 Henri CORNET (Fra) in 1904

21

🏴🏴 Romain MAES (Bel) in 1935

22

🏴 François FABER (Lux) in 1909

🏴🏴 Octave LAPIZE (Fra) in 1910

🏴🏴 Felice GIMONDI (Ita) in 1965

🏴🏴 Laurent FIGNON (Fra) in 1983

NB: Age at Tour finish.

LONGEST GAP BETWEEN TOUR WINS

10 years

🏴🏴 Gino BARTALI (Ita) in 1938 and 1948

MOST TOUR APPEARANCES (SINCE 1947)

17

🇺🇸 George HINCAPIE (USA) (one abandon)

16

🏴 Joop ZOETEMELK (Ned) (no abandons)

🏴 Stuart O'GRADY (Aus) (two abandons)

15

🏴🏴 Lucien VAN IMPE (Bel) (no abandons)

🏴🏴 Guy NULENS (Bel) (two abandons)

🏴 Viatcheslav EKIMOV (Rus) (no abandons)

🏴🏴 Christophe MOREAU (Fra) (three abandons, one exclusion)

🏴 Jens VOIGT (Ger) (three abandons)

14

🏴🏴 André DARRIGADE (Fra) (one abandon)

🏴🏴 Raymond POULIDOR (Fra) (two abandons)

🏴🏴 Sean KELLY (Irl) (two abandons)

13

🏴 Joaquim AGOSTINHO (Por) (one abandon)

🏴 Phil ANDERSON (Aus) (no abandons)

🏴 Gerrie KNETEMANN (Net) (two abandons)

🏴 Henk LUBBERDING (Net) (two abandons)

🏴🏴 Jean DOTTO (Fra) (three abandons)

🏴🏴 Jean-Pierre GENET (Fra) (three abandons)

🏴🏴 François MAHE (Fra) (four abandons)

🏴🏴 Gilbert DUCLOS-LASSALLE (Fra) (three abandons, one elimination)

🏴🏴 Marc WAUTERS (Bel) (four abandons, one elimination)

🏴🏴 Didier ROUS (Fra) (five abandons, one exclusion)

THE ROLL OF HONOUR

1903 *Dist: 2,428 km, Ave Speed: 25.678 km/h*
1. Maurice GARIN (FRA, age 32)
2. Lucien POTHIER (FRA)
3. Fernand AUGEREAU (FRA)

1904 *Dist: 2,429 km, Ave Speed: 26.081 km/h*
1. Henri CORNET (FRA, 19)
2. Jean-Baptiste DORTIGNACQ (FRA)
3. Aloïs CATTEAU (BEL)

1905 *Dist: 2,994 km, Ave Speed: 27.107 km/h*
1. Louis TROUSSELIER (FRA, 24)
2. Hippolyte AUCOUTURIER (FRA)
3. Jean-Baptiste DORTIGNACQ (FRA)

1906 *Dist: 4,637 km, Ave Speed: 24.463 km/h*
1. René POTTIER (FRA, 27)
2. Georges PASSERIEU (FRA)
3. Louis TROUSSELIER (FRA)

1907 *Dist: 4,488 km, Ave Speed: 28.47 km/h*
1. Lucien PETIT-BRETON (FRA, 25)
2. Gustave GARRIGOU (FRA)
3. Émile GEORGET (FRA)

1908 *Dist: 4,488 km, Ave Speed: 28.74 km/h*
1. Lucien PETIT-BRETON (FRA, 26)
2. François FABER (LUX)
3. Georges PASSERIEU (FRA)

1909 *Dist: 4,488 km, Ave Speed: 28.658 km/h*
1. François FABER (LUX, 22)
2. Gustave GARRIGOU (FRA)
3. Jean ALAVOINE (FRA)

1910 *Dist: 4,737 km, Ave Speed: 26.68 km/h*
1. Octave LAPIZE (FRA, 22)
2. François FABER (LUX)
3. Gustave GARRIGOU (FRA)

1911 *Dist: 5,344 km, Ave Speed: 27.332 km/h*
1. Gustave GARRIGOU (FRA, 27)
2. Paul DUBOC (FRA)
3. Émile GEORGET (FRA)

1912 *Dist: 5,319 km, Ave Speed: 27.763 km/h*
1. Odile DEFRAYE (BEL, 24)
2. Eugène CHRISTOPHE (FRA)
3. Gustave GARRIGOU (FRA)

1913 *Dist: 5,388 km, Ave Speed: 27.22 km/h*
1. Philippe THYS (BEL, 23)
2. Gustave GARRIGOU (FRA)
3. Marcel BUYSSE (BEL)

1914 *Dist: 5,405 km, Ave Speed: 26.96 km/h*
1. Philippe THYS (BEL, 24)
2. Henri PÉLISSIER (FRA)
3. Jean ALAVOINE (FRA)

1919 *Dist: 5,560 km, Ave Speed: 24.056 km/h*
1. Firmin LAMBOT (BEL, 33)
2. Jean ALAVOINE (FRA)
3. Eugène CHRISTOPHE (FRA)

1920 *Dist: 5,503 km, Ave Speed: 24.072 km/h*
1. Philippe THYS (BEL, 30)
2. Hector HEUSGHEM (BEL)
3. Firmin LAMBOT (BEL)

1921 *Dist: 5,484 km, Ave Speed: 24.72 km/h*
1. Léon SCIEUR (BEL, 33)
2. Hector HEUSGHEM (BEL)
3. Honoré BARTHÉLÉMY (FRA)

1922 *Dist: 5,375 km, Ave Speed: 24.196 km/h*
1. Firmin LAMBOT (BEL, 36)
2. Jean ALAVOINE (FRA)
3. Félix SELLIER (BEL)

1923 *Dist: 5,386 km, Ave Speed: 24.233 km/h*
1. Henri PELISSIER (FRA, 34)
2. Ottavio BOTTECCHIA (ITA)
3. Romain BELLENGER (FRA)

1924 *Dist: 5,425 km, Ave Speed: 23.971 km/h*
1. Ottavio BOTTECCHIA (ITA, 30)
2. Nicolas FRANTZ (LUX)
3. Lucien BUYSSE (BEL)

1925 *Dist: 5,430 km, Ave Speed: 24.775 km/h*
1. Ottavio BOTTECCHIA (ITA, 31)
2. Lucien BUYSSE (BEL)
3. Bartolomeo AIMO (ITA)

1926 *Dist: 5,745 km, Ave Speed: 24.063 km/h*
1. Lucien BUYSSE (BEL, 33)
2. Nicolas FRANTZ (LUX)
3. Bartolomeo AIMO (ITA)

1927 *Dist: 5,340 km, Ave Speed: 26.931 km/h*
1. Nicolas FRANTZ (LUX, 28)
2. Maurice DEWAELE (BEL)
3. Julien VERVAECKE (BEL)

1928 *Dist: 5,476 km, Ave Speed: 28.4 km/h*
1. Nicolas FRANTZ (LUX, 29)
2. André LEDUCQ (FRA)
3. Maurice DEWAELE (BEL)

1929 *Dist: 5,256 km, Ave Speed: 28.159 km/h*
1. Maurice DEWAELE (BEL, 33)
2. Giuseppe PANCERA (ITA)
3. Joseph DEMUYSERE (BEL)

1930 *Dist: 4,818 km, Ave Speed: 27.978 km/h*
1. André LEDUCQ (FRA, 26)
2. Learco GUERRA (ITA)
3. Antonin MAGNE (FRA)

1931 *Dist: 5,095 km, Ave Speed: 28.758 km/h*
1. Antonin MAGNE (FRA, 27)
2. Joseph DEMUYSERE (BEL)
3. Antonio PESENTI (ITA)

1932 *Dist: 4,520 km, Ave Speed: 29.313 km/h*
1. André LEDUCQ (FRA, 28)
2. Kurt STÖEPEL (GER)
3. Francesco CAMUSSO (ITA)

1933 *Dist: 4,395 km, Ave Speed: 29.724 km/h*
1. Georges SPEICHER (FRA, 26)
2. Learco GUERRA (ITA)
3. Giuseppe MARTANO (ITA)

1934 *Dist: 4,363 km, Ave Speed: 29.633 km/h*
1. Antonin MAGNE (FRA, 30)
2. Giuseppe MARTANO (ITA)
3. Roger LAPÉBIE (FRA)

1935 *Dist: 4,338 km, Ave Speed: 30.65 km/h*
1. Romain MAES (BEL, 22)
2. Ambrogio MORELLI (ITA)
3. Félicien VERVAECKE (BEL)

1936 *Dist: 4,442 km, Ave Speed: 31.108 km/h*
1. Sylvère MAES (BEL, 27)
2. Antonin MAGNE (FRA)
3. Félicien VERVAECKE (BEL)

1937 *Dist: 4,415 km, Ave Speed: 31.768 km/h*
1. Roger LAPÉBIE (FRA, 26)
2. Mario VICINI (ITA)
3. Léo AMBERG (SWI)

1938 *Dist: 4,694 km, Ave Speed: 31.612 km/h*
1. Gino BARTALI (ITA, 24)
2. Félicien VERVAECKE (BEL)
3. Victor COSSON (FRA)

1939 *Dist: 4,224 km, Ave Speed: 31.986 km/h*
1. Sylvère MAES (BEL, 30)
2. René VIETTO (FRA)
3. Lucien VLAEMINCK (BEL)

1947 *Dist: 4,640 km, Ave Speed: 31.311 km/h*
1. Jean ROBIC (FRA, 26)
2. Édouard FACHLEITNER (FRA)
3. Pierre BRAMBILLA (ITA)

1948 *Dist: 4,922 km, Ave Speed: 33.442 km/h*
1. Gino BARTALI (ITA, 34)
2. Albéric SCHOTTE (BEL)
3. Guy LAPÉBIE (FRA)

1949 *Dist: 4,808 km, Ave Speed: 32.121 km/h*
1. Fausto COPPI (ITA, 29)
2. Gino BARTALI (ITA)
3. Jacques MARINELLI (FRA)

1950 *Dist: 4,775 km, Ave Speed: 32.791 km/h*
1. Ferdi KÜBLER (SWI, 31)
2. Constant OCKERS (BEL)
3. Louison BOBET (FRA)

1951 *Dist: 4,697 km, Ave Speed: 32.999 km/h*
1. Hugo KOBLET (SWI, 26)
2. Raphaël GEMINIANI (FRA)
3. Lucien LAZARIDÈS (FRA)

1952 *Dist: 4,827 km, Ave Speed: 31.765 km/h*
1. Fausto COPPI (ITA, 32)
2. Constant OCKERS (BEL)
3. Bernardo RUIZ (SPA)

1953 *Dist: 4,479 km, Ave Speed: 34.616 km/h*
1. Louison BOBET (FRA, 28)
2. Jean MALLÉJAC (FRA)
3. Giancarlo ASTRUA (ITA)

1954 *Dist: 4,669 km, Ave Speed: 33.325 km/h*
1. Louison BOBET (FRA, 29)
2. Ferdi KÜBLER (SWI)
3. Fritz SCHÄR (SWI)

1955 *Dist: 4,476 km, Ave Speed: 34.301 km/h*
1. Louison BOBET (FRA, 30)
2. Jean BRANKART (BEL)
3. Charly GAUL (LUX)

1956 *Dist: 4,498 km, Ave Speed: 36.268 km/h*
1. Roger WALKOWIAK (FRA, 29)
2. Gilbert BAUVIN (FRA)
3. Jan ADRIAENSENS (BEL)

1957 *Dist: 4,665 km, Ave Speed: 34.365 km/h*
1. Jacques ANQUETIL (FRA, 23)
2. Marcel JANSSENS (BEL)
3. Adolf CHRISTIAN (AUT)

1958 *Dist: 4,319 km, Ave Speed: 36.919 km/h*
1. Charly GAUL (LUX, 26)
2. Vito FAVERO (ITA)
3. Raphaël GEMINIANI (FRA)

1959 *Dist: 4,355 km, Ave Speed: 35.183 km/h*
1. Federico BAHAMONTES (SPA, 31)
2. Henry ANGLADE (FRA)
3. Jacques ANQUETIL (FRA)

1960 *Dist: 4,173 km, Ave Speed: 37.21 km/h*
1. Gastone NENCINI (ITA, 30)
2. Graziano BATTISTINI (ITA)
3. Jan ADRIAENSENS (BEL)

1961 *Dist: 4,397 km, Ave Speed: 36.033 km/h*
1. Jacques ANQUETIL (FRA, 27)
2. Guido CARLESI (ITA)
3. Charly GAUL (LUX)

1962 *Dist: 4,274 km, Ave Speed: 37.317 km/h*
1. Jacques ANQUETIL (FRA, 28)
2. Jozef PLANCKAERT (BEL)
3. Raymond POULIDOR (FRA)

1963 *Dist: 4,137 km, Ave Speed: 36.448 km/h*
1. Jacques ANQUETIL (FRA, 29)
2. Federico BAHAMONTES (SPA)
3. José PÉREZ-FRANCÉS (SPA)

1964 *Dist: 4,504 km, Ave Speed: 35.419 km/h*
1. Jacques ANQUETIL (FRA, 30)
2. Raymond POULIDOR (FRA)
3. Federico BAHAMONTES (SPA)

1965 *Dist: 4,177 km, Ave Speed: 35.792 km/h*
1. Felice GIMONDI (ITA, 22)
2. Raymond POULIDOR (FRA)
3. Gianni MOTTA (ITA)

1966 *Dist: 4,322 km, Ave Speed: 36.76 km/h*
1. Lucien AIMAR (FRA, 25)
2. Jan JANSSEN (NED)
3. Raymond POULIDOR (FRA)

1967 *Dist: 4,758 km, Ave Speed: 34.756 km/h*
1. Roger PINGEON (FRA, 27)
2. Julio JIMÉNEZ (SPA)
3. Franco BALMAMION (ITA)

1968 *Dist: 4,492 km, Ave Speed: 33.565 km/h*
1. Jan JANSSEN (NED, 28)
2. Herman VAN SPRINGEL (BEL)
3. Ferdinand BRACKE (BEL)

1969 *Dist: 4,117 km, Ave Speed: 35.409 km/h*
1. Eddy MERCKX (BEL, 24)
2. Roger PINGEON (FRA)
3. Raymond POULIDOR (FRA)

1970 *Dist: 4,254 km, Ave Speed: 35.589 km/h*
1. Eddy MERCKX (BEL, 25)
2. Joop ZOETEMELK (NED)
3. Gösta PETTERSSON (SWE)

1971 *Dist: 3,608 km, Ave Speed: 37.29 km/h*
1. Eddy MERCKX (BEL, 26)
2. Joop ZOETEMELK (NED)
3. Lucien VAN IMPE (BEL)

1972 *Dist: 3,846 km, Ave Speed: 35.516 km/h*
1. Eddy MERCKX (BEL, 27)
2. Felice GIMONDI (ITA)
3. Raymond POULIDOR (FRA)

1973 *Dist: 4,090 km, Ave Speed: 33.407 km/h*
1. Luis OCAÑA (SPA, 28)
2. Bernard THÉVENED (FRA)
3. José Manuel FUENTE (SPA)

1974 *Dist: 4,098 km, Ave Speed: 35.241 km/h*
1. Eddy MERCKX (BEL, 29)
2. Raymond POULIDOR (FRA)
3. Vicente LÓPEZ CARRIL (SPA)

1975 *Dist: 4,000 km, Ave Speed: 34.906 km/h*
1. Bernard THÉVENED (FRA, 27)
2. Eddy MERCKX (BEL)
3. Lucien VAN IMPE (BEL)

1976 *Dist: 4,017 km, Ave Speed: 34.518 km/h*
1. Lucien VAN IMPE (BEL, 30)
2. Joop ZOETEMELK (NED)
3. Raymond POULIDOR (FRA)

1977 *Dist: 4,096 km, Ave Speed: 35.419 km/h*
1. Bernard THÉVENED (FRA, 29)
2. Hennie KUIPER (NED)
3. Lucien VAN IMPE (BEL)

1978 *Dist: 3,908 km, Ave Speed: 36.084 km/h*
1. Bernard HINAULT (FRA, 23)
2. Joop ZOETEMELK (NED)
3. Joaquim AGOSTINHO (POR)

1979 *Dist: 3,765 km, Ave Speed: 36.513 km/h*
1. Bernard HINAULT (FRA, 24)
2. Joop ZOETEMELK (NED)
3. Joaquim AGOSTINHO (POR)

1980 *Dist: 3,946 km, Ave Speed: 36.095 km/h*
1. Joop ZOETEMELK (NED, 33)
2. Hennie KUIPER (NED)
3. Raymond MARTIN (FRA)

1981 *Dist: 3,757 km, Ave Speed: 39.002 km/h*
1. Bernard HINAULT (FRA, 26)
2. Lucien VAN IMPE (BEL)
3. Robert ALBAN (FRA)

1982 *Dist: 3,512 km, Ave Speed: 37.469 km/h*
1. Bernard HINAULT (FRA, 27)
2. Joop ZOETEMELK (NED)
3. Johan VAN DER VELDE (NED)

1983 *Dist: 3,862 km, Ave Speed: 35.914 km/h*
1. Laurent FIGNON (FRA, 22)
2. Angel ARROYO (SPA)
3. Peter WINNEN (NED)

1984 *Dist: 4,021 km, Ave Speed: 35.882 km/h*
1. Laurent FIGNON (FRA, 24)
2. Bernard HINAULT (FRA)
3. Greg LEMOND (USA)

1985 *Dist: 4,127 km, Ave Speed: 36.391 km/h*
1. Bernard HINAULT (FRA, 30)
2. Greg LEMOND (USA)
3. Stephen ROCHE (IRL)

1986 *Dist: 4,083 km, Ave Speed: 36.92 km/h*
1. Greg LEMOND (USA, 25)
2. Bernard HINAULT (FRA)
3. Urs ZIMMERMANN (SWI)

1987 *Dist: 4,039 km, Ave Speed: 34.981 km/h*
1. Stephen ROCHE (IRL, 28)
2. Pedro DELGADO (SPA)
3. Jean-François BERNARD (FRA)

1988 *Dist: 3,282 km, Ave Speed: 38.856 km/h*
1. Pedro DELGADO (SPA, 28)
2. Steven ROOKS (NED)
3. Fabio PARRA (COL)

1989 *Dist: 3,285 km, Ave Speed: 37.481 km/h*
1. Greg LEMOND (USA, 28)
2. Laurent FIGNON (FRA)
3. Pedro DELGADO (SPA)

1990 *Dist: 3,404 km, Ave Speed: 37.521 km/h*
1. Greg LEMOND (USA, 29)
2. Claudio CHIAPPUCCI (ITA)
3. Erik BREUKINK (NED)

1991 *Dist: 3,914 km, Ave Speed: 38.743 km/h*
1. Miguel INDURAIN (SPA, 27)
2. Gianni BUGNO (ITA)
3. Claudio CHIAPPUCCI (ITA)

1992 *Dist: 3,983 km, Ave Speed: 39.504 km/h*
1. Miguel INDURAIN (SPA, 28)
2. Claudio CHIAPPUCCI (ITA)
3. Gianni BUGNO (ITA)

1993 *Dist: 3,714 km, Ave Speed: 38.706 km/h*
1. Miguel INDURAIN (SPA, 29)
2. Tony ROMINGER (SWI)
3. Zenon JASKULA (POL)

1994 *Dist: 3,978 km, Ave Speed: 38.381 km/h*
1. Miguel INDURAIN (SPA, 30)
2. Piotr UGRUMOV (LAT)
3. Marco PANTANI (ITA)

1995 *Dist: 3,635 km, Ave Speed: 39.191 km/h*
1. Miguel INDURAIN (SPA, 31)
2. Alex ZÜLLE (SWI)
3. Bjarne RIIS (DEN)

1996 *Dist: 3,765 km, Ave Speed: 39.237 km/h*
1. Bjarne RIIS (DEN, 32)
2. Jan ULLRICH (GER)
3. Richard VIRENQUE (FRA)

1997 *Dist: 3,944 km, Ave Speed: 39.239 km/h*
1. Jan ULLRICH (GER, 23)
2. Richard VIRENQUE (FRA)
3. Marco PANTANI (ITA)

1998 *Dist: 3,875 km, Ave Speed: 39.983 km/h*
1. Marco PANTANI (ITA, 28)
2. Jan ULLRICH (GER)
3. Bobby JULICH (USA)

1999 *Dist: 3,870 km, Ave Speed: 40.276 km/h*
1. No winner
2. Alex ZÜLLE (SWI)
3. Fernando ESCARTÍN (SPA)

2000 *Dist: 3,662 km, Ave Speed: 39.569 km/h*
1. No winner
2. Jan ULLRICH (GER)
3. Joseba BELOKI (SPA)

2001 *Dist: 3,458 km, Ave Speed: 40.070 km/h*
1. No winner
2. Jan ULLRICH (GER)
3. Joseba BELOKI (SPA)

2002 *Dist: 3,278 km, Ave Speed: 39.920 km/h*
1. No winner
2. Joseba BELOKI (SPA)
3. Raimondas RUMSAS (LIT)

2003 *Dist: 3,427 km, Ave Speed: 40.940 km/h*
1. No winner
2. Jan ULLRICH (GER)
3. Alexandre VINOKOUROV (KAZ)

2004 *Dist: 3,391 km, Ave Speed: 40.553 km/h*
1. No winner
2. Andreas KLODEN (GER)
3. Ivan BASSO (ITA)

2005 *Dist: 3,607 km, Ave Speed: 41.654 km/h*
1. No winner
2. Ivan BASSO (ITA)
3. No third place

2006 *Dist: 3,657 km, Ave Speed: 40.781 km/h*
1. Oscar PEREIRO (SPA, 28)
2. Andreas KLÖDEN (GER)
3. Carlos Sastre (SPA)

2007 *Dist: 3,550 km, Ave Speed: 39.23 km/h*
1. Alberto CONTADOR (SPA, 24)
2. Cadel EVANS (AUS)
3. No third place

2008 *Dist: 3,559.5 km,*
Ave Speed: 40.50 km/h
1. Carlos SASTRE (SPA, 33)
2. Cadel EVANS (AUS)
3. Denis MENCHOV (RUS)

2009 *Dist: 3,459.5 km, Ave Speed: 40.315 km/h*
1. Alberto CONTADOR (SPA, 26)
2. Andy SCHLECK (LUX)
3. Bradley WIGGINS (GBR)*

* Lance Armstrong and Mikel Astarloza were both stripped of their top 10 finishes for doping infringements. In the 2009 edition, the UCI elevated Bradley Wiggins to third place.

2010 *Dist: 3,642 km, Ave Speed: 39.896 km/h*
1. Andy SCHLECK (LUX, 24)**
2. Denis MENCHOV (RUS)
3. Samuel SÁNCHEZ (SPA)

** Alberto Contador finished 39 seconds ahead of Andy Schleck but was stripped of the title after a positive test for clenbuterol. The UCI elevated Andy Schleck to first place.

2011 *Dist: 3,430.5 km, Ave Speed: 39.790 km/h*
1. Cadel EVANS (AUS, 34)
2. Andy SCHLECK (LUX)
3. Fränk SCHLECK (LUX)

2012 *Dist: 3,497 km, Ave Speed: 34.900 km/h*
1. Bradley WIGGINS (GBR, 32)
2. Chris FROOME (GBR)
3. Vincenzo NIBALI (ITA)

INDEX